To Kelly
from
Ed Mc David III
Oct. 18, 1991

SO-BYJ-457

LET GOD SPEAK

LET GOD SPEAK

and

Let Us Listen

Edmund R. McDavid III

Hope Publishing Company
P. O. Box 131447
Birmingham, Alabama 35213

Let God Speak:

Copyright © 1991 by E. R. McDavid III

All rights reserved

All Scripture quoted is from the New International Version.

Scripture taken from the Holy Bible: New International Version. Copyright © 1973, 1978, 1984 by the International Bible Society. Used by permission of Zondervan Bible Publishers.

First printing 1991

Library of Congress Catalog Card Number 91-73632

Cloth: ISBN 0-9630447-0-2
Paper: ISBN 0-9630447-1-0

Published by: Hope Publishing Company
P. O. Box 131447
Birmingham, Alabama 35213

Printed in the United States of America

DEDICATION

This book is dedicated to those individuals who are committed to knowing and serving God. By His grace, may it prove helpful.

ACKNOWLEDGMENTS

A special thanks to my wife Peg, who not only has been a wonderful wife for forty-one years, but who was a tremendous help in bringing this book to fruition. What I scratched out in longhand, she deciphered and put into the computer. She bore with patience the numerous changes and revisions. At the same time she acted as a sounding board for many of my thoughts about doctrine. Her help has been invaluable.

I want to thank my son Mike McDavid, his wife Mikelyn, my daughter Peggy Joseph and her husband Thomas for their encouragement and help. Mikelyn was a real help with punctuation and Peggy with outlines.

My thanks also to my niece Ceci Zerega for taking time to proofread the book.

Leo Hyche was helpful in setting up the computer program and provided much needed instruction in the operation of the computer, which I appreciate.

Emalyn Spencer was faithful to pray for our efforts and this is certainly appreciated.

To others who encouraged and prayed, let me say thanks.

One more acknowledgement remains and that is of my four grandchildren, Taylor and Edmund Jospeh and Lyndsay and Michael McDavid. Their contribution was indirect but a contribution nevertheless: that of being such a joy to their ol' grandpa that it made the task of writing this book easier. All four of them professed Jesus Christ as their Savior and Lord at a very young age. It is my prayer that God will give them the grace to hold fast to their profession and walk close with Him throughout their lives.

CONTENTS

PREFACE

My purpose in writing this book is to encourage others to examine some of the more difficult and controversial doctrines in the Bible. I ask you to temporarily lay aside what you have heard, thought, or read about these issues so that you may look with an open mind at what God says in the Bible. When we read the Bible we must remember that this is what God has said to us.

As we begin our study of these topics, allow me to make my position clear. I will state what I believe the Bible teaches about a particular doctrine and give Scripture references in support of my belief. However, I do not want you to arbitrarily accept my understanding of Scripture. Nor do I want you to reject my understanding because it is different from what you have been thinking or were taught. I ask you to look to God to impress upon your heart and mind what He would have you believe. For this to take place, you must be willing to put His will above your own. Ask Him to reveal His truths to you and then believe what His Word says to you—even if it is difficult.

I now invite you to join me in a study of God's Word. If God is who He claims to be (the only true God, the sovereign Lord of all), then the words He speaks are the most meaningful words we will ever encounter. If we are to have eternal life, if we are to walk with Him, if we are to enjoy the blessings that come from obeying Him, it is imperative that we know what He says. Therefore, let us begin our study with an attentive mind and a willing heart, and Let God Speak.

By faith we believe the Bible is true.

Is there evidence to support this faith?

Has God given us reasons to believe the Bible is His Word to us?

The grass withers and the flowers fall, but the word of our God stands forever. (Isaiah 40:8)

Why Believe the Bible

We will be looking at the Bible to see what it says; therefore, each of us should resolve what we believe about it. Do we believe it is God's Word to us? Is it absolute truth? Is it infallible? Is it inspired by God? I believe that the answer to these questions is yes. If you agree, then the only remaining thing for us is to attempt, by God's grace, to understand what He has said. However, if at this time you cannot answer yes to these questions, let me offer a few thoughts that may be helpful.

Views of Man Concerning the Bible

The atheist does not believe the Bible is reliable because he does not believe God exists. Whether he has come to this conclusion with little or much thought, he is placing himself in opposition to a book that declares there is a God—a book that has stood the test of time and critics, and has been a best seller over the years. He is, in essence, claiming to be more knowledgeable on this question than the millions of people throughout history who have believed there is a God and that the Bible is God's Word.

These millions of believers range from the uneducated to those with a string of degrees.

The atheist also has the problem of trying to explain Creation. He is faced with trying to account for the universe and all that it contains, including man, with one of the theories of evolution. However, in order to do this, he must start with something. He must assume that something already existed—some basic elements. He cannot come up with a satisfactory explanation as to where these came from in the beginning, to say nothing of the fact that his theories have no validity as they are carried further. To be an atheist one must have faith that there is no God, for he cannot prove that God does not exist.

The agnostic, on the other hand, does not deny that there is a God, but does deny that one can know Him. The agnostic does not seem to accept the fact that if God does exist, then as God, He should be able to make Himself known. He does not believe the living revelation of God in Christ or the written revelation of God in the Bible. His is a world of uncertainty. He does not know if there is a God, what He is like if He does exist, if there is a heaven or a hell, and where (if any place) he will go after this life. It behooves the agnostic to do some serious searching for truth about God, and some serious seeking of God. God has told us that if we seek, we will find.

When we move beyond the atheist and the agnostic, we find that most people definitely believe God exists. However, among this group we find widely held differences of opinion about the truth and reliability of the Bible. Some think it is a book written from man's perspective as to what God is like. Some think this in part, but also believe it contains the Word of God. Others believe all of it to be the infallible Word of God. Let us look at some reasons as to why we might come to the conclusion that the Bible is truly God's infallible Word to us.

Historical Evidence Substantiates It's Reliability

As a first step, let us ignore supernatural qualifications and test the reliability of the Bible as we would any other ancient book. We find that we have many more copies of manuscripts written closer to the time of the original writing than probably any other book of antiquity. This would certainly be true of the New Testament.

As a book of history, we find the Bible giving historical accounts of people and events by eyewitnesses, and people who knew and talked with eyewitnesses. We find that archaeological discoveries and nonreligious writings of antiquity confirm and substantiate a number of biblical records. There are references to Christ in early historical writings including that of the Jewish historian Josephus, and the Roman historians Suetonius and Tacitus. Even our system of dating time is B.C. or A.D. (before Christ and the year of our Lord). When we look at the Bible solely as a historical book of antiquity, we find it is unparalleled in evidence and documentation for genuineness and reliability as an accurate rendering of the original record. This being the case, we have good reason to think the Bible says what the writers intended to say.

Over Forty Writers but only One Author

Our next step is to determine if we have reason to believe what the writers say. We find that throughout the Bible there is one central theme: God's redemption of mankind through Jesus Christ. This becomes remarkable when we consider that the Bible was written over a period of approximately 1,500 years by over forty different authors from varied walks of life, ranging from peasant to king, fisherman to scholar, tax collector to military leader, herdsman to doctor. It was written in three different languages: Hebrew, Aramaic, and Greek. Many controversial subjects are covered, yet there is continuity of thought, position, and purpose throughout. This is enough to move one to acknowledge that the Bible is unique, and to cause a thinking person to question how this could come about.

If there were one person who lived during the entire period of 1,500 years who was in a position to influence and direct the authors to write what he chose to have written, we could easily account for it. However, that person would have to be God to be able to do it. And that is exactly how the Bible claims to have come about. God says He wrote the Bible by His Holy Spirit moving upon man to cause him to write what He wanted written. However, this was done without making man a robot and without violating man's will or personality. How God did this we do not know, but then God is God and we are man. His ways are above ours, and the secret things belong to him.

As the heavens are higher than the earth, so are my ways higher than your ways and my thoughts than you thoughts. (Isaiah 55:9)

The secret things belong to the Lord our God, but the things revealed belong to us and to our children forever, that we may follow all the words of this law. (Deuteronomy 29:29)

If God wrote the Bible through mankind, then we have every reason to believe what the authors wrote. Let us look further to see if there are reasons to believe that God did this.

Bible Prophecies

The Bible prophesies many things, and some of these are prophesied hundreds of years before they are due to happen. Everything that the Bible says would happen by the present time, has happened. A track record of one hundred percent thus far gives us every reason to believe the other prophecies will take place on schedule. One example of fulfilled prophecy is that of the utter destruction of Tyre, prophesied by the prophet Ezekiel. Ezekiel was taken captive to Babylon by Nebuchadnezzar around 597 B.C. His prophecy against Tyre appears to have been made between 593 and 571 B.C.

In the eleventh year, on the first day of the month, the word of the Lord came to me: "Son of man, because Tyre has said of Jerusalem, 'Aha! The gate to the nations is broken, and its doors have swung open to me; now that she lies in ruins I will prosper,' therefore this is what the Sovereign Lord says: I am against you, O Tyre, and I will bring many nations against you, like the sea casting up its waves. They will destroy the walls of Tyre and pull down her towers; I will scrape away her rubble and make her a bare rock. Out in the sea she will become a place to spread fishnets, for I have spoken, declares the Sovereign Lord. She will become plunder for the nations, and her settlements on the mainland will be ravaged by the sword. Then they will know that I am the Lord.

"For this is what the Sovereign Lord says: From the north I am going to bring against Tyre Nebuchadnezzar king of Babylon, king of kings, with horses and chariots, with horsemen and a great army. He will ravage your settlements on the mainland with the sword; he will set up siege works against you, build a ramp up to your walls and raise his shields against you. He will direct the blows of his battering rams against your walls and demolish your towers with his weapons. His horses will be so many that they will cover you with dust. Your walls will tremble at the noise of the war horses, wagons and chariots when he enters your gates as men enter a city whose walls have been broken through. The hoofs of his horses will trample all your streets; he will kill your people with the sword, and your strong pillars will fall to the ground. They will plunder your wealth and loot your merchandise; they will break down your walls and demolish your fine houses and throw your stones, timber and rubble into the sea. I will put an end to your noisy songs, and the music of your harps will be heard no more. I will make you a bare rock, and you will become a place to spread fishnets. You will never be rebuilt, for I the Lord have spoken, declares the Sovereign Lord."
(Ezekiel 26:1-14)

After a thirteen-year siege, Nebuchadnezzar destroyed the mainland city of Tyre. However, the people withdrew (carrying treasure with them) to an island possession about one-half mile off shore. A large part of the prophecy had been completed. Tyre had been defeated and left in rubble. The noisy songs and harp music were heard no more. When the Babylonian army left, the Tyrians made no effort to rebuild the mainland city. They had a superb navy and felt secure on their island. Although the city had been reduced to rubble, God had said that the stones, timber, and rubble would be thrown into the sea, and that where the city had stood would be bare rock. The remainder of the prophecy had yet to be fulfilled to protect God's honor.

Over 250 years later the rest of the prophecy was completed. The powerful army of Alexander the Great attacked the island city of Tyre in 332 B.C. Alexander had his men take all the stone, timber, and rubble they could find on the site where mainland Tyre had stood, and throw it into the sea in order to build a causeway out to the island.

Both the <u>Encyclopedia Britannica</u> and <u>World Book</u> tell of the building of the causeway, which was approximately 200 feet wide. Arrian, a Greek historian, tells us that the Tyrians made use of their navy, mounting attacks on Alexander's forces building the causeway. Alexander, realizing that he needed ships, pressed into service ships from people he had conquered. This, plus the fact that he also had soldiers in his army who were conquered subjects, could account for the Bible saying God would bring many nations against Tyre. Or the fact that the island city was rebuilt and attacked by other armies over a period of hundreds of years, could account for it. The prophecy was fulfilled. The mainland city of Tyre was destroyed and left as bare rock. Philip Myers, a secular historian, tells us that fishermen spread their nets there today. At present, there is a city named Tyre, but it is not located on the same site as the original. It is not the Tyre of our prophecy, but just another city that happens to have the same name.

John Beck tells us that the island city continued to be besieged and rebuilt until, after 1600 years, it fell, never to be rebuilt again.

Another example of Bible prophecy is found in the 28th chapter of Deuteronomy. God tells the Israelites what will happen to them if they are disobedient. They will be scattered among the nations, suffer hardships, etc. One of the things that will happen is that they will be sent back to Egypt in ships, to be sold as slaves.

The Lord will send you back in ships to Egypt on a journey I said you should never make again. There you will offer yourselves for sale to your enemies as male and female slaves, but no one will buy you. (Deuteronomy 28:68)

This prophecy was made approximately 1400 years before the fall of Jerusalem at the hands of the Roman Titus. Josephus, the Jewish historian, was there with the Romans when they besieged Jerusalem and when it fell. He records that a man named Fronto was appointed to determine the fate of the Jews that were taken alive. Some were put to death, some sent to the provinces to be killed by sword or beast for entertainment, some reserved for the triumph, and some sent to Egypt to work in the mines. It seems that there were so many being sold as slaves that the market was glutted. There are other historians who refer to this, including Wilkinson and Milman. Prophecy of this nature is overwhelming evidence that the Bible is God's Word, because no one but God could accurately predict such a happening 1400 years before it took place.

There are countless prophecies in the Bible like the two we have looked at. However, we will not pursue others. These two should suffice as examples to us that the Bible is God's inspired Word. We will, however, look at a few of the many prophecies and their fulfillment concerning Jesus Christ. This we do, not only to further solidify our confidence that the Bible is the Word of God, but to also strengthen our confidence that Jesus is the promised Messiah, and that no one but Jesus could be the Messiah. To insure that there is no mistake about the fact that He is sovereign and that He speaks through the Bible, God tells us what will happen, and then, at the appointed time, He brings it to pass.

I foretold the former things long ago, my mouth announced them and I made them known; then suddenly I acted, and they came to pass ... Therefore I told you these things long ago; before they happened I announced them to you. (Isaiah 48:3,5a)

When they had carried out all that was written about him, they took him down from the tree and laid him in a tomb. (Acts 13:29)

But this has all taken place that the writings of the prophets might be fulfilled. (Matthew 26:56a)

Prophecies About Christ Fulfilled

Scholars say there are more than 300 prophecies about Jesus in the Old Testament. Let us look at just a few of these and see their fulfillment in the New Testament.

Seed of a Woman

Prophecy	Fulfillment
And I will put enmity between you and the woman and between your offspring and hers.... (Genesis 3:15a)	**But when the time had fully come, God sent his Son, born of a woman, born under law....** (Galatians 4:4)

Seed of Abraham

Prophecy	Fulfillment
Abraham will surely become a great and powerful nation, and all nations on earth will be blessed through him. (Genesis 18:18)	And you are heirs of the prophets and of the covenant God made with your fathers. He said to Abraham, "Through your offspring all peoples on earth will be blessed." (Acts 3:25)

Place of Birth

Prophecy	Fulfillment
But you, Bethlehem Ephrathah, though you are small among the clans of Judah, out of you will come for me one who will be ruler over Israel, whose origins are from of old, from ancient times. (Micah 5:2)	After Jesus was born in Bethlehem in Judea, during the time of King Herod, Magi from the east came to Jerusalem.... (Matthew 2:1)

Born of a Virgin

Prophecy	Fulfillment
Therefore the Lord himself will give you a sign: The virgin will be with child and will give birth to a son, and will call him Immanuel. (Isaiah 7:14)	This is how the birth of Jesus Christ came about: His mother Mary was pledged to be married to Joseph, but before they came together, she was found to be with child through the Holy Spirit. (Matthew 1:18)

All this took place to fulfill what the Lord had said through the prophet: "The virgin will be with child and will give birth to a son, and they will call him Immanuel"—which means, "God with us." (Matthew 1:22-23) |

Prophet Like Moses

Prophecy	Fulfillment
The Lord your God will raise up for you a prophet like me from among your brothers. You must listen to him. (Deuteronomy 18:15)	After the people saw the miraculous sign that Jesus did, they began to say, "Surely this is the Prophet who is to come into the world." (John 6:14)
	Then a cloud appeared and enveloped them, and a voice came from the cloud: "This is my Son, whom I love. Listen to him!" (Mark 9:7)

His Rejection

Prophecy	Fulfillment
He was despised and rejected by men, a man of sorrows, and familiar with suffering. Like one from whom men hide their faces he was despised, and we esteemed him not. (Isaiah 53:3)	He came to that which was his own, but his own did not receive him. (John 1:11)

His Triumphal Entry

Prophecy	Fulfillment
Rejoice greatly, O Daughter of Zion! Shout, Daughter of Jerusalem! See, your king comes to you, righteous and having salvation, gentle and riding on a donkey, on a colt, the foal of a donkey. (Zechariah 9:9)	They took palm branches and went out to meet him, shouting, "Hosanna!" "Blessed is he who comes in the name of the Lord!" "Blessed is the King of Israel!" Jesus found a young donkey and sat upon it, as it is written, "Do not be afraid, O Daughter of Zion; see, your king is coming, seated on a donkey's colt." (John 12:13-14)

Betrayed by Judas

Prophecy	Fulfillment
Even my close friend, whom I trusted, he who shared my bread, has lifted up his heel against me. (Psalm 41:9)	Then Judas Iscariot, one of the Twelve, went to the chief priests to betray Jesus to them. (Mark 14:10)

Beaten and Spat Upon

Prophecy	Fulfillment
I offered my back to those who beat me, my cheeks to those who pulled out my beard; I did not hide my face from mocking and spitting. (Isaiah 50:6)	Then some began to spit at him; they blindfolded him, struck him with their fists, and said, "Prophesy!" And the guards took him and beat him. (Mark 14:65)

Hated Without Cause

Prophecy	Fulfillment
Those who hate me without reason outnumber the hairs of my head; many are my enemies without cause, those who seek to destroy me. I am forced to restore what I did not steal. (Psalm 69:4)	He who hates me hates my Father as well. If I had not done among them what no one else did, they would not be guilty of sin. But now they have seen these miracles, and yet they have hated both me and my Father. But this is to fulfill what is written in their Law: "They hated me without reason." (John 15:23-25)

Hands and Feet Pierced

Prophecy	Fulfillment
Dogs have surrounded me; a band of evil men has encircled me, they have pierced my hands and my feet. (Psalm 22:16)	Then he said to Thomas, "Put your finger here; see my hands. Reach out your hand and put it into my side. Stop doubting and believe." (John 20:27)

Mocked and Ridiculed

Prophecy	Fulfillment
But I am a worm and not a man, scorned by men and despised by the people. All who see me mock me; they hurl insults, shaking their heads: "He trusts in the Lord; let the Lord rescue him. Let him deliver him, since he delights in him." (Psalm 22:6-8)	Those who passed by hurled insults at him, shaking their heads and saying, "You who are going to destroy the temple and built it in three days, save yourself. Come down from the cross, if you are the Son of God!" (Matthew 27:39-40)

Given Vinegar

Prophecy	Fulfillment
They put gall in my food and gave me vinegar for my thirst. (Psalm 69:21)	A jar of wine vinegar was there, so they soaked a sponge in it, put the sponge on a stalk of the hyssop plant, and lifted it to Jesus' lips. (John 19:29)

His Side to be Pierced

Prophecy	Fulfillment
They will look on me, the one they have pierced.... (Zechariah 12:10b)	Instead, one of the soldiers pierced Jesus' side with a spear, bringing a sudden flow of blood and water. (John 19:34)

Cast Lots for His Clothes

Prophecy	Fulfillment
They divide my garments among them and cast lots for my clothing. (Psalm 22:18)	And they crucified him. Dividing up his clothes, they cast lots to see what each would get. (Mark 15:24)

Not Break His Bones

Prophecy	Fulfillment
He protects all his bones, not one of them will be broken. (Psalm 34:20)	The soldiers therefore came and broke the legs of the first man who had been crucified with Jesus, and then those of the other. But when they came to Jesus and found that he was already dead, they did not break his legs. (John 19:32-33)

His Resurrection

Prophecy	Fulfillment
...because you will not abandon me to the grave, nor will you let your Holy One see decay. (Psalm 16:10)	Then go quickly and tell his disciples: "He has risen from the dead and is going ahead of you into Galilee. There you will see him. Now I have told you." So the women hurried away from the tomb, afraid yet filled with joy, and ran to tell his disciples. Suddenly Jesus met them. "Greetings," he said. They came to him, clasped his feet and worshiped him. (Matthew 28:7-9)

His Ascension

Prophecy	Fulfillment
When you ascended on high, you led captives in your train; you received gifts from men, even from the rebellious—that you, O Lord God, might dwell there. (Psalm 68:18)	When he had led them out to the vicinity of Bethany, he lifted up his hands and blessed them. While he was blessing them, he left them and was taken up into heaven. (Luke 24:50-51)

These Old Testament prophecies were made over a period of time that ranged from 1400 to 400 years before the birth of Christ. Their fulfillment, recorded in the New Testament, covers a span of approximately 34 years. If the odds against someone being able to accurately predict the above prophecies were calculated according to the science of probability, I imagine they would be so large that we would have trouble understanding them. If the odds were calculated for someone to accurately predict all the Old Testament prophecies concerning Christ, the odds against it happening would be so astronomical that most of us would be unable to even relate to them. Fulfilled prophecy is evidence that demands our attention and pushes our reasoning powers to conclude that the Bible is the Word of God and that Christ is the promised Messiah.

The Testimony of the Writers

I believe another compelling reason for believing the Bible is the testimony of its writers. Often if we have the word of two or three witnesses to something, we feel that is sufficient—particularly if, in our opinion, we think the witnesses are reliable. Here we have over forty writers telling us what God has said and done. We certainly have every reason to believe they are reliable. We have no reason to doubt their honesty, integrity, intentions or motivations in writing what they did. We have every reason to believe they saw what they said they saw, and did what they said they did. Moreover, we have all the more reason to believe them when we find two or more of them claiming to have seen the same thing, such as the resurrected Christ.

These writers were flesh and blood people with family, friends, and loved ones—just as we are. Many of them suffered much in the way of physical and mental persecution for what they believed and said. A number of the Old Testament prophets were killed by stoning, etc., and tradition says that all of the apostles, except John, were martyred. Why would these people write as they did when it undoubtedly cost most of them very much, and often led to an early and violent death? Christ was crucified for His claims. Why in the world would anyone come right behind Him and claim to be a follower of His, and to have seen and talked with the resurrected Christ, if it were not so?

Throughout history, many people have died for causes that they thought were noble. However, the apostles did not die for a cause they thought worthy. They were in a position to be certain of their cause. They either knew they had seen the risen Christ or they knew they had not. If Christ did not rise from the dead, then

He was a liar and a fraud; therefore, Christianity was useless. If He did rise, then He was truly the Messiah. They claimed to have seen the risen Christ, and were willing to die for His sake, and for His cause. The trouble and danger that awaited those who made such claims was obvious. However, we have two fishermen (Peter and John), a tax collector (Matthew), and a well-educated pharisee (Paul) among those who wrote and preached about the resurrected Christ. We have two writers (James and Jude) who, scholars think, were half-brothers of Christ, and who were not believers or followers of Christ until after the Resurrection. The apostle Paul was a persecutor of the church before his conversion, which took place when the resurrected Christ appeared to him on the road to Damascus.

We are not told if Luke, who was a physician, saw the resurrected Christ, but one thing is for sure—he certainly believed in Him. Luke knew the apostles, and often traveled with Paul. If he did not see Christ in person, he saw Him through the eyes of the apostles and all the eyewitnesses that he interviewed before writing the books of Luke and Acts. Luke is considered to have been a very conscientious and thorough historian, and his writing indicates that he was a well-educated man.

These were sensible men committed to a cause they knew to be true—because they were committed to the person who is the Truth. Impulsive Peter who, in fear, denied Christ three times before the Crucifixion, boldly preached Christ after the Resurrection to those he accused of having a part in Christ's death.

> Men of Israel, listen to this: Jesus of Nazareth was a man accredited by God to you by miracles, wonders and signs, which God did among you through him, as you yourselves know. This man was handed over to you by God's set purpose and foreknowledge; and you, with the help of wicked men, put him to death by nailing him to the cross. (Acts 2:22-23)

He told them that Christ had been raised to life and that there were witnesses to that fact.

> God has raised this Jesus to life, and we are all witnesses of the fact. (Acts 2:32)

The witnesses that Peter speaks of are certainly the Apostles, but probably include the one hundred and twenty in the Upper Room.

Paul speaks of Christ appearing to more than 500 people at one time, and says that most of them were still living.

> For what I received I passed on to you as of first importance: that Christ died for our sins according to the Scriptures, that he was buried, that he was raised on the third day according to the Scriptures, and that he appeared to Peter, and then to the Twelve. After that, he appeared to more than five hundred of the brothers at the same time, most of whom are still living, though some have fallen asleep. Then he appeared to James, then to all the apostles.... (1 Corinthians 15:3-7)

The apostle John, who some think may have been a first cousin to Jesus, tells us about seeing, hearing, and touching Christ.

> That which was from the beginning, which we have heard, which we have seen with our eyes, which we have looked at and our hands have touched—this we proclaim concerning the Word of life. The life appeared; we have seen it and testify to it, and we proclaim to you the eternal life, which was with the Father and has appeared to us. We proclaim to you what we have seen and heard, so that you also may have fellowship with us. And our fellowship is with the Father and with his Son, Jesus Christ. (1 John 1:1-3)

This was written about 90 A.D. Therefore, in verse 3, John not only was speaking of fellowship with Christ, before the cross and during His time on earth after the Resurrection, but also present fellowship with the ascended Christ.

Peter tells us that what he and others are saying about Christ is not make-believe. It is very real. They were there.

> We did not follow cleverly invented stories when we told you about the power and coming of our Lord Jesus Christ, but we were eyewitnesses of his majesty. (2 Peter 1:16)

The resurrected Christ told Peter that when he was old he would be put to death, and it would glorify God.

"I tell you the truth, when you were younger you dressed yourself and went where you wanted; but when you are old you will stretch out your hands, and someone else will dress you and lead you where you do not want to go." Jesus said this to indicate the kind of death by which Peter would glorify God. Then he said to him, "Follow me!" (John 21:18-19)

Many years later when Peter realized this time was near, he wrote about it. Tradition says that Peter was crucified.

I think it is right to refresh your memory as long as I live in the tent of this body, because I know that I will soon put it aside, as our Lord Jesus Christ has made clear to me.
(2 Peter 1:13-14)

In his second letter to the Corinthians, we read about some of the hardships Paul underwent.

Five times I received from the Jews the forty lashes minus one. Three times I was beaten with rods, once I was stoned, three times I was shipwrecked, I spent a night and a day in the open sea, I have been constantly on the move. I have been in danger from rivers, in danger from bandits, in danger from my own countrymen, in danger from Gentiles; in danger in the city, in danger in the country, in danger at sea; and in danger from false brothers. I have labored and toiled and have often gone without sleep; I have known hunger and thirst and have often gone without food; I have been cold and naked.
(2 Corinthians 11:24-27)

Paul, like Peter, knew when his time of death was near, and mentioned this in a letter to Timothy.

For I am already being poured out like a drink offering, and the time has come for my departure. I have fought the good fight, I have finished the race, I have kept the faith. Now there is in store for me the crown of righteousness, which the Lord, the righteous Judge, will award to me on that day—and not only to me, but also to all who have longed for his appearing.
(2 Timothy 4:6-8)

Beyond the suffering and martyr's deaths of so many of the prophets and apostles, we have to look at the suffering and violent deaths of others who were imprisoned, thrown to the lions, or burned at the stake, etc. The writers of the Bible were not only jeopardizing their own lives but those of their families, friends, and loved ones. The historian Eusebius tells us that grandsons of Jude were brought before Emperor Domitian on charges of sedition because they were Christians, but apparently were released because they appeared to be just poor Syrian peasants. The writers of the Bible encouraged people to live for God, and give witness to Jesus knowing that it could bring persecution on them. An example of this is found in Paul's second letter to Timothy.

So do not be ashamed to testify about our Lord, or ashamed of me his prisoner. But join with me in suffering for the gospel, by the power of God.... (2 Timothy 1:8)

We see that Paul was not only willing to suffer for the sake of the resurrected Christ but he also asked others to do so. Timothy was like a son to Paul (some think he was his spiritual son) and Paul asked him to suffer for the Gospel.

When we look at the evidence and examine the facts, logic and reason tell us that the writers of the Bible believed what they wrote. Logic and reason also tell us that we should believe what they wrote. By not believing, one is, in essence, denying the facts, disregarding the evidence, and disparaging the character of those writers. In a sense, a nonbeliever is claiming to know more about what happened 2,000 to 3,000 years ago than those who were there. From the time of Moses to the time of Christ, there were many people who witnessed the miracles that are so hard for some to believe today. Those living at that time could have refuted them if they had not happened. However, in the case of the Jews, we find that they believed what Moses and others wrote, and were very careful to see that it was recorded and passed down to each generation.

Let us not overlook the fact that those who first believed Moses had been with Moses. They had come out of Egypt, had seen the Red Sea part, and had been fed manna from heaven. Those born after the crossing of the Red Sea would have been told about it. They would have heard of the slavery in Egypt—not from one or two people, but from many. If these events did not happen, it stands to reason the nation of Israel would not have lived and worshiped according to the Law of Moses. However, the writings of Moses are treasured by Christian and Jew alike. Both consider Moses to be a great prophet. (The Christian Old Testament contains the same Scriptures as the Jewish Torah.)

> **Since then, no prophet has risen in Israel like Moses, whom the Lord knew face to face....** (Deuteronomy 34:10)

The same situation that applied to the miracles of Moses' time applied to the miracles of Christ. There were many who would have been in a position to refute what the New Testament writers wrote, if what they said was not true. People did not deny the miracles of Christ—they denied that He was the Messiah. The miracles of feeding the five thousand and the four thousand men, plus women and children, would certainly be the type of miracles that could be checked out in the community. Between the two miracles, there were surely many young adults as well as children present who could testify to them years later.

Paul, when he stood before Festus and King Agrippa, told them that things concerning Christ (His life, death, and Resurrection) were public knowledge. These were things that were known. They had not been kept secret.

> **But I have had God's help to this very day, and so I stand here and testify to small and great alike. I am saying nothing beyond what the prophets and Moses said would happen—that the Christ would suffer and, as the first to rise from the dead, would proclaim light to his own people and to the Gentiles.**
>
> **At this point Festus interrupted Paul's defense. "You are out of your mind, Paul!" he shouted. "Your great learning is driving you insane."**
>
> **"I am not insane, most excellent Festus," Paul replied. "What I am saying is true and reasonable. The king is familiar with these things, and I can speak freely to him. I am convinced that none of this has escaped his notice, because it was not done in a corner."** (Acts 26:22-26)

We can be confident that Christ did much that we have no record of, but that the people of His day witnessed.

> **This is the disciple who testifies to these things and who wrote them down. We know that his testimony is true.**

> Jesus did many other things as well. If everyone of them were written down, I suppose that even the whole world would not have room for the books that would be written.
> (John 21:24-25)

John says his testimony is true. Polycarp, one of the early church fathers, certainly believed him. Polycarp was a disciple of the apostle John, and he also knew others who had seen Christ. Polycarp had a disciple named Ireneus who wrote a letter to a person named Florinus. In his letter, Ireneus speaks of how Polycarp would tell of what he had learned from John and the others about Christ, and that what he had learned agreed with Scripture. Even the Jewish historian Josephus (born around 37 A.D.), although not a believer, wrote about Christ doing wonderful works. He wrote that after the Crucifixion, Christ appeared alive to His disciples on the third day. Josephus also refers to James, the brother of Jesus, being brought before the Sanhedrin.

The Bible Claims to be the Word of God

Another thing that deserves our most serious consideration is the fact that the Bible claims to be the Word of God. The writers of the Bible claim it is written at the direction, under the control, and in the power of God the Holy Spirit. They claim it is the inspired Word of God. When Christ walked on earth, the Jewish Scriptures (the Christian's Old Testament) was the Bible. The fact that He referred to the Old Testament indicates that Christ recognized it as the Word of God.

> He said to them, "How foolish you are, and how slow of heart to believe all that the prophets have spoken! Did not the Christ have to suffer these things and then enter his glory?" And beginning with Moses and all the Prophets, he explained to them what was said in all the Scriptures concerning himself.
> (Luke 24:25-27)

> He said to them, "This is what I told you while I was still with you: Everything must be fulfilled that is written about me in the Law of Moses, the Prophets and the Psalms."
> Then he opened their minds so they could understand the Scriptures. He told them, "This is what is written: The Christ

will suffer and rise from the dead on the third day, and repentance and forgiveness of sins will be preached in his name to all nations, beginning at Jerusalem." (Luke 24:44-47)

Furthermore, we find examples in the New Testament of Christ quoting the Old Testament, as the Word of God to be obeyed.

Jesus answered, "It is written: 'Man does not live on bread alone, but on every word that comes from the mouth of God.'" (Matthew 4:4)

Jesus answered him, "It is also written: 'Do not put the Lord your God to the test.'" (Matthew 4:7)

Jesus said to him, "Away from me, Satan! For it is written: 'Worship the Lord your God, and serve him only.'" (Matthew 4:10)

Some Pharisees came to him to test him. They asked, "Is it lawful for a man to divorce his wife for any and every reason?"
    "Haven't you read," he replied, "that at the beginning the Creator 'made them male and female,' and said, 'For this reason a man will leave his father and mother and be united to his wife, and the two will become one flesh'? So they are no longer two, but one. Therefore what God has joined together, let man not separate." (Matthew 19:3-6)

We find the apostles quoting the Old Testament as the Word of God.

Do not take revenge, my friends, but leave room for God's wrath, for it is written: "It is mine to avenge; I will repay," says the Lord. (Romans 12:19)

...for it is written: "Be holy, because I am holy." (1 Peter 1:16)

As it is written: "See, I lay in Zion a stone that causes men to stumble and a rock that makes them fall, and the one who trusts in him will never be put to shame." (Romans 9:33)

The Scripture foresaw that God would justify the Gentiles by faith, and announced the gospel in advance to Abraham: "All nations will be blessed through you." (Galatians 3:8)

For the Scripture says to Pharaoh: "I raised you up for this very purpose, that I might display my power in you and that my name might be proclaimed in all the earth." (Romans 9:17)

We tell you the good news: What God promised our fathers he has fulfilled for us, their children, by raising up Jesus. As it is written in the second Psalm: "You are my Son; today I have become your Father." The fact that God raised him from the dead, never to decay, is stated in these words: "I will give you the holy and sure blessings promised to David." So it is stated elsewhere: "You will not let your Holy One see decay." For when David had served God's purpose in his own generation, he fell asleep; he was buried with his fathers and his body decayed. But the one whom God raised from the dead did not see decay. (Acts 13:32-37)

The Old Testament writers themselves indicated that they were writing what God had told them to write.

He said: "Son of man, I am sending you to the Israelites, to a rebellious nation that has rebelled against me; they and their fathers have been in revolt against me to this very day. The people to whom I am sending you are obstinate and stubborn. Say to them, 'This is what the Sovereign Lord says.' And whether they listen or fail to listen—for they are a rebellious house—they will know that a prophet has been among them. (Ezekiel 2:3-5)

Then Moses went up to God, and the Lord called to him from the mountain and said, "This is what you are to say to the house of Jacob and what you are to tell the people of Israel...." (Exodus 19:3)

Then the Lord said to Joshua: "Tell the Israelites to designate the cities of refuge, as I instructed you through Moses, so that anyone who kills a person accidentally and unintentionally may flee there and find protection from the avenger of blood." (Joshua 20:1-3)

"For my thoughts are not your thoughts, neither are your ways
my ways," declares the Lord. (Isaiah 55:8)

The word of the Lord came to me, saying, "Before I formed you
in the womb I knew you, before you were born I set you apart;
I appointed you as a prophet to the nations." "Ah, Sovereign
Lord," I said, "I do not know how to speak; I am only a child."
     But the Lord said to me, "Do not say, 'I am only a child.'
You must go to everyone I send you to and say whatever I
command you. Do not be afraid of them, for I am with you and
will rescue you," declares the Lord. (Jeremiah 1:4-7)

Therefore, the Lord says: "I am planning disaster against this
people, from which you cannot save yourselves. You will no
longer walk proudly, for it will be a time of calamity."
(Micah 2:3)

Then the Lord replied: "Write down the revelation and make
it plain on tablets so that a herald may run with it."
(Habakkuk 2:2)

"At that time I will gather you; at that time I will bring you
home. I will give you honor and praise among all the peoples
of the earth when I restore your fortunes before your very
eyes," says the Lord. (Zephaniah 3:20)

"Surely the day is coming; it will burn like a furnace. All the
arrogant and every evildoer will be stubble, and that day that
is coming will set them on fire," says the Lord Almighty.
(Malachi 4:1)

God warns the people through the prophet Zechariah not to
be like their forefathers.

In the eighth month of the second year of Darius, the word of
the Lord came to the prophet Zechariah son of Berekiah, the
son of Iddo:
     "The Lord was very angry with your forefathers. Therefore
tell the people: This is what the Lord Almighty says: 'Return
to me,' declares the Lord Almighty, 'and I will return to you,'
says the Lord Almighty. Do not be like your forefathers, to
whom the earlier prophets proclaimed: This is what the Lord
Almighty says: 'Turn from your evil ways and your evil
practices.' But they would not listen or pay attention to me,

declares the Lord. Where are your forefathers now? And the prophets, do they live forever? But did not my words and my decrees, which I commanded my servants the prophets, overtake your forefathers?

Then they repented and said, 'The Lord Almighty has done to us what our ways and practices deserve, just as he determined to do.'" (Zechariah 1:1-6)

Their forefathers and the earlier prophets had died. However, God raises the question of whether or not His Word, that had come through the earlier prophets concerning their forefathers, had come true. The question is raised knowing that the people must answer yes; because Israel had suffered much in the way of captivity and exile. This had been prophesied by more than one prophet as far back as the time of Moses.

The Lord will scatter you among the peoples, and only a few of you will survive among the nations to which the Lord will drive you. (Deuteronomy 4:27)

Zechariah reminds his listeners that this happened because of the disobedience of their forefathers. They would not listen to the words of the Holy Spirit spoken through the prophets.

But they refused to pay attention; stubbornly they turned their backs and stopped up their ears. They made their hearts as hard as flint and would not listen to the law or to the words that the Lord Almighty had sent by his Spirit through the earlier prophets. So the Lord Almighty was very angry.

"When I called, they did not listen; so when they called, I would not listen,' says the Lord Almighty. 'I scattered them with a whirlwind among all the nations, where they were strangers. The land was left so desolate behind them that no one could come or go. This is how they made the pleasant land desolate.'" (Zechariah 7:11-14)

The New Testament writers acknowledge that the Holy Spirit wrote the Old Testament.

When they heard this, they raised their voices together in prayer to God. "Sovereign Lord," they said, "you made the heaven and the earth and the sea, and everything in them. You spoke by the Holy Spirit through the mouth of your servant,

our father David: 'Why do the nations rage and the peoples
plot in vain? The kings of the earth take their stand and the
rulers gather together against the Lord and against his
Anointed One.' (Acts 4:24-26)

They disagreed among themselves and began to leave after
Paul had made this final statement: "The Holy Spirit spoke the
truth to your forefathers when he said through Isaiah the
prophet: 'Go to this people and say, "You will be ever hearing
but never understanding; you will be ever seeing but never
perceiving."'" (Acts 28:25-26)

So, as the Holy Spirit says: "Today, if you hear his voice, do
not harden your hearts as you did in the rebellion, during the
time of testing in the desert...." (Hebrews 3:7-8)

The Holy Spirit also testifies to us about this. First he says:
"This is the covenant I will make with them after that time,
says the Lord. I will put my laws in their hearts, and I will
write them on their minds." Then he adds: "Their sins and
lawless acts I will remember no more." (Hebrews 10:15-17)

Concerning this salvation, the prophets, who spoke of the grace
that was to come to you, searched intently and with the
greatest care, trying to find out the time and circumstances to
which the Spirit of Christ in them was pointing when he
predicted the sufferings of Christ and the glories that would
follow. It was revealed to them that they were not serving
themselves but you, when they spoke of the things that have
now been told you by those who have preached the gospel to
you by the Holy Spirit sent from heaven. Even angels long to
look into these things. (1 Peter 1:10-12)

Above all, you must understand that no prophecy of Scripture
came about by the prophet's own interpretation. For prophecy
never had its origin in the will of man, but men spoke from
God as they were carried along by the Holy Spirit.
(2 Peter 1:20-21)

After the apostles had written, certain of their writings were
included in Scripture. These, along with other writings, were
considered to be the Word of God and became our New

Testament. The apostle Paul tells us that all Scripture is God-breathed. That includes both the Old and New Testaments.

All Scripture is God-breathed and is useful for teaching, rebuking, correcting and training in righteousness....
(2 Timothy 3:16)

Peter refers to Paul's writings as Scripture by including them with the other Scriptures.

Bear in mind that our Lord's patience means salvation, just as our dear brother Paul also wrote you with the wisdom that God gave him. He writes the same way in all his letters, speaking in them of these matters. His letters contain some things that are hard to understand, which ignorant and unstable people distort, as they do the other Scriptures, to their own destruction. (2 Peter 3:15-16)

Paul claimed to speak as taught by the Holy Spirit.

This is what we speak, not in words taught us by human wisdom but in words taught by the Spirit, expressing spiritual truths in spiritual words. (1 Corinthians 2:13)

I already gave you a warning when I was with you the second time. I now repeat it while absent: On my return I will not spare those who sinned earlier or any of the others, since you are demanding proof that Christ is speaking through me. He is not weak in dealing with you, but is powerful among you.
(2 Corinthians 13:2-3)

And we also thank God continually because, when you received the word of God, which you heard from us, you accepted it not as the word of men, but as it actually is, the word of God, which is at work in you who believe. (1 Thessalonians 2:13)

By faith, we believe the Bible is the Word of God; however, our faith and belief are based on sound reasons and solid evidence. For many of those who do not believe, the problem is not a lack of reasons or insufficient evidence—they simply choose not to believe. I hope that any who are so inclined will pause and rethink their position.

Is God truly sovereign over everything?

Why is there sin and suffering?

Did Noah get all those animals into the Ark?

If God has ordained all that happens, why pray?

The Lord has established his throne in
heaven, and his kingdom rules over all.
(Psalm 103:19)

The Sovereignty of God

Most Christians, and even many non-Christians, believe that God
is omnipotent (all powerful), omnipresent (present in all places at
all times), and omniscient (all knowing); thus they would say they
believe in the sovereignty of God. However, many have never given
much thought to what this means. Some would qualify the meaning
of sovereignty by putting restrictions on what God can or does do.
There are others who would say (and I am in this group) that
God's sovereignty is complete, total and absolute. In our study, I
believe we will find that this is what is taught in the Bible.

Sovereignty in Creation

God created the heavens, the earth, and all the creatures—
including man. He did this in His sovereignty and in a manner of
His choosing. Over the centuries man has theorized how the
Universe came into existence. However, rather than accept the
theories of man, who was not around when the earth was formed,
let us look at the only account of Creation by one who was there.
God was not only there, He did the creating. Here is His report:

In the beginning God created the heavens and the earth. Now the earth was formless and empty, darkness was over the surface of the deep, and the Spirit of God was hovering over the waters.

And God said, "Let there be light," and there was light. God saw that the light was good, and he separated the light from the darkness. God called the light "day," and the darkness he called "night." And there was evening, and there was morning—the first day.

And God said, "Let there be an expanse between the waters to separate water from water." So God made the expanse and separated the water under the expanse from the water above it. And it was so. God called the expanse "sky." And there was evening, and there was morning—the second day.

And God said, "Let the water under the sky be gathered to one place, and let dry ground appear." And it was so. God called the dry ground "land," and the gathered waters he called "seas." And God saw that it was good.

Then God said, "Let the land produce vegetation: seed-bearing plants and trees on the land that bear fruit with seed in it, according to their various kinds." And it was so. The land produced vegetation: plants bearing seed according to their kinds and trees bearing fruit with seed in it according to their kinds. And God saw that it was good. And there was evening, and there was morning—the third day.

And God said, "Let there be lights in the expanse of the sky to separate the day from the night, and let them serve as signs to mark seasons and days and years, and let them be lights in the expanse of the sky to give light on the earth." And it was so. God made two great lights—the greater light to govern the day and the lesser light to govern the night. He also made the stars. God set them in the expanse of the sky to give light on the earth, to govern the day and the night, and to separate light from darkness. And God saw that it was good. And there was evening, and there was morning—the fourth day.

And God said, "Let the water teem with living creatures, and let birds fly above the earth across the expanse of the sky." So God created the great creatures of the sea and every living and moving thing with which the water teems, according to their kinds, and every winged bird according to its kind. And God saw that it was good. God blessed them and said, "Be fruitful and increase in number and fill the water in the seas, and let the birds increase on the earth." And there was evening, and there was morning—the fifth day.

And God said, "Let the land produce living creatures according to their kinds: livestock, creatures that move along the ground, and wild animals, each according to its kind." And it was so. God made the wild animals according to their kinds, the livestock according to their kinds, and all the creatures that move along the ground according to their kinds. And God saw that it was good.

Then God said, "Let us make man in our image, in our likeness, and let them rule over the fish of the sea and the birds of the air, over the livestock, over all the earth, and over all the creatures that move along the ground."

So God created man in his own image, in the image of God he created him; male and female he created them. God blessed them and said to them, "Be fruitful and increase in number; fill the earth and subdue it. Rule over the fish of the sea and the birds of the air and over every living creature that moves on the ground."

Then God said, "I give you every seed-bearing plant on the face of the whole earth and every tree that has fruit with seed in it. They will be yours for food. And to all the beasts of the earth and all the birds of the air and all the creatures that move on the ground—everything that has the breath of life in it—I give every green plant for food." And it was so.

God saw all that he had made, and it was very good. And there was evening, and there was morning—the sixth day. (Genesis Chapter 1)

Thus the heavens and the earth were completed in all their vast array.

By the seventh day God had finished the work he had been doing; so on the seventh day he rested from all his work. And God blessed the seventh day and made it holy, because on it he rested from all the work of creating that he had done.

This is the account of the heavens and the earth when they were created.

When the Lord God made the earth and the heavens—and no shrub of the field had yet appeared on the earth and no plant of the field had yet sprung up, for the Lord God had not sent rain on the earth and there was no man to work the ground, but streams came up from the earth and watered the whole surface of the ground—the Lord God formed the man from the dust of the ground and breathed into his nostrils the breath of life, and the man became a living being.

Now the Lord God had planted a garden in the east, in Eden; and there he put the man he had formed. And the Lord God made all kinds of trees grow out of the ground—trees that were pleasing to the eye and good for food. In the middle of the garden were the tree of life and the tree of the knowledge of good and evil.

A river watering the garden flowed from Eden; from there it was separated into four headwaters. The name of the first is the Pishon; it winds through the entire land of Havilah, where there is gold. (The gold of that land is good; aromatic resin and onyx are also there.) The name of the second river is the Gihon; it winds through the entire land of Cush. The name of the third river is the Tigris; it runs along the east side of Asshur. And the fourth river is the Euphrates.

The Lord God took the man and put him in the Garden of Eden to work it and take care of it. And the Lord God commanded the man, "You are free to eat from any tree in the garden; but you must not eat from the tree of the knowledge of good and evil, for when you eat of it you will surely die."

The Lord God said, "It is not good for the man to be alone. I will make a helper suitable for him."

Now the Lord God had formed out of the ground all the beasts of the field and all the birds of the air. He brought them to the man to see what he would name them; and whatever the man called each living creature, that was its name. So the man gave names to all the livestock, the birds of the air and all the beasts of the field.

But for Adam no suitable helper was found. So the Lord God caused the man to fall into a deep sleep; and while he was sleeping, he took one of the man's ribs and closed up the place with flesh. Then the Lord God made a woman from the rib he had taken out of the man, and he brought her to the man.

The man said, "This is now bone of my bones and flesh of my flesh; she shall be called 'woman,' for she was taken out of man."

For this reason a man will leave his father and mother and be united to his wife, and they will become one flesh. The man and his wife were both naked, and they felt no shame. (Genesis Chapter 2)

God not only created the elements, He also controls all the elements that are so frequently referred to as "Mother Nature." He sent the flood of Noah's day, He caused the earth to open up and swallow a number of people in Moses' day.

> But if the Lord brings about something totally new, and the earth opens its mouth and swallows them, with everything that belongs to them, and they go down alive into the grave, then you will know that these men have treated the Lord with contempt.
> As soon as he finished saying all this, the ground under them split apart and the earth opened its mouth and swallowed them.... (Numbers 16:30-32a)

And He held back rain for three and one-half years when Elijah prayed.

> Elijah was a man just like us. He prayed earnestly that it would not rain, and it did not rain on the land for three and a half years. (James 5:17)

God can be very selective in His control of the elements, as we see in the following verses:

> Throughout Egypt hail struck everything in the fields—both men and animals; it beat down everything growing in the fields and stripped every tree. The only place it did not hail was the land of Goshen, where the Israelites were. (Exodus 9:25-26)

> I also withheld rain from you when the harvest was still three months away. I sent rain on one town, but withheld it from another. One field had rain; another had none and dried up. (Amos 4:7)

God created everything, including Satan and all his demonic beings. Nothing happened by chance. There is not an atom, a particle of matter, an amoeba, an animal, a person, or a spirit-being that came into existence outside of God. Nothing exists that God did not make.

> For by him all things were created: things in heaven and on earth, visible and invisible, whether thrones or powers or rulers or authorities; all things were created by him and for him. (Colossians 1:16)

In the beginning was the Word, and the Word was with God,
and the Word was God. He was with God in the beginning.
Through him all things were made; without him nothing was
made that has been made. (John 1:1-3)

Purpose for Creation

God has a purpose for His Creation and that purpose is to
bring honor and glory to Himself.

Then the Lord said to Moses, "Why are you crying out to me?
Tell the Israelites to move on. Raise your staff and stretch out
your hand over the sea to divide the water so that the
Israelites can go through the sea on dry ground. I will harden
the hearts of the Egyptians so that they will go in after them.
And I will gain glory through Pharaoh and all his army,
through his chariots and his horsemen. The Egyptians will
know that I am the Lord when I gain glory through Pharaoh,
his chariots and his horsemen." (Exodus 14:15-18)

All the nations you have made will come and worship before
you, O Lord; they will bring glory to your name.
(Psalm 86:9)

This is to my Father's glory, that you bear much fruit, showing
yourselves to be my disciples. (John 15:8)

They raise their voices, they shout for joy; from the west they
acclaim the Lord's majesty. Therefore in the east give glory to
the Lord; exalt the name of the Lord, the God of Israel, in the
islands of the sea. From the ends of the earth we hear singing:
"Glory to the Righteous One." (Isaiah 24:14-16a)

Suddenly a great company of the heavenly host appeared with
the angel, praising God and saying, "Glory to God in the
highest, and on earth peace to men on whom his favor rests."
(Luke 2:13-14)

May the God who gives endurance and encouragement give you
a spirit of unity among yourselves as you follow Christ Jesus,
so that with one heart and mouth you may glorify the God and
Father of our Lord Jesus Christ. (Romans 15:5-6)

...in order that we, who were the first to hope in Christ, might be for the praise of his glory. (Ephesians 1:12)

Jesus said this to indicate the kind of death by which Peter would glorify God. (John 21:19a)

...so that you may be able to discern what is best and may be pure and blameless until the day of Christ, filled with the fruit of righteousness that comes through Jesus Christ—to the glory and praise of God. (Philippians 1:10-11)

You are worthy, our Lord and God, to receive glory and honor and power, for you created all things, and by your will they were created and have their being. (Revelation 4:11)

God has a plan for carrying out His purpose.

...according to his eternal purpose which he accomplished in Christ Jesus our Lord. (Ephesians 3:11)

And we know that in all things God works for the good of those who love him, who have been called according to his purpose. (Romans 8:28)

In him we were also chosen, having been predestined according to the plan of him who works out everything in conformity with the purpose of his will.... (Ephesians 1:11)

Let all the earth fear the Lord; let all the people of the world revere him. For he spoke, and it came to be; he commanded, and it stood firm. The Lord foils the plans of the nations; he thwarts the purposes of the peoples. But the plans of the Lord stand firm forever, the purposes of his heart through all generations. (Psalm 33:8-11)

God is all powerful.

No one from the east or the west or from the desert can exalt a man. But it is God who judges: He brings one down, he exalts another. (Psalm 75:6-7)

The lot is cast into the lap, but its every decision is from the Lord. (Proverbs 16:33)

When a trumpet sounds in a city, do not the people tremble?
When disaster comes to a city, has not the Lord caused it?
(Amos 3:6)

This is what the Lord says, he who appoints the sun to shine
by day, who decrees the moon and stars to shine by night, who
stirs up the sea so that its waves roar—the Lord Almighty is
his name.... (Jeremiah 31:35)

He changes times and seasons; he sets up kings and deposes
them. He gives wisdom to the wise and knowledge to the
discerning. (Daniel 2:21)

Is it not from the mouth of the Most High that both calamities
and good things come? (Lamentations 3:38)

The king's heart is in the hand of the Lord; he directs it like
a watercourse wherever he pleases. (Proverbs 21:1)

For who in the skies above can compare with the Lord? Who
is like the Lord among the heavenly beings? In the council of
the holy ones God is greatly feared; he is more awesome than
all who surround him. (Psalm 89:6-7)

For nothing is impossible with God. (Luke 1:37)

God is all knowing.

"Can anyone hide in secret places so that I cannot see him?"
declares the Lord. (Jeremiah 23:24a)

For a man's ways are in full view of the Lord, and he examines
all his paths. (Proverbs 5:21)

The eyes of the Lord are everywhere, keeping watch on the
wicked and the good. (Proverbs 15:3)

But the Lord said to Samuel, "Do not consider his appearance
or his height, for I have rejected him. The Lord does not look
at the things man looks at. Man looks at the outward
appearance, but the Lord looks at the heart." (1 Samuel 16:7)

O Lord, you have searched me and you know me. You know
when I sit and when I rise; you perceive my thoughts from

afar. You discern my going out and my lying down; you are familiar with all my ways. Before a word is on my tongue you know it completely, O Lord. (Psalm 139:1-4)

...for the Lord searches every heart and understands every motive behind the thoughts. (1 Chronicles 28:9b)

Do not be like them, for your Father knows what you need before you ask him. (Matthew 6:8)

God is everywhere.

Where can I go from your Spirit? Where can I flee from your presence? If I go up to the heavens, you are there; if I make my bed in the depths, you are there. (Psalm 139:7-8)

"Am I only a God nearby," declares the Lord, "and not a God far away?" (Jeremiah 23:23)

"Do not I fill heaven and earth?" declares the Lord. (Jeremiah 23:24b)

God's plan will come about just as He has determined; no one can prevent it from happening.

...for dominion belongs to the Lord and he rules over the nations. (Psalm 22:28)

With my great power and outstretched arm I made the earth and its people and the animals that are on it, and I give it to anyone I please. (Jeremiah 27:5)

Which of all these does not know that the hand of the Lord has done this? In his hand is the life of every creature and the breath of all mankind. (Job 12:9-10)

May the nations be glad and sing for joy, for you rule the peoples justly and guide the nations of the earth. (Psalm 67:4)

The Lord has established his throne in heaven, and his kingdom rules over all. (Psalm 103:19)

See now that I myself am He! There is no god besides me. I
put to death and I bring to life, I have wounded and I will
heal, and no one can deliver out of my hand.
(Deuteronomy 32:39)

Remember the former things, those of long ago; I am God, and
there is no other; I am God, and there is none like me. I make
known the end from the beginning, from ancient times, what
is still to come. I say: My purpose will stand, and I will do all
that I please. From the east I summon a bird of prey; from a
far-off land, a man to fulfill my purpose. What I have said,
that will I bring about; what I have planned, that will I do.
(Isaiah 46:9-11)

Our God is in heaven; he does whatever pleases him.
(Psalm 115:3)

As the rain and the snow come down from heaven, and do not
return to it without watering the earth and making it bud and
flourish, so that it yields seed for the sower and bread for the
eater, so is my word that goes out from my mouth: It will not
return to me empty, but will accomplish what I desire and
achieve the purpose for which I sent it. (Isaiah 55:10-11)

Misconceptions of God's Sovereignty

A man I know believes that after God made the world, and
the people in it, He sat back and let things take their own course—
just as you put a wind-up toy train on a table and let it run around.
You only interfere with the train to keep it from falling off the
table. This man's idea is that God only interferes with His Creation
when it is necessary to keep it from "falling off the table." This
concept of the sovereignty of God is interesting, and to a number
of people it seems logical.

There are those who think God is interested in only the big
events in this world, or the big events in their lives. They believe
He is not to be bothered with the day-in and day-out routine of
life. As a result, they hesitate to go to God in prayer about "minor
things" because they feel He is not concerned or does not have
time for them.

There are probably people who feel they are so unimportant
that God does not concern Himself with anything that takes place

in their lives. These people are not necessarily saying that God cannot, but rather that God chooses not to involve Himself in a certain life or a certain event, at a given time. However, if a person reaches an important position in life, or some important event takes place in the world, then God may choose to step in and take some type of action.

If everyone were left only to their own appraisal of things, we can understand how some could reach these conclusions, but God does not leave us to figure this out on our own. Instead, He has drawn us a clear picture from Scripture. How can one feel his life is unimportant to God, no matter what his position is, when he reads:

> For you created my inmost being; you knit me together in my mother's womb. I praise you because I am fearfully and wonderfully made; your works are wonderful, I know that full well. My frame was not hidden from you when I was made in the secret place. When I was woven together in the depths of the earth, your eyes saw my unformed body. All the days ordained for me were written in your book before one of them came to be. (Psalm 139:13-16)

> And even the very hairs of your head are all numbered. (Matthew 10:30)

These verses teach us that God's sovereignty extends to every aspect of our lives. Before we were conceived, He had determined what we would look like, what we would be, what we would do, and the number of days we would have on this earth. Whatever happens to us and whatever happens because of us is all part of God's plan. These verses make it clear that God is concerned with every detail of our lives and knows even the number of hairs on our heads. He is telling us the degree to which He is involved in our lives. The following verses teach the same concept:

> Before I formed you in the womb I knew you, before you were born I set you apart; I appointed you as a prophet to the nations. (Jeremiah 1:5)

> I know, O Lord, that a man's life is not his own; it is not for man to direct his steps. (Jeremiah 10:23)

I lie down and sleep; I wake again, because the Lord sustains me. (Psalm 3:5)

In his heart a man plans his course, but the Lord determines his steps. (Proverbs 16:9)

...for every animal of the forest is mine, and the cattle on a thousand hills. I know every bird in the mountains, and the creatures of the field are mine. (Psalm 50:10-11)

Sovereignty and Sin

These verses teach the complete, total, and absolute sovereignty of God. Everything that happens in this world happens because God directs it or because God permits it to happen. This means that everything that happens is part of God's overall plan. Nothing can happen unless it fits His plan. This raises the question of sin. If God is sovereign over all things, how did sin get into the world? Since God did not keep sin out of the world, does that mean He approves of sin? The answer is clear in the Scriptures— He does not.

You are not a God who takes pleasure in evil; with you the wicked cannot dwell. (Psalm 5:4)

Your eyes are too pure to look on evil; you cannot tolerate wrong. (Habakkuk 1:13a)

When tempted, no one should say, "God is tempting me." For God cannot be tempted by evil, nor does he tempt anyone.... (James 1:13)

For the eyes of the Lord are on the righteous and his ears are attentive to their prayer, but the face of the Lord is against those who do evil. (1 Peter 3:12)

If your right eye causes you to sin, gouge it out and throw it away. It is better for you to lose one part of your body than for your whole body to be thrown into hell. (Matthew 5:29)

However, it pleases God to permit sin. The phrase "pleases God" does not mean that God is happy with sin or that He condones sin. Rather, it means that sin fits His plan—He has His reasons for permitting sin. If He did not know it was the right thing to do, He would not allow sin in the world. Had He chosen to do so, He could have kept sin out. However, He has chosen to use the sinful acts of man to accomplish His purpose, as in the case with Joseph. Joseph knew that it was God who had put him in Egypt. However, God used Joseph's brothers as His instruments to do this. It was a sinful act on the part of the brothers, but God used it to accomplish good.

> Then Joseph said to his brothers, "Come close to me." When they had done so, he said, "I am your brother Joseph, the one you sold into Egypt! And now, do not be distressed and do not be angry with yourselves for selling me here, because it was to save lives that God sent me ahead of you. For two years now there has been famine in the land, and for the next five years there will not be plowing and reaping. But God sent me ahead of you to preserve for you a remnant on earth and to save your lives by a great deliverance.
> So then, it was not you who sent me here, but God. He made me father to Pharaoh, lord of his entire household and ruler of all Egypt." (Genesis 45:4-8)

> But Joseph said to them, "Don't be afraid. Am I in the place of God? You intended to harm me, but God intended it for good to accomplish what is now being done, the saving of many lives." (Genesis 50:19-20)

We see God's sovereign hand as He sends the Assyrians to war against Israel as punishment for Israel's disobedience. This is a clear example of the paradox of God's sovereignty and man's freedom of choice. God does not cause the Assyrians to sin by attacking and plundering Israel, but He has decreed that they will. However, they choose to attack, and therefore, they are responsible for their choice. God says He will punish them for doing it.

> The Lord will bring on you and on your people and on the house of your father a time unlike any since Ephraim broke away from Judah—he will bring the king of Assyria.
> (Isaiah 7:17)

"Woe to the Assyrian, the rod of my anger, in whose hand is the club of my wrath! I send him against a godless nation, I dispatch him against a people who anger me, to seize loot and snatch plunder, and to trample them down like mud in the streets. But this is not what he intends, this is not what he has in mind; his purpose is to destroy, to put an end to many nations. 'Are not my commanders all kings?' he says. 'Has not Calno fared like Carchemish? Is not Hamath like Arpad, and Samaria like Damascus? As my hand seized the kingdoms of the idols, kingdoms whose images excelled those of Jerusalem and Samaria—shall I not deal with Jerusalem and her images as I dealt with Samaria and her idols?'"

When the Lord has finished all his work against Mount Zion and Jerusalem, he will say, "I will punish the king of Assyria for the willful pride of his heart and the haughty look in his eyes. For he says:

'By the strength of my hand I have done this, and by my wisdom, because I have understanding. I removed the boundaries of nations, I plundered their treasures; like a mighty one I subdued their kings. As one reaches into a nest, so my hand reached for the wealth of the nations; as men gather abandoned eggs, so I gathered all the countries; not one flapped a wing, or opened its mouth to chirp.'" Does the ax raise itself above him who swings it, or the saw boast against him who uses it? As if a rod were to wield him who lifts it up, or a club brandish him who is not wood! Therefore, the Lord, the Lord Almighty, will send a wasting disease upon his sturdy warriors; under his pomp a fire will be kindled like a blazing flame. The Light of Israel will become a fire, their Holy One a flame; in a single day it will burn and consume his thorns and his briers. The splendor of his forests and fertile fields it will completely destroy, as when a sick man wastes away. And the remaining trees of his forests will be so few that a child could write them down. In that day the remnant of Israel, the survivors of the house of Jacob, will no longer rely on him who struck them down but will truly rely on the Lord, the Holy One of Israel. A remnant will return, a remnant of Jacob will return to the Mighty God. Though your people, O Israel, be like the sand by the sea, only a remnant will return. Destruction has been decreed, overwhelming and righteous. The Lord, the Lord Almighty, will carry out the destruction decreed upon the whole land. Therefore, this is what the Lord, the Lord Almighty, says: "O my people who live in Zion, do not be afraid of the Assyrians, who beat you with a rod and lift up a club against you, as Egypt did. Very soon my anger against you will end and my wrath will be directed to their destruction." The Lord Almighty will lash them with a whip, as when he struck down Midian at the rock of Oreb; and he will raise his staff over the waters, as he did in Egypt. In that day their burden will be lifted from your shoulders, their yoke from your neck; the yoke will be broken because you have grown so fat. (Isaiah 10:5-27)

Sovereignty and Satan

Even Satan cannot do anything without God's permission. Whatever he is allowed to do is part of God's plan—otherwise God would not allow it to happen. The affliction of Job is an example of this. God granted Satan permission to afflict Job; however, Satan's affliction of Job was only to the degree God allowed.

One day the angels came to present themselves before the Lord, and Satan also came with them. The Lord said to Satan, "Where have you come from?"

Satan answered the Lord, "From roaming through the earth and going back and forth in it."

Then the Lord said to Satan, "Have you considered my servant Job? There is no one on earth like him; he is blameless and upright, a man who fears God and shuns evil."

"Does Job fear God for nothing?" Satan replied. "Have you not put a hedge around him and his household and everything he has? You have blessed the work of his hands, so that his flocks and herds are spread throughout the land. But stretch out your hand and strike everything he has, and he will surely curse you to your face."

The Lord said to Satan, "Very well, then, everything he has is in your hands, but on the man himself do not lay a finger."

Then Satan went out from the presence of the Lord. (Job 1:6-12)

Then the Lord said to Satan, "Have you considered my servant Job? There is no one on earth like him; he is blameless and upright, a man who fears God and shuns evil. And he still maintains his integrity, though you incited me against him to ruin him without any reason."

"Skin for skin!" Satan replied. "A man will give all he has for his own life. But stretch out your hand and strike his flesh and bones, and he will surely curse you to your face."

The Lord said to Satan, "Very well, then he is in your hands; but you must spare his life."

So Satan went out from the presence of the Lord and afflicted Job with painful sores from the soles of his feet to the top of his head. (Job 2:3-7)

Sovereignty and Suffering

We know that God restored Job physically, made him twice as wealthy as before, and gave him seven sons and three beautiful daughters. The Bible tells us, **"The Lord blessed the latter part of Job's life more than the first"** (Job 42:12a). Most Christians do not suffer as Job did and are not restored as he was. However, in His sovereignty, God makes suffering work to the good of His people. Therefore, Christians are to face trials and suffering knowing that all things work together for their good.

Consider it pure joy, my brothers, whenever you face trials of many kinds, because you know that the testing of your faith develops perseverance. Perseverance must finish its work so that you may be mature and complete, not lacking anything. (James 1:2-4)

Dear friends, do not be surprised at the painful trial you are suffering, as though something strange were happening to you. But rejoice that you participate in the sufferings of Christ, so that you may be overjoyed when his glory is revealed. If you are insulted because of the name of Christ, you are blessed, for the Spirit of glory and of God rests on you. If you suffer, it should not be as a murderer or thief or any other kind of criminal, or even as a meddler. However, if you suffer as a Christian, do not be ashamed, but praise God that you bear that name. For it is time for judgment to begin with the family of God; and if it begins with us, what will the outcome be for those who do not obey the gospel of God? And, "If it is hard for the righteous to be saved, what will become of the ungodly and the sinner?"

So then, those who suffer according to God's will should commit themselves to their faithful Creator and continue to do good. (1 Peter 4:12-19)

We do not want you to be uninformed, brothers, about the hardships we suffered in the province of Asia. We were under great pressure, far beyond our ability to endure, so that we despaired even of life. Indeed, in our hearts we felt the sentence of death. But this happened that we might not rely on ourselves but on God, who raises the dead.
(2 Corinthians 1:8-9)

For it has been granted to you on behalf of Christ not only to believe on him, but also to suffer for him....
(Philippians 1:29)

Now if we are children, then we are heirs—heirs of God and co-heirs with Christ, if indeed we share in his sufferings in order that we may also share in his glory. (Romans 8:17)

Sovereignty and Persecution

Persecution for their belief in Christ is a form of trial or suffering which Christians must undergo. This too could not happen if it did not fit God's plan—if it had not been decreed by God. He uses persecution to test us, to increase our faith, and to draw us closer to Himself. As Christians, we can expect persecution to one degree or another.

We ought always to thank God for you, brothers, and rightly so, because your faith is growing more and more, and the love every one of you has for each other is increasing. Therefore, among God's churches we boast about your perseverance and faith in all the persecutions and trials you are enduring.

All this is evidence that God's judgment is right, and as a result you will be counted worthy of the kingdom of God, for which you are suffering. God is just: He will pay back trouble to those who trouble you and give relief to you who are troubled, and to us as well. This will happen when the Lord Jesus is revealed from heaven in blazing fire with his powerful angels. He will punish those who do not know God and do not obey the gospel of our Lord Jesus. They will be punished with everlasting destruction and shut out from the presence of the Lord and from the majesty of his power on the day he comes to be glorified in his holy people and to be marveled at among all those who have believed. This includes you, because you believed our testimony to you. (2 Thessalonians 1:3-10)

Blessed are you when people insult you, persecute you and
falsely say all kinds of evil against you because of me. Rejoice
and be glad, because great is your reward in heaven, for in the
same way they persecuted the prophets who were before you.
(Matthew 5:11-12)

Remember the words I spoke to you: 'No servant is greater
than his master.' If they persecuted me, they will persecute you
also. If they obeyed my teaching, they will obey yours also.
(John 15:20)

In fact, everyone who wants to live a godly life in Christ Jesus
will be persecuted.... (2 Timothy 3:12)

As we study the Bible, we find that the Apostle Paul, known
as Saul before his conversion, was one of the greatest persecutors
of the church.

For I am the least of the apostles and do not even deserve to
be called an apostle, because I persecuted the church of God.
(1 Corinthians 15:9)

When they heard this, they were furious and gnashed their
teeth at him. But Stephen, full of the Holy Spirit, looked up to
heaven and saw the glory of God, and Jesus standing at the
right hand of God.
    "Look," he said, "I see heaven open and the Son of Man
standing at the right hand of God."
    At this they covered their ears and, yelling at the top of
their voices, they all rushed at him, dragged him out of the city
and began to stone him. Meanwhile, the witnesses laid their
clothes at the feet of a young man named Saul.
    While they were stoning him, Stephen prayed, "Lord
Jesus, receive my spirit." Then he fell on his knees and cried
out, "Lord, do not hold this sin against them." When he had
said this, he fell asleep. And Saul was there, giving approval to
his death. (Acts 7:54-60)

On that day a great persecution broke out against the church
at Jerusalem, and all except the apostles were scattered
throughout Judea and Samaria. Godly men buried Stephen
and mourned deeply for him. But Saul began to destroy the
church. Going from house to house, he dragged off men and
women and put them in prison. (Acts 8:1-3)

We see an account of Paul's conversion in the Book of Acts:

Meanwhile, Saul was still breathing out murderous threats against the Lord's disciples. He went to the high priest and asked him for letters to the synagogues in Damascus, so that if he found any there who belonged to the Way, whether men or women, he might take them as prisoners to Jerusalem. As he neared Damascus on his journey, suddenly a light from heaven flashed around him. He fell to the ground and heard a voice say to him, "Saul, Saul, why do you persecute me?"

"Who are you, Lord?" Saul asked.

"I am Jesus, whom you are persecuting," he replied. "Now get up and go into the city, and you will be told what you must do."

The men traveling with Saul stood there speechless; they heard the sound but did not see anyone. Saul got up from the ground, but when he opened his eyes he could see nothing. So they led him by the hand into Damascus. For three days he was blind, and did not eat or drink anything.

In Damascus there was a disciple named Ananias. The Lord called to him in a vision, "Ananias!"

"Yes, Lord," he answered.

The Lord told him, "Go to the house of Judas on Straight Street and ask for a man from Tarsus named Saul, for he is praying. In a vision he has seen a man named Ananias come and place his hands on him to restore his sight."

"Lord," Ananias answered, "I have heard many reports about this man and all the harm he has done to your saints in Jerusalem. And he has come here with authority from the chief priests to arrest all who call on your name."

But the Lord said to Ananias, "Go! This man is my chosen instrument to carry my name before the Gentiles and their kings and before the people of Israel. I will show him how much he must suffer for my name."

Then Ananias went to the house and entered it. Placing his hands on Saul, he said, "Brother Saul, the Lord—Jesus, who appeared to you on the road as you were coming here—has sent me so that you may see again and be filled with the Holy Spirit." Immediately, something like scales fell from Saul's eyes, and he could see again. He got up and was baptized, and after taking some food, he regained his strength.

Saul spent several days with the disciples in Damascus. At once he began to preach in the synagogues that Jesus is the Son of God. All those who heard him were astonished and

asked, "Isn't he the man who raised havoc in Jerusalem among those who call on this name? And hasn't he come here to take them as prisoners to the chief priests?" Yet Saul grew more and more powerful and baffled the Jews living in Damascus by proving that Jesus is the Christ. (Acts 9:1-22)

God's sovereignty is seen throughout the Bible, and it is certainly evident in this passage of Scripture. God ordained that Paul would be saved and that he would preach the Gospel (verse 15). When we read the New Testament we begin to see how greatly Paul was used to do this, just as God had planned. We also see that Paul suffered much in upholding the name of Christ, just as Christ had declared (verse 16).

I only know that in every city the Holy Spirit warns me that prison and hardships are facing me. (Acts 20:23)

Five times I received from the Jews the forty lashes minus one. Three times I was beaten with rods, once I was stoned, three times I was shipwrecked, I spent a night and a day in the open sea, I have been constantly on the move. I have been in danger from rivers, in danger from bandits, in danger from my own countrymen, in danger from Gentiles; in danger in the city, in danger in the country, in danger at sea; and in danger from false brothers. I have labored and toiled and have often gone without sleep; I have known hunger and thirst and have often gone without food; I have been cold and naked.
(2 Corinthians 11:24-27)

And of this gospel I was appointed a herald and an apostle and a teacher. That is why I am suffering as I am.
(2 Timothy 1:11-12a)

Sovereignty in Election

In the passage about Paul's conversion, we see God's grace in Election. Paul was a man who not only wanted nothing to do with Christ but who was actually persecuting Him. Suddenly, he had a total change of heart and in no time was risking his life to tell others of the wonders of Christ. This was a result of regeneration by God's Holy Spirit.

Natural man (unregenerate man) cannot understand the things of God, and, in fact, he thinks they are foolish (1 Cor. 2:14). In this state, man will not accept Christ as Savior and Lord because he is unable to believe the truth of the Gospel.

Paul is a good example of this. Prior to conversion, he was very religious (a pharisee) and very well educated. Though he knew the Scriptures, he did not understand the truth of them. But at the time, place, and circumstances of God's choosing, the Holy Spirit opened Paul's understanding and worked in his heart and mind to move him to believe and trust Christ. This was done without violating Paul's will. Paul confirms this in his epistle to the Ephesians, and goes on to point out that God chose (elected) him to be saved, before the creation of the world.

> **Praise be to the God and Father of our Lord Jesus Christ, who has blessed us in the heavenly realms with every spiritual blessing in Christ. For he chose us in him before the creation of the world to be holy and blameless in his sight. In love he predestined us to be adopted as his sons through Jesus Christ, in accordance with his pleasure and will—to the praise of his glorious grace, which he has freely given us in the One he loves. (Ephesians 1:3-6)**

As sovereign Lord, God not only chose certain people to be saved, but He chose one nation to receive special favors and to be an example to the rest of the nations. This nation, of course, was Israel.

> **For you are a people holy to the Lord your God. The Lord your God has chosen you out of all the peoples on the face of the earth to be his people, his treasured possession. The Lord did not set his affection on you and choose you because you were more numerous than other peoples, for you were the fewest of all peoples. But it was because the Lord loved you and kept the oath he swore to your forefathers that he brought you out with a mighty hand and redeemed you from the land of slavery, from the power of Pharaoh king of Egypt. (Deuteronomy 7:6-8)**

> **Hear this word the Lord has spoken against you, O people of Israel—against the whole family I brought up out of Egypt: "You only have I chosen of all the families of the earth; therefore I will punish you for all your sins." (Amos 3:1-2)**

> He has revealed his word to Jacob, his laws and decrees to
> Israel. He has done this for no other nation; they do not know
> his laws. (Psalm 147:19-20)

> These twelve Jesus sent out with the following instructions: "Do
> not go among the Gentiles or enter any town of the
> Samaritans. Go rather to the lost sheep of Israel."
> (Matthew 10:5-6)

The fact that Israel is an elect (chosen) nation does not mean
that all the people of Israel are elect people. The nation was
elected to have God's Word, God's help and God's blessing. There
was a time when Israel was the only nation that enjoyed these
privileges. With the exception of an occasional Gentile who
converted to their religion, the Jews were the only people being
saved for hundreds of years. However, even then, only the
individuals whom God had purposed to save were saved. In all the
earth, only the Elect have been saved in the past; only the Elect
are being saved at present; and only the Elect will be saved in the
future. For further information, see the chapter on Election.

Promises—Threats—Prophecies

In the Bible (particularly in the Old Testament), we see God
making promises, issuing threats, and prophesying the future of
individuals, nations, and the world. No promise, no threat, and no
prophesy has failed to be fulfilled at the appointed time. This track
record can only lead us to believe that all the others will be
fulfilled at their designated times. I believe it will help us to better
understand God's sovereignty if we look for the promises, threats,
and prophesies as we read the Bible. The following verses include
some examples:

> The Lord had said to Abram, "Leave your country, your people
> and your father's household and go to the land I will show you.
>   "I will make you into a great nation and I will bless you;
> I will make your name great, and you will be a blessing. I will
> bless those who bless you, and whoever curses you I will curse;
> and all peoples on earth will be blessed through you."
> (Genesis 12:1-3)

Abram fell facedown, and God said to him, "As for me, this is
my covenant with you: You will be the father of many nations.
No longer will you be called Abram; your name will be
Abraham, for I have made you a father of many nations. I will
make you very fruitful; I will make nations of you, and kings
will come from you. I will establish my covenant as an
everlasting covenant between me and you and your descendants
after you for the generations to come, to be your God and the
God of your descendants after you. The whole land of Canaan,
where you are now an alien, I will give as an everlasting
possession to you and your descendants after you; and I will be
their God." (Genesis 17:3-8)

Then Moses went out and spoke these words to all Israel: "I
am now a hundred and twenty years old and I am no longer
able to lead you. The Lord has said to me, 'You shall not cross
the Jordan.' The Lord your God himself will cross over ahead
of you. He will destroy these nations before you, and you will
take possession of their land. Joshua also will cross over ahead
of you, as the Lord said. And the Lord will do to them what he
did to Sihon and Og, the kings of the Amorites, whom he
destroyed along with their land. The Lord will deliver them to
you, and you must do to them all that I have commanded you.
Be strong and courageous. Do not be afraid or terrified
because of them, for the Lord your God goes with you; he will
never leave you nor forsake you." (Deuteronomy 31:1-6)

The Reubenites, the Gadites and the half-tribe of Manasseh
had 44,760 men ready for military service—able-bodied men
who could handle shield and sword, who could use a bow, and
who were trained for battle. They waged war against the
Hagrites, Jetur, Naphish and Nodab. They were helped in
fighting them, and God handed the Hagrites and all their
allies over to them, because they cried out to him during the
battle. He answered their prayers, because they trusted in him.
They seized the livestock of the Hagrites—fifty thousand
camels, two hundred fifty thousand sheep and two thousand
donkeys. They also took one hundred thousand people captive,
and many others fell slain, because the battle was God's. And
they occupied the land until the exile. (1 Chronicles 5:18-22)

See, I will stir up against them the Medes, who do not care for
silver and have no delight in gold. Their bows will strike down
the young men; they will have no mercy on infants nor will

they look with compassion on children. Babylon, the jewel of kingdoms, the glory of the Babylonians' pride, will be overthrown by God like Sodom and Gomorrah. She will never be inhabited or lived in through all generations; no Arab will pitch his tent there, no shepherd will rest his flocks there. But desert creatures will lie there, jackals will fill her houses; there the owls will dwell, and there the wild goats will leap about. Hyenas will howl in her strongholds, jackals in her luxurious palaces. Her time is at hand, and her days will not be prolonged. (Isaiah 13:17-22)

Whenever Israel went out to fight, the hand of the Lord was against them to defeat them, just as he had sworn to them. They were in great distress. (Judges 2:15)

This is what the Lord says: As I have brought all this great calamity on this people, so I will give them all the prosperity I have promised them. (Jeremiah 32:42)

Not one of all the Lord's good promises to the house of Israel failed; every one was fulfilled. (Joshua 21:45)

The Lord Almighty has sworn, "Surely, as I have planned, so it will be, and as I have purposed, so it will stand. I will crush the Assyrian in my land; on my mountains I will trample him down. His yoke will be taken from my people, and his burden removed from their shoulders.

"This is the plan determined for the whole world; this is the hand stretched out over all nations. For the Lord Almighty has purposed, and who can thwart him? His hand is stretched out, and who can turn it back? (Isaiah 14:24-27)

All this happened to King Nebuchadnezzar. Twelve months later, as the king was walking on the roof of the royal palace of Babylon, he said, "Is not this the great Babylon I have built as the royal residence, by my mighty power and for the glory of my majesty?"

The words were still on his lips when a voice came from heaven, "This is what is decreed for you, King Nebuchadnezzar: Your royal authority has been taken from you. You will be driven away from people and will live with the wild animals; you will eat grass like cattle. Seven times will pass by for you until you acknowledge that the Most High is sovereign over the kingdoms of men and gives them to anyone he wishes."

Immediately what had been said about Nebuchadnezzar was fulfilled. He was driven away from people and ate grass like cattle. His body was drenched with the dew of heaven until his hair grew like the feathers of an eagle and his nails like the claws of a bird.

At the end of that time, I, Nebuchadnezzar, raised my eyes toward heaven, and my sanity was restored. Then I praised the Most High; I honored and glorified him who lives forever. His dominion is an eternal dominion; his kingdom endures from generation to generation. All the peoples of the earth are regarded as nothing. He does as he pleases with the powers of heaven and the peoples of the earth. No one can hold back his hand or say to him: "What have you done?"

At the same time that my sanity was restored, my honor and splendor were returned to me for the glory of my kingdom. My advisers and nobles sought me out, and I was restored to my throne and became even greater than before. Now I, Nebuchadnezzar, praise and exalt and glorify the King of heaven, because everything he does is right and all his ways are just. And those who walk in pride he is able to humble. (Daniel 4:28-37)

Before the spies lay down for the night, she went up on the roof and said to them, "I know that the Lord has given this land to you and that a great fear of you has fallen on us, so that all who live in this country are melting in fear because of you. We have heard how the Lord dried up the water of the Red Sea for you when you came out of Egypt, and what you did to Sihon and Og, the two kings of the Amorites east of the Jordan, whom you completely destroyed. When we heard of it, our hearts melted and everyone's courage failed because of you, for the Lord your God is God in heaven above and on the earth below. Now then, please swear to me by the Lord that you will show kindness to my family, because I have shown kindness to you. Give me a sure sign that you will spare the lives of my father and mother, my brothers and sisters, and all who belong to them, and that you will save us from death."

"Our lives for your lives!" the men assured her. "If you don't tell what we are doing, we will treat you kindly and faithfully when the Lord gives us the land." (Joshua 2:8-14)

Sovereignty and Animals

The God who made the birds and animals is also the God who feeds them. He controls the length of time they have on earth and the rate at which they are replenished.

> Look at the birds of the air; they do not sow or reap or store away in barns, and yet your heavenly Father feeds them. (Matthew 6:26a)

> He makes springs pour water into the ravines; it flows between the mountains. They give water to all the beasts of the field; the wild donkeys quench their thirst. The birds of the air nest by the waters; they sing among the branches. (Psalm 104:10-11)

> He makes grass grow for the cattle.... (Psalm 104:14)

> The lions roar for their prey and seek their food from God. (Psalm 104:21)

> How many are your works, O Lord! In wisdom you made them all; the earth is full of your creatures. There is the sea, vast and spacious, teeming with creatures beyond number—living things both large and small. There the ships go to and fro, and the leviathan, which you formed to frolic there.
> These all look to you to give them their food at the proper time. When you give it to them, they gather it up; when you open your hand, they are satisfied with good things. When you hide your face, they are terrified; when you take away their breath, they die and return to the dust. When you send your Spirit, they are created, and you renew the face of the earth. (Psalm 104:24-30)

In His sovereignty, God put a fear of man in all the animals and creatures that He created. He will also hold accountable any animal that kills a human.

> The fear and dread of you will fall upon all the beasts of the earth and all the birds of the air, upon every creature that moves along the ground, and upon all the fish of the sea; they are given into your hands.
> And for your lifeblood I will surely demand an accounting. I will demand an accounting from every animal. And from each

man, too, I will demand an accounting for the life of his fellow
man. (Genesis 9:2,5)

God uses animals to accomplish His purposes. He allows them
to do what is in their natures, or sometimes causes them to do
what is out of character.

From there Elisha went up to Bethel. As he was walking along
the road, some youths came out of the town and jeered at him.
"Go on up, you baldhead!" they said. "Go on up, you baldhead!"
He turned around, looked at them and called down a curse on
them in the name of the Lord. Then two bears came out of the
woods and mauled forty-two of the youths. (2 Kings 2:23-24)

My God sent his angel, and he shut the mouths of the lions.
They have not hurt me, because I was found innocent in his
sight. Nor have I ever done any wrong before you, O king.
(Daniel 6:22)

Then the Lord said to Jacob, "Go back to the land of your
fathers and to your relatives, and I will be with you."
    So Jacob sent word to Rachel and Leah to come out to the
fields where his flocks were. He said to them, "I see that your
father's attitude toward me is not what it was before, but the
God of my father has been with me. You know that I've worked
for your father with all my strength, yet your father has
cheated me by changing my wages ten times. However, God has
not allowed him to harm me. If he said, 'The speckled ones will
be your wages,' then all the flocks gave birth to speckled
young; and if he said, 'The streaked ones will be your wages,'
then all the flocks bore streaked young. So God has taken away
your father's livestock and has given them to me.
(Genesis 31:3-9)

Then the word of the Lord came to Elijah: "Leave here, turn
eastward and hide in the Kerith Ravine, east of the Jordan.
You will drink from the brook, and I have ordered the ravens
to feed you there."
    So he did what the Lord had told him. He went to the
Kerith Ravine, east of the Jordan, and stayed there. The
ravens brought him bread and meat in the morning and bread
and meat in the evening, and he drank from the brook.
(1 Kings 17:2-6)

> So Moses said, "This is what the Lord says: 'About midnight I will go throughout Egypt. Every firstborn son in Egypt will die, from the firstborn son of Pharaoh, who sits on the throne, to the firstborn son of the slave girl, who is at her hand mill, and all the firstborn of the cattle as well. There will be loud wailing throughout Egypt—worse than there has ever been or ever will be again. But among the Israelites not a dog will bark at any man or animal.' Then you will know that the Lord makes a distinction between Egypt and Israel." (Exodus 11:4-7)

Note how the Lord controlled the animals that entered the Ark. It would seem impossible for Noah to round up the pairs of animals and get them into the Ark. God did not burden him with this task. Noah was commanded to take them, but it was God who caused them to come to Noah and to enter the Ark.

> I am going to bring floodwaters on the earth to destroy all life under the heavens, every creature that has the breath of life in it. Everything on earth will perish. But I will establish my covenant with you, and you will enter the ark—you and your sons and your wife and your sons' wives with you. You are to bring into the ark two of all living creatures, male and female, to keep them alive with you. Two of every kind of bird, of every kind of animal and of every kind of creature that moves along the ground will come to you to be kept alive. (Genesis 6:17-20)

> Pairs of all creatures that have the breath of life in them came to Noah and entered the ark. The animals going in were male and female of every living thing, as God had commanded Noah. Then the Lord shut him in. (Genesis 7:15-16)

Sovereignty and Man

God gives life, and He brings death. He afflicts and He heals. Both Christians and non-Christians are allotted a certain number of days on this earth, according to God's plan for them. No one will depart this earth a day sooner nor stay a day longer than God has determined.

> The Lord said to him, "Who gave man his mouth? Who makes him deaf or mute? Who gives him sight or makes him blind? Is it not I, the Lord?" (Exodus 4:11)

Jesus replied, "Go back and report to John what you hear and see: The blind receive sight, the lame walk, those who have leprosy are cured, the deaf hear, the dead are raised, and the good news is preached to the poor." (Matthew 11:4-5)

Then they brought him a demon-possessed man who was blind and mute, and Jesus healed him, so that he could both talk and see. (Matthew 12:22)

Now listen, you who say, "Today or tomorrow we will go to this or that city, spend a year there, carry on business and make money." Why, you do not even know what will happen tomorrow. What is your life? You are a mist that appears for a little while and then vanishes. Instead, you ought to say, "If it is the Lord's will, we will live and do this or that." (James 4:13-15)

The God who made the world and everything in it is the Lord of heaven and earth and does not live in temples built by hands. And he is not served by human hands, as if he needed anything, because he himself gives all men life and breath and everything else. From one man he made every nation of men, that they should inhabit the whole earth; and he determined the times set for them and the exact places where they should live. (Acts 17:24-26)

We see that God can declare that the Israelites will be slaves for four hundred years, and further declare that at the end of that time they not only will gain their freedom, but they will come out with much wealth. Only One who is absolutely sovereign can declare an event such as this and also bring it about. Furthermore, He does it without violating man's will. Everyone does as he wills to do, yet everyone will "will" to do that which God has ordained. The Egyptians are an example of this, as they give the Israelites silver and gold.

As the sun was setting, Abram fell into a deep sleep, and a thick and dreadful darkness came over him. Then the Lord said to him, "Know for certain that your descendants will be strangers in a country not their own, and they will be enslaved and mistreated four hundred years. But I will punish the nation they serve as slaves, and afterward they will come out with great possessions." (Genesis 15:12-14)

> Now the Lord had said to Moses, "I will bring one more plague on Pharaoh and on Egypt. After that, he will let you go from here, and when he does, he will drive you out completely. Tell the people that men and women alike are to ask their neighbors for articles of silver and gold." (Exodus 11:1-2)

> The Israelites did as Moses instructed and asked the Egyptians for articles of silver and gold and for clothing. The Lord had made the Egyptians favorably disposed toward the people, and they gave them what they asked for; so they plundered the Egyptians. (Exodus 12:35-36)

> He brought out Israel, laden with silver and gold, and from among their tribes no one faltered. (Psalm 105:37)

Paul realized that God is sovereign over the heart and mind. He certainly believed God worked in peoples hearts and minds to cause them to think, feel, and act. This is evident by the way he thanked God for the people, for the faith the people had, and for the way they acted. He also asked God to strengthen their love and their attitude of heart.

> First, I thank my God through Jesus Christ for all of you, because your faith is being reported all over the world. (Romans 1:8)

> How can we thank God enough for you in return for all the joy we have in the presence of our God because of you?
> (1 Thessalonians 3:9)

> Now may our God and Father himself and our Lord Jesus clear the way for us to come to you. May the Lord make your love increase and overflow for each other and for everyone else, just as ours does for you. (1 Thessalonians 3:11-12)

Sovereignty in Dispersing Spiritual Gifts

Another area where we see God's sovereign hand is in the dispensing of spiritual gifts to His people. God knows the plan, He knows what is needed, and He determines whom He will equip with which gifts to get the job done.

These gifts are not something we can come up with on our own, no matter how hard we try. They are gifts from God's Holy Spirit and He alone decides which will be given to whom. All Christians have at least one spiritual gift and some may have two or more. These gifts are given for the common good of the Body of Christ—to be used in the service of Christ.

> Now about spiritual gifts, brothers, I do not want you to be ignorant. You know that when you were pagans, somehow or other you were influenced and led astray to mute idols. Therefore I tell you that no one who is speaking by the Spirit of God says, "Jesus be cursed," and no one can say, "Jesus is Lord," except by the Holy Spirit.
>
> There are different kinds of gifts, but the same Spirit. There are different kinds of service, but the same Lord. There are different kinds of working, but the same God works all of them in all men.
>
> Now to each one the manifestation of the Spirit is given for the common good. To one there is given through the Spirit the message of wisdom, to another the message of knowledge by means of the same Spirit, to another faith by the same Spirit, to another gifts of healing by that one Spirit, to another miraculous powers, to another prophecy, to another distinguishing between spirits, to another speaking in different kinds of tongues, and to still another the interpretation of tongues. All these are the work of one and the same Spirit, and he gives them to each one, just as he determines.
> (1 Corinthians 12:1-11)

> For by the grace given me I say to every one of you: Do not think of yourself more highly than you ought, but rather think of yourself with sober judgment, in accordance with the measure of faith God has given you. Just as each of us has one body with many members, and these members do not all have the same function, so in Christ we who are many form one body, and each member belongs to all the others. We have different gifts, according to the grace given us. If a man's gift is prophesying, let him use it in proportion to his faith. If it is serving, let him serve; if it is teaching, let him teach; if it is encouraging, let him encourage; if it is contributing to the needs of others, let him give generously; if it is leadership, let him govern diligently; if it is showing mercy, let him do it cheerfully. (Romans 12:3-8)

Each one should use whatever gift he has received to serve others, faithfully administering God's grace in its various forms. (1 Peter 4:10)

Though spiritual gifts are given to the Christian, there are many other blessings that are shared by all men—Christian and non-Christian alike. The sun, moon, a beautiful starry night, lakes and rivers, a cool breeze—all are part of what is called common grace. These are given for the benefit and pleasure of all.

He causes his sun to rise on the evil and the good, and sends rain on the righteous and the unrighteous. (Matthew 5:45b)

Sovereignty and Individuals

When we get to a personal level we see that, in His sovereignty, God has given some people the ability to excel in sports, some a talent for music, others a head for business, etc. Some people have more ability than others and there are some who have little or none. In God's sovereignty, He has not endowed us with equal ability.

He also has placed us, from birth, into different families, cultures, and countries. Often these varying and unequal conditions and circumstances appear to favor those who are not God's people. Frequently the differences are great.

This is cause for concern to some Christians who question God's justice. They look around and see many people who could not care less about God doing very well on this earth. On the other hand, they see many Christians struggling with a variety of problems. This gives them cause to raise the question, If God really is who He says He is, why does He allow this to happen?

Many people have a critical attitude of how God orders His Creation. They think He is unfair in the bestowing of His blessings.

Who is Qualified to Question God's Sovereignty?

I think it is all right to wonder "why" God causes something to happen, or permits it to happen. However, it should be done with an acknowledgement that what God does is right and just—that it is the best thing. It is the perfect thing in the sense of being part of God's perfect plan. If we wonder in this manner, we are not questioning what God does, but rather wondering in amazement at how He carries out His plan for all of His Creation.

However, if we question what God does with an attitude of disagreeing with Him, of thinking that He has done wrong, and of thinking that He is unmerciful or unloving—then we are in sin. We must remember that whatever the Christian's circumstances, in God's sovereignty they are working for his good (Romans 8:28). He is being blessed by God, and at death he will go to be with God. This is not the case for the non-Christian.

The Apostle Paul speaks of the end of the non-Christian. He says they will not inherit the kingdom of God. If they do not inherit the kingdom of God, that leaves only one other place for them to spend eternity—hell.

Do you not know that the wicked will not inherit the kingdom of God? Do not be deceived: Neither the sexually immoral nor idolaters nor adulterers nor male prostitutes nor homosexual offenders nor thieves nor the greedy nor drunkards nor slanderers nor swindlers will inherit the kingdom of God. (1 Corinthians 6:9-10)

Those whom Paul refers to as the wicked are those who have not trusted Christ as Savior and Lord. In this passage, Paul cautions those who profess Christ not to deceive themselves. We are not to think we can live life, willfully committing these sins (or other sins), and inherit the kingdom of God. We cannot sow to the flesh and reap to the Spirit. If we live in willful sin, we deceive ourselves, and our profession of Christ is in question. We may find we are numbered among the wicked.

Sometimes, as Christians, we seem to expect things to go our way, as though God owes us something. In reality, we all come into this world as sinners, born with a sinful nature and under the penalty of Adam's first sin—eating fruit from the forbidden tree.

Therefore, just as sin entered the world through one man, and death through sin, and in this way death came to all men, because all sinned.... (Romans 5:12)

According to God's Word we are sinners and deserve to go to hell.

I said, "O Lord, have mercy on me; heal me, for I have sinned against you." (Psalm 41:4)

Surely I was sinful at birth, sinful from the time my mother conceived me. (Psalm 51:5)

For our offenses are many in your sight, and our sins testify against us. Our offenses are ever with us, and we acknowledge our iniquities.... (Isaiah 59:12)

You know my folly, O God; my guilt is not hidden from you. (Psalm 69:5)

For whoever keeps the whole law and yet stumbles at just one point is guilty of breaking all of it. (James 2:10)

If we claim to be without sin, we deceive ourselves and the truth is not in us. (1 John 1:8)

...for all have sinned and fall short of the glory of God.... (Romans 3:23)

For the wages of sin is death.... (Romans 6:23)

The Son of Man will send out his angels, and they will weed out of his kingdom everything that causes sin and all who do evil. They will throw them into the fiery furnace, where there will be weeping and gnashing of teeth. (Matthew 13:41-42)

There will be weeping there, and gnashing of teeth, when you see Abraham, Isaac and Jacob and all the prophets in the kingdom of God, but you yourselves thrown out. (Luke 13:28)

We see from the above verses how emphatically God declares that we are sinners and, as such, we deserve hell. That raises the question of what, if anything, can we do to change that. In His sovereignty, God has provided a way to change our situation through our acceptance of His son Jesus Christ as Savior and Lord. Once we accept Christ, by God's mercy and because of our relationship with Christ, we will go to heaven. (For further information, see the chapter on Salvation.)

There are people who have no problem accepting the fact of heaven and hell, but they do have a problem with what takes place in this present world and in their own lives in particular. These people often get upset with God over something that happens and are quick to blame Him for their troubles or their suffering.

It is true that God has decreed all that takes place, and it is also true that God could take away their troubles and suffering. But it is equally true that their troubles and suffering are brought on by sin, beginning with Adam's and including their own—man is responsible for his sin. The penalty for sin, as we have seen, is hell.

Some people speak of hell on earth, but for those who do not accept Christ the worst is yet to come. If hell is the worst thing that can happen to us and if hell is what we deserve, then, at present (no matter what our circumstances), we are getting better than we deserve. We have no right to complain to God or question Him.

Realizing that someone may disagree with this fact, I will ask the question, Why? Are you going to tell God He is wrong? Do you know better than God? Are you wiser, more loving, more merciful than God? Are you qualified to counsel God? If so, then perhaps you could answer the questions that God asked Job.

Then the Lord answered Job out of the storm. He said: "Who is this that darkens my counsel with words without knowledge? Brace yourself like a man; I will question you, and you shall answer me. Where were you when I laid the earth's foundation? Tell me, if you understand. Who marked off its dimensions? Surely you know! Who stretched a measuring line across it? On what were its footings set, or who laid its cornerstone—while the morning stars sang together and all the angels shouted for joy? Who shut up the sea behind doors when it burst forth from the womb, when I made the clouds its garment and wrapped it in thick darkness, when I fixed limits for it and set its doors and bars in place, when I said, 'This far you may come and no farther; here is where your proud waves halt'? Have you ever given orders to the morning, or shown the dawn its place, that it might take the earth by the edges and shake the wicked out of it? The earth takes shape like clay under a seal; its features stand out like those of a garment. The wicked are denied their light, and their upraised arm is broken. Have you journeyed to the springs of the sea or walked in the recesses of the deep? Have the gates of death been shown to you? Have you seen the gates of the shadow of death?

Have you comprehended the vast expanses of the earth? Tell me, if you know all this." (Job 38:1-18)

The Lord said to Job: "Will the one who contends with the Almighty correct him? Let him who accuses God answer him!" (Job 40:1-2)

Then Job replied to the Lord: "I know that you can do all things; no plan of yours can be thwarted. You asked, 'Who is this that obscures my counsel without knowledge?' Surely I spoke of things I did not understand, things too wonderful for me to know. You said, 'Listen now, and I will speak; I will question you, and you shall answer me.' My ears had heard of you but now my eyes have seen you. Therefore I despise myself and repent in dust and ashes." (Job 42:1-6)

Sovereignty and Adam's Sin

You may agree that God is all powerful and completely sovereign, but question why Adam's sin should condemn us. If so, you are not alone. For many centuries this question has been raised and discussed by theologians, believers, and unbelievers around the world. It is a valid question; however, it is one to which no answer will be acceptable—unless our hearts are bowed before God Almighty. We must be able to say in sincerity, "Thy will be done." For it really makes no difference what our theological explanations are, nor whether or not our finite minds can grasp the complexity of it all. It matters not that we agree or disagree with what was done. The fact remains—God purposed it would be this way. As with all things, we must acknowledge that God's will is perfect.

Most Christian theologians agree that Adam is the federal head of the human race, and as such his sin of eating forbidden fruit from the tree of knowledge of good and evil was binding upon all mankind. The Bible teaches that we are held accountable for Adam's sin just as though we had committed it ourselves (example: Romans Chapter 5). The way a president represents his country would be a rough idea of how Adam represented us. A president can make agreements with others that commit and bind the people of his country to carry them out. A lawyer, who has power of attorney, can represent an individual or corporation, binding them to contracts. In a given situation, one family member may represent the rest of the family in negotiations. The captain of a football team calls the toss of the coin, and the team wins or loses the toss along with the captain.

Someone may say, Yes, but these people were elected or appointed by others and I did not appoint Adam. That is true, but God appointed Adam. Eve ate of the forbidden fruit, yet God says it was through Adam that sin entered the world. Adam was the first of the human race, and Eve was made from a part of Adam's body; therefore all mankind is descended from the one blood line of Adam.

Before the Fall, Adam and Eve did not have sinful natures, but they did after the Fall. That sinful nature has been passed down through all mankind—this is the reason we sin. We are not sinners because we sin; we sin because we are sinners—man's human nature is sinful. If Adam had not fallen and there was no death, no sickness, no heartaches, most people would be glad God had chosen Him to represent us. But knowing what happened, some people think they should have an opportunity to resist the temptation themselves and stand or fall on how they do. If you think that way, I would ask the question, Do you sin? You surely must answer, Yes, for we all sin. Then I would ask, Why do you sin?

When we were saved, we were saved from going to hell. The power of sin in our lives was broken. If we abide in Christ and let the Holy Spirit control our lives, we will not sin. As Christians, we all live for periods of time when we feel we have been walking with the Lord without conscious sin. Then that sin of commission or omission takes place. But we did not have to sin. As long as the Holy Spirit is in control of our lives, we will not sin. However, there comes a time when we realize we have taken over control and have sinned.

Now for anyone who feels he or she should have stood the test in place of Adam, I would ask you a question. If God were to choose a Christian who sinned the least to represent the human race, would that person be you? Are you more qualified, are you more obedient, do you walk closer with God than any other Christian that ever lived? Would you be more fit to represent mankind than the Apostle Paul or one of the other apostles? Are you more qualified than Moses, Isaiah, or Jeremiah? Do you live a more obedient life than Stephen, who was stoned, or those

Christians who were fed to the lions? Would your track record look better to God than all of these?

If not, it would be better to have God pick someone who loved Him more and walked closer to Him to represent you and the rest of mankind. We can have confidence that God's choosing to have Adam represent the human race was not only the best choice—it was the perfect choice. God's will, plan and purpose are all perfect. Everything God does is good and right—He can do no wrong. Furthermore, as God is sovereign, it was foreordained that Adam would fall (even though Adam did so of his own will).

Sovereignty and the Cross of Christ

It was also foreordained that Christ would come, die on the cross, and be resurrected. To bring this about, someone had to put Christ to death; moreover, there had to be a chain of events leading up to the crucifixion.

> **Men of Israel, listen to this: Jesus of Nazareth was a man accredited by God to you by miracles, wonders and signs, which God did among you through him, as you yourselves know. This man was handed over to you by God's set purpose and foreknowledge; and you, with the help of wicked men, put him to death by nailing him to the cross. (Acts 2:22-23)**

> **Indeed Herod and Pontius Pilate met together with the Gentiles and the people of Israel in this city to conspire against your holy servant Jesus, whom you anointed. They did what your power and will had decided beforehand should happen. (Acts 4:27-28)**

Some may object to Adam, but no one objects to the fact that Christ died on the cross to pay for our sins—He took our punishment upon Himself. All Christians agree that this is wonderful and that it is a great blessing. It truly is the greatest and most wonderful blessing God has bestowed on mankind. It was all part of God's plan and came about exactly as He planned. Nonetheless, it was a sinful act on the part of those who did it. God ordained it, but He is not responsible for the sin of those who committed the act. They are responsible and will be held accountable by God Almighty. Even though his betrayal was part of God's plan, Judas will have to answer for his deed.

> Then Jesus replied, "Have I not chosen you, the Twelve? Yet one of you is a devil!" (John 6:70)

> When evening came, Jesus was reclining at the table with the Twelve. And while they were eating, he said, "I tell you the truth, one of you will betray me." They were very sad and began to say to him one after the other, "Surely not I, Lord?"
> Jesus replied, "The one who has dipped his hand into the bowl with me will betray me. The Son of Man will go just as it is written about him. But woe to that man who betrays the Son of Man! It would be better for him if he had not been born."
> Then Judas, the one who would betray him, said, "Surely not I, Rabbi?"
> Jesus answered, "Yes, it is you." (Matthew 26:20-25)

> While he was still speaking, Judas, one of the Twelve, arrived. With him was a large crowd armed with swords and clubs, sent from the chief priests and the elders of the people. Now the betrayer had arranged a signal with them: "The one I kiss is the man; arrest him."
> Going at once to Jesus, Judas said, "Greetings, Rabbi!" and kissed him.
> Jesus replied, "Friend, do what you came for."
> Then the men stepped forward, seized Jesus and arrested him. With that, one of Jesus' companions reached for his sword, drew it out and struck the servant of the high priest, cutting off his ear.
> "Put your sword back in its place," Jesus said to him, "for all who draw the sword will die by the sword. Do you think I cannot call on my Father, and he will at once put at my disposal more than twelve legions of angels? But how then would the Scriptures be fulfilled that say it must happen in this way?"
> At that time Jesus said to the crowd, "Am I leading a rebellion, that you have come out with swords and clubs to capture me? Every day I sat in the temple courts teaching, and you did not arrest me. But this has all taken place that the writings of the prophets might be fulfilled...."
> (Matthew 26:47-56)

> While I was with them, I protected them and kept them safe by
> that name you gave me. None has been lost except the one
> doomed to destruction so that Scripture would be fulfilled.
> (John 17:12)

Before the world was made, God planned for Christ to come, to suffer, and to die for our sins. This was foretold in Scripture hundreds of years before it happened. Although it was foreordained by God, those who crucified Christ were responsible for the act. We cannot understand how this works, but it is the teaching of the Bible. We are not expected to understand everything in God's Word, but we are expected to believe what God tells us.

> Oh, the depth of the riches of the wisdom and knowledge of
> God! How unsearchable his judgments, and his paths beyond
> tracing out! "Who has known the mind of the Lord? Or who
> has been his counselor?" (Romans 11:33-34)

> Trust in the Lord with all your heart and lean not on your own
> understanding.... (Proverbs 3:5)

> "For my thoughts are not your thoughts, neither are your ways
> my ways," declares the Lord. "As the heavens are higher than
> the earth, so are my ways higher than your ways and my
> thoughts than your thoughts." (Isaiah 55:8-9)

When we study God's Word with a yielded heart and mind, we can know that He will reveal to us the truth of those doctrines He would have us understand—in His own time. However, He has not seen fit to explain to us many things that are above and beyond our understanding. The Trinity is the classical example of this.

The Bible teaches that there is one God who is three persons. We do not understand this. But the Bible is God's Word, and we believe God; therefore we do not have a problem with the Trinity.

For the same reasons, we should not have a problem with other difficult doctrines. For most Christians, the doctrine of the Trinity is probably easier to accept than the doctrine of the Sovereignty of God. The former is only a matter of believing about God; whereas the latter is often a point of contention with God. Too often Christians expect God to do things their way, and rebel when He does not. It is as if they think God is not aware of their situation, or else He is not concerned with doing anything about it. Some may question that He is even able to help them. They may feel that their situation is so awful that not even God can do anything about it. But, according to the Bible, they are wrong in their thinking.

God Controls Smallest to Largest Detail

Nothing exists or comes about apart from God's plan. If it did, then God would not be all powerful. His plan would be subject to change by others; therefore He would not be sovereign. Anyone who could alter God's plan, even to the slightest degree, would have to be more powerful than God—Scripture tells us no one is.

> All the peoples of the earth are regarded as nothing. He does as he pleases with the powers of heaven and the peoples of the earth. No one can hold back his hand or say to him: "What have you done?" (Daniel 4:35)

> "You are my witnesses," declares the Lord, "and my servant whom I have chosen, so that you may know and believe me and understand that I am he. Before me no god was formed, nor will there be one after me. I, even I, am the Lord, and apart from me there is no savior. I have revealed and saved and proclaimed—I, and not some foreign god among you. You are my witnesses," declares the Lord, "that I am God. Yes, and from ancient days I am he. No one can deliver out of my hand. When I act, who can reverse it?" (Isaiah 43:10-13)

> This is what the Lord says—Israel's King and Redeemer, the Lord Almighty: I am the first and I am the last; apart from me there is no God. Who then is like me? Let him proclaim it. Let him declare and lay out before me what has happened since I established my ancient people, and what is yet to come—yes, let him foretell what will come. Do not tremble, do not be afraid. Did I not proclaim this and foretell it long ago? You are my witnesses. Is there any God besides me? No, there is no other Rock; I know not one. (Isaiah 44:6-8)

God made the beginning, declared the end, and controls all that is in the middle. He controls the big events and the minute events. There are no accidents in this world and no such thing as luck—good or bad. There is also no such thing as injury or illness that happens by chance. No one is born blind or deaf by chance; intelligence or ability is not by chance; heads of government do not get there by chance. God controls the oceans, the wind and the rain. He controls the insects and the growth of vegetation. He controls individuals and nations, and He will sit in judgment of them.

The Lord brings death and makes alive; he brings down to the grave and raises up. (1 Samuel 2:6)

I form the light and create darkness, I bring prosperity and create disaster; I, the Lord, do all these things. (Isaiah 45:7)

By myself I have sworn, my mouth has uttered in all integrity a word that will not be revoked: Before me every knee will bow; by me every tongue will swear. (Isaiah 45:23)

Yours, O Lord, is the greatness and the power and the glory and the majesty and the splendor, for everything in heaven and earth is yours. Yours, O Lord, is the kingdom; you are exalted as head over all. (1 Chronicles 29:11)

For we know him who said, "It is mine to avenge; I will repay," and again, "The Lord will judge his people." It is a dreadful thing to fall into the hands of the living God. (Hebrews 10:30-31)

Then I saw a great white throne and him who was seated on it. Earth and sky fled from his presence, and there was no place for them. And I saw the dead, great and small, standing before the throne, and books were opened. Another book was opened, which is the book of life. The dead were judged according to what they had done as recorded in the books. The sea gave up the dead that were in it, and death and Hades gave up the dead that were in them, and each person was judged according to what he had done. Then death and Hades were thrown into the lake of fire. The lake of fire is the second death. If anyone's name was not found written in the book of life, he was thrown into the lake of fire. (Revelation 20:11-15)

I believe the teaching of Scripture is clear—God controls all things. He controls how fast the grass grows. Suppose it grew five feet a day—we would all be in trouble. Or suppose it rained every day or never rained at all. God's Word says even a sparrow does not fall to the ground without God knowing it.

Are not two sparrows sold for a penny? Yet not one of them will fall to the ground apart from the will of your Father. (Matthew 10:29)

This does not mean that God only knows when the sparrow will fall, but cannot keep it from falling or cause it to fall sooner. It means the sparrow falls at a time and place and under the circumstances God has decreed. If it is due to disease or injury, that is in the plan. If a man shoots it, that too is in the plan. For the man to shoot the sparrow, God must have control over the man, the sparrow, the people who manufacture the gun, and the people who sell it. If the sparrow is sitting on a tree limb at the time it is shot, then God must have control over all factors to cause the tree to grow in that place, at that time.

There would be a seemingly infinite number of things that would have to happen to bring this event about. In fact it had to start at Creation, for without Creation there would be no earth, no man, no sparrow, etc. If this event actually happened, it would be because God had ordained it before He ever made the earth. He ordained all the steps and events leading up to it. It is the same with all that takes place in God's Creation. If one man shoots another or saves another from drowning, it is all part of the sovereign plan.

Sovereignty and Man's Freedom of Choice

In examining the fact of God's sovereignty we need to be careful not to lose sight of another fact that is equally true—man is free to choose. In reality, man is almost in a constant state of choosing as he goes through his daily living. Dressing, eating, working, watching TV, reading, and playing are only a few of the many areas in which man chooses what, how, where, when, etc. He is free to think good thoughts or evil ones. When faced with making decisions, whether trivial or important, man chooses that which he wills to choose. Often, when the desire to do one thing and the need to do another come into conflict, he may feel he is forced to choose the need. However, this is not the case. He is not forced, but he thinks it is better to choose the need—so he freely wills to do so. God's Word tells us we are free to choose. Furthermore, it puts before us the choice of choosing life or death.

> This day I call heaven and earth as witnesses against you that I have set before you life and death, blessings and curses. Now choose life, so that you and your children may live and that you may love the Lord your God, listen to his voice, and hold fast to him. (Deuteronomy 30:19-20a)

> But if serving the Lord seems undesirable to you, then choose for yourselves this day whom you will serve.... (Joshua 24:15)

> Then they will call to me but I will not answer; they will look for me but will not find me. Since they hated knowledge and did not choose to fear the Lord.... (Proverbs 1:28-29)

We see that man is free to choose, but he is also accountable for his choices. He is responsible for his thoughts, decisions, and actions. These are results of the will of man. Man is not a robot. He is free to choose whatever pleases him, and he does so in every case. Therefore, we are to blame when we sin—it is the way of our flesh. We cannot fix the blame on the world or Satan. The world can entice us and Satan can tempt us, but we are responsible for yielding. There is no such thing as "the devil made me do it." He may lure us, deceive us, and tempt us; however, he cannot make us sin. He can influence us to sin, if we let him. He can lead us into sin, if we follow him—but he cannot make us sin. Satan is one of the most powerful creatures God created—much more powerful than man. The Scriptures tell us to resist the devil and be strong in the Lord.

> Submit yourselves, then, to God. Resist the devil, and he will flee from you. (James 4:7)

> Finally, be strong in the Lord and in his mighty power. Put on the full armor of God so that you can take your stand against the devil's schemes. For our struggle is not against flesh and blood, but against the rulers, against the authorities, against

the powers of this dark world and against the spiritual forces of evil in the heavenly realms. (Ephesians 6:10-12)

The Scriptures also tell us it is out of our hearts that sinful thoughts and deeds arise.

For out of the heart come evil thoughts, murder, adultery, sexual immorality, theft, false testimony, slander. (Matthew 15:19)

Sovereignty and Prayer

Because God's sovereignty extends to everything, we could continue to indefinitely explore one topic after another. However, let us bring our study to a close with a look at one final subject. It is a most important one—God's sovereignty in prayer.

I think we can agree from our study so far that what takes place has been decreed by God and it is certain to come about. Yet, we Christians talk in terms of prayer changing things, and it does. Through prayer our lives and our circumstances are changed in a very real way. However, God's eternal decree is not changed. Changes that occur as a result of prayer are changes that were decreed. When changes do not take place in response to prayer, it is because they were not decreed. The way God has decreed a life or an event to be is the way it is going to be, no matter how much prayer to the contrary. From God's perspective, the purpose of prayer is not that we should change Him, but rather that He should change us. From our perspective, one basic reason for praying is to cause God to change His mind and actions. However, God tells us in Scripture that He does not change His mind.

He who is the Glory of Israel does not lie or change his mind; for he is not a man, that he should change his mind. (1 Samuel 15:29)

I the Lord do not change. (Malachi 3:6a)

There are those places in Scripture where God says that He will do or not do something, and then He appears to change His mind. There are times when it seems that He reacts after He has done something as though He is sorry He did it—as though He had not known what the end result of His action would be. This is all for our benefit. It is God putting things on a level we can understand. Examples of this are as follows:

> The Lord saw how great man's wickedness on the earth had become, and that every inclination of the thoughts of his heart was only evil all the time. The Lord was grieved that he had made man on the earth, and his heart was filled with pain. So the Lord said, "I will wipe mankind, whom I have created, from the face of the earth—men and animals, and creatures that move along the ground, and birds of the air—for I am grieved that I have made them." (Genesis 6:5-7)

> He said to them, "This is what the Lord, the God of Israel, to whom you sent me to present your petition, says: 'If you stay in this land, I will build you up and not tear you down; I will plant you and not uproot you, for I am grieved over the disaster I have inflicted on you.'" (Jeremiah 42:9-10)

> Rend your heart and not your garments. Return to the Lord your God, for he is gracious and compassionate, slow to anger and abounding in love, and he relents from sending calamity. (Joel 2:13)

> Then he issued a proclamation in Nineveh: "By the decree of the king and his nobles: Do not let any man or beast, herd or flock, taste anything; do not let them eat or drink. But let man and beast be covered with sackcloth. Let everyone call urgently on God. Let them give up their evil ways and their violence. Who knows? God may yet relent and with compassion turn from his fierce anger so that we will not perish." When God saw what they did and how they turned from their evil ways, he had compassion and did not bring upon them the destruction he had threatened. (Jonah 3:7-10)

Relative to the above verses, we know that before God made the world He decreed what man would do. And, of course, He knew what He would do in carrying out His decree. Therefore, there is no change of mind or heart on God's part—though it may appear so to us. He makes no mistakes.

Man is the one who makes the mistakes and is continually having a change of heart and mind. Imperfect man, in an imperfect world, finds himself faced with problems or situations that he cannot resolve; therefore he turns to the One who can—the sovereign God. Whether it is a request for the salvation of a friend, the healing of a family member, or food for the poor, the one praying knows the outcome is in God's hands. From man's perspective, until the issue has been settled, there is always a possibility that God can be persuaded to grant the favor. And as long as man is not praying contrary to God's principles, I believe we can accept that as fact. However, to repeat what we must never lose sight of, this possibility is only from man's perspective. From God's perspective, the decision to grant or deny the request was made in His decree before He made the world. We are told in Acts 15:18 that all of God's works are known to Him from the beginning of the world.

When we look at the story of King Hezekiah, we see where prayer appears to have caused God to change His mind and give Hezekiah a longer life than planned. We read where God tells Hezekiah he is going to die. Hezekiah then prays, and God, in response to his prayer, gives Hezekiah fifteen more years to live.

> In those days Hezekiah became ill and was at the point of death. The prophet Isaiah son of Amoz went to him and said, "This is what the Lord says: Put your house in order, because you are going to die; you will not recover."
>
> Hezekiah turned his face to the wall and prayed to the Lord, "Remember, O Lord, how I have walked before you faithfully and with wholehearted devotion and have done what is good in your eyes." And Hezekiah wept bitterly.
>
> Before Isaiah had left the middle court, the word of the Lord came to him: "Go back and tell Hezekiah, the leader of my people, 'This is what the Lord, the God of your father David, says: I have heard your prayer and seen your tears; I will heal you. On the third day from now you will go up to the temple of the Lord. I will add fifteen years to your life. And I will deliver you and this city from the hand of the king of Assyria. I will defend this city for my sake and for the sake of my servant David.'"
>
> Then Isaiah said, "Prepare a poultice of figs." They did so and applied it to the boil, and he recovered. (2 Kings 20:1-7)

This is not a case of a man's prayer changing God's decree, but rather God's decree causing a man to pray as a means of fulfilling the decree. God had planned for Hezekiah to have the additional fifteen years, but the only way he would have them was to pray—and it was certain he would pray.

Can you imagine what might have taken place if the fifteen years, instead of being part of the eternal decree, had been a spur-of-the-moment decision on God's part? Think of the changes that would have had to have taken place in the lives of so many people around Hezekiah. They would have lived one way if Hezekiah had died, but their lives were different because he lived. Imagine over a fifteen-year period the number of lives God would have had to revise, to fit into the new plan, and the continued fallout that would have spread throughout time—the course of history would have been changed.

Go a step further and imagine what would happen if God were constantly changing His plan, in response to the prayers of people around the world. In time, what was taking place would not even resemble His original plan. We can be thankful that God's plan does not conform to our prayers, but rather our prayers conform to God's plan.

Although the Israelites were the prime recipients of salvation for hundreds of years, God had decreed that, at a point in time, He would have the Gospel taken to the Gentiles. One of the means He used was the prayer of a Gentile named Cornelius. We are not told what he prayed, but we are told his prayer was heard by God. The man God chose to send to Cornelius was the Apostle Peter, who was a Jew. It is interesting to read the account of this and see God's sovereign hand at work in carrying out His decree.

> At Caesarea there was a man named Cornelius, a centurion in what was known as the Italian Regiment. He and all his family were devout and God-fearing; he gave generously to those in need and prayed to God regularly. One day at about three in the afternoon he had a vision. He distinctly saw an angel of God, who came to him and said, "Cornelius!"
>
> Cornelius stared at him in fear. "What is it, Lord?" he asked.
>
> The angel answered, "Your prayers and gifts to the poor have come up as a memorial offering before God. Now send men to Joppa to bring back a man named Simon who is called Peter. He is staying with Simon the tanner, whose house is by the sea."
>
> When the angel who spoke to him had gone, Cornelius called two of his servants and a devout soldier who was one of

his attendants. He told them everything that had happened and sent them to Joppa.

About noon the following day as they were on their journey and approaching the city, Peter went up on the roof to pray. He became hungry and wanted something to eat, and while the meal was being prepared, he fell into a trance. He saw heaven opened and something like a large sheet being let down to earth by its four corners. It contained all kinds of four-footed animals, as well as reptiles of the earth and birds of the air. Then a voice told him, "Get up, Peter. Kill and eat."

"Surely not, Lord!" Peter replied. "I have never eaten anything impure or unclean."

The voice spoke to him a second time, "Do not call anything impure that God has made clean."

This happened three times, and immediately the sheet was taken back to heaven.

While Peter was wondering about the meaning of the vision, the men sent by Cornelius found out where Simon's house was and stopped at the gate. They called out, asking if Simon who was known as Peter was staying there.

While Peter was still thinking about the vision, the Spirit said to him, "Simon, three men are looking for you. So get up and go downstairs. Do not hesitate to go with them, for I have sent them."

Peter went down and said to the men, "I'm the one you're looking for. Why have you come?"

The men replied, "We have come from Cornelius the centurion. He is a righteous and God-fearing man, who is respected by all the Jewish people. A holy angel told him to have you come to his house so that he could hear what you have to say." Then Peter invited the men into the house to be his guests.

The next day Peter started out with them, and some of the brothers from Joppa went along. The following day he arrived in Caesarea. Cornelius was expecting them and had called together his relatives and close friends. As Peter entered the house, Cornelius met him and fell at his feet in reverence. But Peter made him get up. "Stand up," he said, "I am only a man myself."

Talking with him, Peter went inside and found a large gathering of people. He said to them: "You are well aware that it is against our law for a Jew to associate with a Gentile or visit him. But God has shown me that I should not call any man impure or unclean. So when I was sent for, I came without raising any objection. May I ask why you sent for me?"

Cornelius answered: "Four days ago I was in my house praying at this hour, at three in the afternoon. Suddenly a man in shining clothes stood before me and said, 'Cornelius, God has heard your prayer and remembered your gifts to the poor. Send to Joppa for Simon who is called Peter. He is a guest in the home of Simon the tanner, who lives by the sea.' So I sent for you immediately, and it was good of you to come. Now we are all here in the presence of God to listen to everything the Lord has commanded you to tell us."

Then Peter began to speak: "I now realize how true it is that God does not show favoritism but accepts men from every nation who fear him and do what is right. You know the message God sent to the people of Israel, telling the good news of peace through Jesus Christ, who is Lord of all. You know what has happened throughout Judea, beginning in Galilee after the baptism that John preached—how God anointed Jesus of Nazareth with the Holy Spirit and power, and how he went around doing good and healing all who were under the power of the devil, because God was with him.

We are witnesses of everything he did in the country of the Jews and in Jerusalem. They killed him by hanging him on a tree, but God raised him from the dead on the third day and caused him to be seen. He was not seen by all the people, but by witnesses whom God had already chosen—by us who ate and drank with him after he rose from the dead. He commanded us to preach to the people and to testify that he is the one whom God appointed as judge of the living and the dead. All the prophets testify about him that everyone who believes in him receives forgiveness of sins through his name."

While Peter was still speaking these words, the Holy Spirit came on all who heard the message. The circumcised believers who had come with Peter were astonished that the gift of the Holy Spirit had been poured out even on the Gentiles. For they heard them speaking in tongues and praising God.

Then Peter said, "Can anyone keep these people from being baptized with water? They have received the Holy Spirit just as we have." So he ordered that they be baptized in the name of Jesus Christ. Then they asked Peter to stay with them for a few days. (Acts chapter 10)

The apostles and the brothers throughout Judea heard that the Gentiles also had received the word of God. So when Peter went up to Jerusalem, the circumcised believers criticized him and said, "You went into the house of uncircumcised men and ate with them."

Peter began and explained everything to them precisely as it had happened: "I was in the city of Joppa praying, and in a trance I saw a vision. I saw something like a large sheet being let down from heaven by its four corners, and it came down to where I was. I looked into it and saw four-footed animals of the earth, wild beasts, reptiles, and birds of the air. Then I heard a voice telling me, "Get up, Peter. Kill and eat."

I replied, 'Surely not, Lord! Nothing impure or unclean has ever entered my mouth.'

The voice spoke from heaven a second time, 'Do not call anything impure that God has made clean.' This happened three times, and then it was all pulled up to heaven again.

Right then three men who had been sent to me from Caesarea stopped at the house where I was staying. The Spirit told me to have no hesitation about going with them. These six brothers also went with me, and we entered the man's house. He told us how he had seen an angel appear in his house and say, 'Send to Joppa for Simon who is called Peter. He will bring you a message through which you and all your household will be saved.'

As I began to speak, the Holy Spirit came on them as he had come on us at the beginning. Then I remembered what the Lord had said: 'John baptized with water, but you will be baptized with the Holy Spirit.' So if God gave them the same gift as he gave us, who believed in the Lord Jesus Christ, who was I to think that I could oppose God?"

When they heard this, they had no further objections and praised God, saying, "So then, God has granted even the Gentiles repentance unto life." (Acts 11:1-18)

God's sovereignty in prayer is another one of those paradoxes of Scripture where God has decreed how it will be; yet man is free to choose what he will pray. In Scripture, we find God attaches conditions to prayer. He tells us if we will do this then He will do that, and if we do not do this He will do something else. It is up to us to heed God's promises and admonitions. The following verses are examples:

The Lord is far from the wicked but he hears the prayer of the righteous. (Proverbs 15:29)

If I had cherished sin in my heart, the Lord would not have listened.... (Psalm 66:18)

If a man shuts his ears to the cry of the poor, he too will cry out and not be answered. (Proverbs 21:13)

The eyes of the Lord are on the righteous and his ears are attentive to their cry.... (Psalm 34:15)

...if my people, who are called by my name, will humble themselves and pray and seek my face and turn from their wicked ways, then will I hear from heaven and will forgive their sin and will heal their land. (2 Chronicles 7:14)

But your iniquities have separated you from your God; your sins have hidden his face from you, so that he will not hear. (Isaiah 59:2)

Forgive us our debts, as we also have forgiven our debtors. (Matthew 6:12)

Husbands, in the same way be considerate as you live with your wives, and treat them with respect as the weaker partner and as heirs with you of the gracious gift of life, so that nothing will hinder your prayers. (1 Peter 3:7)

When you spread out your hands in prayer, I will hide my eyes from you; even if you offer many prayers, I will not listen. Your hands are full of blood; wash and make yourselves clean. Take your evil deeds out of my sight! Stop doing wrong.... (Isaiah 1:15-16)

Therefore confess your sins to each other and pray for each other so that you may be healed. The prayer of a righteous man is powerful and effective. (James 5:16)

Throughout Scripture, God gives us instructions and examples on how to pray. Sometimes we Christians have a problem because we look at one instruction or one example and try to make that the only criteria for prayer. We must fit Scripture with Scripture to maintain the context of what is being taught. Therefore, let us look at some more verses and see if, together, they will give us a clearer

picture of God's sovereignty in prayer. We know that God tells us
not to pray vain repetitions.

> And when you pray, do not keep on babbling like pagans, for
> they think they will be heard because of their many words.
> (Matthew 6:7)

However, we see that God does tell us to be persistent in prayer.

> Then Jesus told his disciples a parable to show them that they
> should always pray and not give up. He said: "In a certain
> town there was a judge who neither feared God nor cared
> about men. And there was a widow in that town who kept
> coming to him with the plea, 'Grant me justice against my
> adversary.'
> For some time he refused. But finally he said to himself,
> 'Even though I don't fear God or care about men, yet because
> this widow keeps bothering me, I will see that she gets justice,
> so that she won't eventually wear me out with her coming!'"
> And the Lord said, "Listen to what the unjust judge says.
> And will not God bring about justice for his chosen ones, who
> cry out to him day and night? Will he keep putting them off?
> I tell you, he will see that they get justice, and quickly.
> However, when the Son of Man comes, will he find faith on the
> earth?" (Luke 18:1-8)

> ...pray continually; give thanks in all circumstances, for this is
> God's will for you in Christ Jesus. (1 Thessalonians 5:17-18)

We find God telling us that when we pray we are not to
doubt, but we are to believe that we will receive what we pray
for—then we will receive it.

> "Have faith in God," Jesus answered. "I tell you the truth, if
> anyone says to this mountain, 'Go, throw yourself into the sea,'
> and does not doubt in his heart but believes that what he says
> will happen, it will be done for him. Therefore I tell you,
> whatever you ask for in prayer, believe that you have received
> it, and it will be yours." (Mark 11:22-24)

> If any of you lacks wisdom, he should ask God, who gives
> generously to all without finding fault, and it will be given to
> him. But when he asks, he must believe and not doubt, because

> he who doubts is like a wave of the sea, blown and tossed by
> the wind. That man should not think he will receive anything
> from the Lord.... (James 1:5-7)

There are material as well as spiritual blessings which we do
not receive because we fail to ask God for them. There are also
times when, even though we do ask God, we do not receive what
we ask for because we ask for the wrong things, or for the wrong
reasons.

> You do not have, because you do not ask God. When you ask,
> you do not receive, because you ask with wrong motives, that
> you may spend what you get on your pleasures. (James 4:2b-3)

We are told if we are obedient to God we will receive
whatever we ask.

> Dear friends, if our hearts do not condemn us, we have
> confidence before God and receive from him anything we ask,
> because we obey his commands and do what pleases him.
> (1 John 3:21-22)

If we remain in Christ, we can ask whatever we wish.

> If you remain in me and my words remain in you, ask whatever
> you wish, and it will be given you. (John 15:7)

God will give us whatever we ask if we ask in the name of Christ.

> In that day you will no longer ask me anything. I tell you the
> truth, my Father will give you whatever you ask in my name.
> (John 16:23)

If we ask according to God's will, He will give us our requests.

> This is the confidence we have in approaching God: that if we
> ask anything according to his will, he hears us. And if we know
> that he hears us—whatever we ask—we know that we have
> what we asked of him. (1 John 5:14-15)

From these verses we learn that meeting certain conditions
and having a correct attitude are very important in receiving what

we ask. However, for the moment, let us look again at the last three passages. If we meet perfectly the conditions of John 15:7, what would our prayer requests be like? They would be like the requests Christ would make for us. We would, by faith, be living under His control and, in obedience, be praying according to His words and commands. Our attitude would be "not my will but Thine!"

What does it mean to pray in the name of Christ (John 16:23)? It certainly is not a special code, nor is it a name that anyone can use to receive from God anything they desire. If that were the case, men could use it as a means of satisfying their greed. But that is not the case. Praying in the name of Christ is equivalent to asking what Christ would have us ask. Christ said He came not to do His will but the will of His Father (John 6:38). Anything He would ask would conform to God's will; therefore, anything we ask in His name must conform to God's will, or Christ will not put His stamp of approval on it.

Next, we come to 1 John 5:14-15. Here we are told that if we pray according to God's will our prayers will be answered. It is implied that if we do not, our prayers will not be answered. This is what John 15:7 and John 16:23 tell us. However, here it is expressed in a manner that leaves no room for misunderstanding.

As we look at the other verses, in light of these last three, we can better understand God's sovereignty in prayer. We begin to see that our purpose in prayer is not to change God's will—it is to pray God's will. Man is not even qualified to govern his own life—why would he think he is capable of pointing out to God what needs to be done? Man does not know what the next minute holds. God knows what the vast span of centuries will bring—He is the source of all true wisdom. Our prayer (the very fact that we pray) reminds us of our dependency on God to provide our needs, and honors Him by acknowledging this truth. He tells us He knows our needs before we ask Him.

Do not be like them, for your Father knows what you need before you ask him. (Matthew 6:8)

As we fit together the different verses on prayer, a clear picture begins to come into focus. Our first consideration is that we must pray if we expect to receive. We must pray for the right things and from a heart which is rightly motivated. Our lives must reflect obedience and be pleasing to God. Our prayers must be offered in faith—not in faith that God will give us anything we ask, but faith that He will give us what He knows is best. (What parent would give a small child a poisonous snake just because he asked?) The more we walk in submission to God's will, the more faith we will have that we are praying His will.

We see that there are times when we need to persist in prayer. We may pray for the salvation of a loved one for ten years and grow weary of praying when nothing happens. However, it may be God's will for us to pray for twenty years.

One thing becomes clear as we compare verse with verse and fit them together—we must pray according to God's will to receive what we request. We know that the prayers of all men, whether granted or denied, are prayed because of God's decree. However, this does not mean that all prayer, including Christian prayer, is in accordance with God's will concerning a particular person or situation. Prayer for God to save someone who is not one of the Elect is not in accordance with God's decree for that person. It is true that God wishes that none should perish (2 Peter 3:9). However, all but the Elect will perish according to God's decree. Therefore, if we pray for a person who is non-Elect (and we certainly do not know who is Elect or non-Elect), then we cannot be praying for something that God intends to grant. We would not be praying according to God's will, in the sense of asking for something that He will grant. On the other hand, if we pray for one of the Elect to be saved, our prayer will be granted because we are praying according to God's will in the sense that this is something He will grant.

We do not receive by changing God's decree but rather by conforming to it. When we pray for something that God grants, we have conformed to His decree and prayed according to His will. Two examples of prayer requests that were decreed, and not granted (because it was not God's will to grant them), were prayed by King David and the Apostle Paul.

> Then David said to Nathan, "I have sinned against the Lord."
> Nathan replied, "The Lord has taken away your sin. You are not going to die. But because by doing this you have made the enemies of the Lord show utter contempt, the son born to you will die."

> After Nathan had gone home, the Lord struck the child that Uriah's wife had borne to David, and he became ill. David pleaded with God for the child. He fasted and went into his house and spent the nights lying on the ground. The elders of his household stood beside him to get him up from the ground, but he refused, and he would not eat any food with them.
> On the seventh day the child died. (2 Samuel 12:13-18a)

> To keep me from becoming conceited because of these surpassingly great revelations, there was given me a thorn in my flesh, a messenger of Satan, to torment me. Three times I pleaded with the Lord to take it away from me. But he said to me, "My grace is sufficient for you, for my power is made perfect in weakness." Therefore I will boast all the more gladly about my weaknesses, so that Christ's power may rest on me. (2 Corinthians 12:7-9)

There are times when some people pray for one team to win a sports contest and others pray for the opposing team. In the case of a tie, neither group receives their request. If one team wins, those praying for that team were praying for something that God had decreed would happen—a request that He would grant. The group of people praying for the team that lost were praying for something that God had not decreed to happen. The same situation, I feel sure, has occurred in wars. Both sides thinking God is with them, and both praying to Him for victory.

Let us look at prayers prayed by a person who always prayed according to God's will. That person, of course, is Jesus Christ.

> After Jesus said this, he looked toward heaven and prayed:
> "Father, the time has come. Glorify your Son, that your Son may glorify you. For you granted him authority over all people that he might give eternal life to all those you have given him. Now this is eternal life: that they may know you, the only true God, and Jesus Christ, whom you have sent. I have brought you glory on earth by completing the work you gave me to do. And now, Father, glorify me in your presence with the glory I had with you before the world began." (John 17:1-5)

> Going a little farther, he fell with his face to the ground and prayed, "My Father, if it is possible, may this cup be taken from me. Yet not as I will, but as you will." (Matthew 26:39)

When we seek God, should we not seek all that He is and all that He would have us to be? Our purpose for being is to glorify God through persevering in faith and obedience, and being conformed to the image of Christ. Only God knows what is needed to make this a reality—He knows what He is going to do in and through our lives. He knows when and how He is going to do it. Our prayers must conform to His will. Prayers prayed in the flesh will not do this. Only as we pray in the power of the Holy Spirit will this happen.

> However, as it is written: "No eye has seen, no ear has heard, no mind has conceived what God has prepared for those who love him" but God has revealed it to us by his Spirit. The Spirit searches all things, even the deep things of God. For who among men knows the thoughts of a man except the man's spirit within him? In the same way no one knows the thoughts of God except the Spirit of God. (1 Corinthians 2:9-11)

> Those who live according to the sinful nature have their minds set on what that nature desires; but those who live in accordance with the Spirit have their minds set on what the Spirit desires. (Romans 8:5)

> But you, dear friends, build yourselves up in your most holy faith and pray in the Holy Spirit. (Jude 20)

If we will do as the psalmist says and commit our ways to the Lord, trust in Him and delight ourselves in Him (Psalm 37), we will find that our wills increasingly conform to His will. Our prayers and our answers to prayers will reflect this.

Sovereignty vs Fatalism

At this point, let me caution you not to confuse God's sovereignty with fatalism. Fatalism is the belief that whatever will be, will be. In other words, some power has determined what will be, and nothing can change it. In this respect, fatalism and God's sovereignty are similar. However, there is an important difference—fatalism does not allow for second causes.

God has decreed all that will happen, and His having done so ensures that it will come about. However, He has also decreed the means by which it will happen, and these means are referred to as second causes.

If someone is sick and dying, the fatalist says it is meant to be and leaves it at that. In God's sovereignty, we turn to Him in prayer. From the Christian perspective, He may heal the person as He did King Hezekiah. If the fatalist believes there is a heaven, his approach would be this: If you are meant to go to heaven, you will go. Moreover, if you are not meant to go, you will not go. In God's sovereignty, we know that the Elect will go to heaven. However, though this is true, it is equally true that it will only come about through second causes such as preaching, missions, witnessing, etc. If fatalism were carried to the extreme, a fatalist could stand on the shore of a lake and watch a person drown—without attempting to save him. One who believes in God's sovereignty would attempt to help the person—knowing the outcome was in God's hands.

It does not take long to see that fatalism is not scriptural and therefore not compatible with Christian doctrine. On the other hand, God's sovereignty is a wonderful and comforting doctrine. It is comfort and encouragement beyond comparison to know that God has decreed all that happens, and knowing that all that happens to Christians is working to our good (to conform us more to the image of Christ and to ensure that we will persevere and endure to the end).

And we know that in all things God works for the good of those who love him, who have been called according to his purpose. For those God foreknew he also predestined to be conformed to the likeness of his Son, that he might be the firstborn among many brothers. (Romans 8:28-29)

Praise be to the God and Father of our Lord Jesus Christ! In his great mercy he has given us new birth into a living hope through the resurrection of Jesus Christ from the dead, and into an inheritance that can never perish, spoil or fade—kept in heaven for you, who through faith are shielded by God's power until the coming of the salvation that is ready to be revealed in the last time. In this you greatly rejoice, though now for a little while you may have had to suffer grief in all kinds of trials. These have come so that your faith—of greater worth than gold, which perishes even though refined by fire—may be proved genuine and may result in praise, glory and honor when Jesus Christ is revealed. Though you have not

seen him, you love him; and even though you do not see him now, you believe in him and are filled with an inexpressible and glorious joy, for you are receiving the goal of your faith, the salvation of your souls. (1 Peter 3-9)

As we seek to live our lives in the full realization of the absolute sovereignty of God, let us remember two vital points we have discussed:

1.   From God's perspective, He has decreed all that will come to pass, and nothing can change His decree.

2.   From our perspective, our attitude toward God, our actions in front of God, and our prayers to God will evoke either assistance or opposition, rewards or penalties, favor or disfavor, blessings or curses from Him. It is up to us.

Sovereignty Brings Freedom and Comfort

Believing in the totality of God's sovereignty, what should our reaction be? Having knowledge that God is sovereign is one thing, but having the wisdom to act on that knowledge is another. One thing is certain: We should seek to know what His will for our lives is and then seek to do it.

Our belief in God's sovereignty frees us from many of the world's bonds. We no longer have to contend with the numerous superstitions that affect so many people. We are not concerned about having bad luck if we walk under a ladder, break a mirror, or if a black cat crosses our path. These are a few of the traditional superstitions—I feel sure there are many others.

Also, we are not prone to develop our own peculiar superstitions. As a teenage boy, I had one. My family lived in a two-story home, and every time I would go up or down the stairs, I felt I had to tap the banister three times with my hand. If I got to the top or the bottom of the stairs and realized I had forgotten to tap it, I would go back and do it. I do not remember the specifics of why I felt the need to tap the banister, other than I thought things would go better for me if I did.

There are intelligent people who would laugh at the thought that a wooden idol could have influence over them, yet they will seriously consult Ouija boards, crystal balls, and tarot cards in making decisions. These objects have no life, no intelligence, no power, no meaning unless they are utilized by Satan and his demonic beings. Then their influence is destructive to the user and often to others.

Many people waste their time and money in an attempt to discover something about their future through the use of fortune tellers, astrology, and the channeling of the New Age Movement. In doing this, they not only ignore the One who holds their future in His hand, but they make themselves detestable to God.

> **Let no one be found among you who sacrifices his son or daughter in the fire, who practices divination or sorcery, interprets omens, engages in witchcraft, or casts spells, or who is a medium or spiritist or who consults the dead. Anyone who does these things is detestable to the Lord....**
> (Deuteronomy 18:10-12)

Believing in God's sovereignty also frees us from the problem of trying to figure out how God created the earth and all the creatures on it—we accept what God says He did. The world cannot accept God's account, so man tries to reason out an explanation. Of the explanations he has come up with, evolution is by far the most popular. Because evolution is pushed by so many in the fields of science and education, some people who profess to be Christians have embraced the theory. They acknowledge that God created the earth and all the creatures in it but rationalize that He chose to do it through evolution. This flies right into the face of sound Bible doctrine and destroys true Christian theology.

It is not just a question of how man got here (though that is important), but it is the far-reaching effects of what can we believe if man was not created according to the biblical account? If the story of Creation in Genesis cannot be believed, can we believe the rest of the Book? Why not throw out the account of Noah and The Flood? By getting rid of the creation of man, as stated in Genesis, we can get rid of being under the first sin of Adam. We can also be rid of our sinful nature or else blame it on an amoeba, a bird, or a baboon. We can throw out the teaching of Paul and others who quoted Genesis and obviously believed what it said. We can

forget about Abraham, Isaac, and Jacob, for their accounts are in
Genesis. We can pretend the Israelites were never in Egypt
because the account of how they got there is recorded in Genesis.
Then we move on to where this finally leads us—to question that
Christ is who He says He is. We can forget the references to Christ
in Genesis, and also the teachings that are based on those
references by the writers of the Bible. And when we see that Christ
quotes from Genesis (Matt. 19:4), we can question His motivation
in doing so. And when He refers to Noah and The Flood (Matt.
24:37) we can have grave and serious doubts about Him. If we
cannot believe Him about these things, how can we believe Him at
all? We apostatize and turn to a "man-made Christianity"—maybe
even total disbelief.

There are many who worship the god of their imagination.
They do not want to bow before the living God and acknowledge
His sovereignty, so they create a god of their own—one they can
control. What their god will do is determined by what they think
he should do. This god allows them to live as they choose because
his morals are no higher than their own. They do not hear their
god say, "Be ye holy for I am holy." Their god does not require
them to receive Jesus Christ as Savior and Lord for the forgiveness
of their sins. This may seem to be working out fine for the
moment, but a day of reckoning is coming when it will be too late
to change—their destiny will already be determined.

> **I told you that you would die in your sins; if you do not believe
> that I am the one I claim to be, you will indeed die in yours
> sins. (John 8:24)**

> **Whoever believes in the Son has eternal life, but whoever
> rejects the Son will not see life, for God's wrath remains on
> him. (John 3:36)**

Under God's wrath, they will acknowledge the Christ of the
Bible. God says that every knee will bow and every tongue confess
that Jesus Christ is Lord. If you do not acknowledge Christ as your
Savior and Lord in this world, you will acknowledge Him as the
Judge who condemns you in the next.

> **And being found in appearance as a man, he humbled himself
> and became obedient to death—even death on a cross!**

Therefore God exalted him to the highest place and gave him the name that is above every name, that at the name of Jesus every knee should bow, in heaven and on earth and under the earth, and every tongue confess that Jesus Christ is Lord, to the glory of God the Father. (Philippians 2:8-11)

Let us be thankful that God is sovereign, and say with Isaiah:

...all that we have accomplished you have done for us. (Isaiah 26:12)

God's sovereignty is complete, total and absolute. By God's grace, may our minds acknowledge this truth, may our hearts believe this truth, and may our mouths confess this truth.

What is salvation?

How do you get it?

Does hell exist?

Do the unsaved go there?

Salvation

The Most Important Subject

The doctrine of Salvation is the most important subject any person will ever encounter. Nuclear war, space travel, cures for cancer and AIDS are issues of great importance; however, by comparison, they pale in significance to the issue of how one gets to heaven. These issues are temporal, and no matter what their outcome, they are of short duration. But the question of salvation is a question of where one will spend eternity—in heaven or in hell. There is no other place for us to go when our spirits leave this earth, and they will leave. Eternity is not a thousand, a million, or even a billion years—it is forever. Considering this, does the reader not believe that salvation should be the topic of conversation with everyone? I marvel at the lack of interest on the part of so many concerning the question, What must I do to be saved?

The President and the Congress of the United States spend much time meeting and planning to handle issues which affect all of us. And, of course, this is necessary. But have you ever wondered why they do not spend time looking into the issue of salvation, in order to impart information to the citizens of the country? Why does the media not spend time addressing the subject? In fact, if the issue is as important as the Bible says it is, why do countries of the world not lay aside their differences and work together to try to understand God's plan of salvation?

Man's Lack of Interest

The Bible tells us why. It tells us that natural man (man without God's Spirit—unregenerate man) thinks he is too wise to believe the plan of salvation. The message of the Gospel is foolishness to him. However, God tells us that it is the wisdom of the world that is foolish.

> **For the message of the cross is foolishness to those who are perishing, but to us who are being saved it is the power of God. For it is written: "I will destroy the wisdom of the wise; the intelligence of the intelligent I will frustrate."**
>
> **Where is the wise man? Where is the scholar? Where is the philosopher of this age? Has not God made foolish the wisdom of the world? For since in the wisdom of God the world through its wisdom did not know him, God was pleased through the foolishness of what was preached to save those who believe. (1 Corinthians 1:18-21)**

Because the things of God are foolishness to natural man, he sees little need to spend time or energy in pursuit of them. He may present a pious appearance by his external actions and religious activity, but he does not seek to know the true God.

> **...there is no one who understands, no one who seeks God.** (Romans 3:11)

Although man does not seek to know God, throughout history he has felt a need to worship something or someone; therefore, he has made up his own religion. He has worshiped the sun, moon, man, animals and many other things that appealed to his unregenerate mind. He has even been foolish enough to carve idols out of wood and then bow down and worship them. For man to look to these gods for help is like a two-year-old boy asking an imaginary playmate to pull him in a wagon.

Most people in today's sophisticated world would agree that it is foolish to worship imaginary gods, but many of these same people are doing exactly that. They are worshiping a god of their imagination or a god that someone else imagined. They are even expecting that god to get them into heaven. They have not considered that their god is imaginary and without a foundation. If they would compare their counterfeit with the real God they would see the flaws, just as the flaws of counterfeit money show up when contrasted with the real thing. However, rather than study the Bible to see what God says about Himself, they will go along with something they hear—something that sounds good to them. After all, many people believe in finding a religion they can be "comfortable" with. As a result, man makes up all types of religions—including so-called Christian religions. We see many of these being practiced today.

The Lord says: "These people come near to me with their mouth and honor me with their lips, but their hearts are far from me. Their worship of me is made up only of rules taught by men." (Isaiah 29:13)

God says these manmade religions lead to spiritual death.

There is a way that seems right to a man, but in the end it leads to death. (Proverbs 16:25)

Regardless of man's complacency, rebellion, and determination to go his own way, God, because of His love and mercy, has made a way for man to be saved. Furthermore, it is the only way of salvation—through Jesus Christ.

Jesus answered, "I am the way and the truth and the life. No one comes to the Father except through me." (John 14:6)

Let us look at what God says about this vital subject. If you have never understood or believed God's plan of salvation, then let us prayerfully and seriously devote ourselves to its consideration. We need to contemplate it in its entirety, asking God to open our understanding and to give us the faith with which to believe it. Now is the time to do this, because God tells us to seek Him while He may be found.

Seek the Lord while he may be found; call on him while he is near. (Isaiah 55:6)

As God's fellow workers we urge you not to receive God's grace in vain. For he says, "In the time of my favor I heard you, and in the day of salvation I helped you." I tell you, now is the time of God's favor, now is the day of salvation.
(2 Corinthians 6:1-2)

The Fall and it's Consequences

What then does God say about salvation? Let us look at the picture from the beginning. In the book of Genesis, we see that the first two people on earth were Adam and Eve. God created them in a state of innocence and placed them in the Garden of Eden.

He told them they were free to eat from any tree in the garden, except the tree of knowledge of good and evil. They were commanded not to eat from this tree and were told that if they did they would surely die. We know from reading the account that they did eat from it and thus disobeyed God. Satan tempted Eve and she ate; then she gave some fruit of the tree to Adam, and he ate (Genesis 3:1-19). God's sentence of death was then enacted. This is referred to as the "Fall of Man," or the "Fall."

Two types of death took place as a result of the Fall. Adam and Eve were doomed to die physically; though their deaths would not take place for a number of years, they would surely die. The other death—spiritual death—took place immediately.

Whereas before the Fall, Adam and Eve had enjoyed fellowship with God in a state of innocence (no sin and no inclination to sin; no guilt and no reason to feel guilty), after the Fall they were separated from Him. They no longer had fellowship with Him. They had fallen from their state of innocence; there was sin and the inclination to sin, guilt and reason to feel guilty.

Furthermore, Adam, as head of the human race, represented all of mankind. When he fell, all mankind fell with him. We are all born under the penalty of Adam's first sin.

Therefore, just as sin entered the world through one man, and death through sin, and in this way death came to all men, because all sinned.... (Romans 5:12)

As a result, we come into the world separated from God—spiritually dead. The sinful nature which Adam and Eve had after the Fall is passed down through all generations. Therefore, all mankind is born with a sinful nature.

> Surely I was sinful at birth, sinful from the time my mother conceived me. (Psalm 51:5)

> When they sin against you—for there is no one who does not sin.... (2 Chronicles 6:36a)

> All of us have become like one who is unclean, and all our righteous acts are like filthy rags; we all shrivel up like a leaf, and like the wind our sins sweep us away. (Isaiah 64:6)

> As for you, you were dead in your transgressions and sins, in which you used to live when you followed the ways of this world and of the ruler of the kingdom of the air, the spirit who is now at work in those who are disobedient. All of us also lived among them at one time, gratifying the cravings of our sinful nature and following its desires and thought. Like the rest, we were by nature objects of wrath. (Ephesians 2:1-3)

Sin separates man from God—this separation is spiritual death.

> For the wages of sin is death.... (Romans 6:23)

> The mind of sinful man is death.... (Romans 8:6)

Separated from God, man does not understand the things of God.

> The man without the Spirit does not accept the things that come from the Spirit of God, for they are foolishness to him, and he cannot understand them because they are spiritually discerned. (1 Corinthians 2:14)

He has a passive indifference toward God or is in active rebellion toward Him.

> Why should you be beaten anymore? Why do you persist in rebellion? Your whole head is injured, your whole heart afflicted. (Isaiah 1:5)

We all, like sheep, have gone astray, each of us has turned to his own way; and the Lord has laid on him the iniquity of us all. (Isaiah 53:6)

...the sinful mind is hostile to God. (Romans 8:7)

I have listened attentively, but they do not say what is right. No one repents of his wickedness, saying, "What have I done?" Each pursues his own course like a horse charging into battle. (Jeremiah 8:6)

A man's own folly ruins his life, Yet his heart rages against the Lord. (Proverbs 19:3)

This wrong attitude toward God springs forth from man's sinful nature. This nature continues to produce sin which brings God's wrath on man in this world and in the world to come.

The wrath of God is being revealed from heaven against all the godlessness and wickedness of men who suppress the truth by their wickedness, since what may be known about God is plain to them, because God has made it plain to them. For since the creation of the world God's invisible qualities—his eternal power and divine nature—have been clearly seen, being understood from what has been made, so that men are without excuse.

For although they knew God, they neither glorified him as God nor gave thanks to him, but their thinking became futile and their foolish hearts were darkened. Although they claimed to be wise, they became fools and exchanged the glory of the immortal God for images made to look like mortal man and birds and animals and reptiles.

Therefore God gave them over in the sinful desires of their hearts to sexual impurity for the degrading of their bodies with one another. They exchanged the truth of God for a lie, and worshiped and served created things rather than the Creator—who is forever praised. Amen.

Because of this, God gave them over to shameful lusts. Even their women exchanged natural relations for unnatural ones. In the same way the men also abandoned natural relations with women and were inflamed with lust for one another. Men committed indecent acts with other men, and received in themselves the due penalty for their perversion.

Furthermore, since they did not think it worthwhile to retain the knowledge of God, he gave them over to a depraved mind, to do what ought not to be done. They have become filled with every kind of wickedness, evil, greed and depravity. They are full of envy, murder, strife, deceit and malice. They are gossips, slanderers, God-haters, insolent, arrogant and boastful; they invent ways of doing evil; they disobey their parents; they are senseless, faithless, heartless, ruthless. Although they know God's righteous decree that those who do such things deserve death, they not only continue to do these very things but also approve of those who practice them. (Romans 1:18-32)

But because of your stubbornness and your unrepentant heart, you are storing up wrath against yourself for the day of God's wrath, when his righteous judgment will be revealed. (Romans 2:5)

Man without Christ is a lost sinner and without hope of going to heaven. Even if he could stop sinning at this moment (which he cannot), he would still be condemned to hell. God's requirement is perfection, and man has the sin of Adam, in addition to his own sins, against him. The fact that we are sinners is established. To deny that we are sinners, in the light of Scripture, is to call God a liar.

If we claim to be without sin, we deceive ourselves and the truth is not in us. (1 John 1:8)

There is not a righteous man on earth who does what is right and never sins. (Ecclesiastes 7:20)

Who can say, "I have kept my heart pure; I am clean and without sin?" (Proverbs 20:9)

...for all have sinned and fall short of the glory of God.... (Romans 3:23)

Wages of Sin

We see from God's Word that we are sinners, but what does that mean? To most people who do not know Christ, it means very little. Through the hardening of his heart and the searing of his conscience, man becomes insensitive to sin. He has a tendency to minimize and rationalize, not only the evil of sin, but also the consequences of it. He reaches a point where he cannot imagine God sending anyone to hell for the "little" sins one commits. In fact, from his view, it would be unjust, and a loving God would not do it. He often reaches a point where he either believes God will not carry out punishment or he doubts that there really is a hell.

Perhaps you think this way. If so, I would ask, How did you arrive at this conclusion? What do you base it on? Can you back it up from Scripture?

Let us look at God's Word to see what He says about sin and sinners. He tells us the wages of sin is death (Romans 6:23). This means that sin deserves death, because wages are something you receive for something you do. God says the ox is entitled to eat in payment for its work and the worker is entitled to his wages.

> **For the Scripture says, "Do not muzzle the ox while it is treading out the grain," and "The worker deserves his wages."** (1 Timothy 5:18)

Man's wages change with the times, but the wages of sin have not changed since the beginning of man's existence. A man may get away with not paying another his wages, but no man gets away with sin. Sin does not go unpaid.

> **...The soul who sins is the one who will die.** (Ezekiel 18:4b)

> **...and you may be sure that your sin will find you out.** (Numbers 32:23)

Even Satan will pay up in "the lake of fire." God's justice will be carried out.

> **And the devil, who deceived them, was thrown into the lake of burning sulfur, where the beast and the false prophet had been thrown. They will be tormented day and night for ever and ever.** (Revelation 20:10)

Considering that "the wages of sin is death," let us look closer at what is meant by death as a wage of sin and how man is affected by it. The death referred to is spiritual separation from God.

...remember that at that time you were separate from Christ, excluded from citizenship in Israel and foreigners to the covenants of the promise, without hope and without God in the world. (Ephesians 2:12)

They are darkened in their understanding and separated from the life of God because of the ignorance that is in them due to the hardening of their hearts. (Ephesians 4:18)

We come into the world spiritually dead, separated from God. Most people are born, live, and die separated from God. Attempting to understand the meaning of life, coping with problems, and facing death is a heavy load to bear when separated from God. However, we want to turn our attention to what this separation means once we have departed from this world. Our bodies may be in the ground, but our spirits will go to either heaven or hell.

Way to Hell is Easy

Let us first look into how one goes to hell, and then we will discuss how one gets to heaven. To go to hell is easy—we do not have to do anything. We come into the world as sinners who are separated from God. If we do nothing to change that, we will leave the world in the same condition. Those who are separated from God are spiritually dead; when they physically die they remain spiritually dead in the next world. In the eyes of a holy God, a spiritually dead sinner is wicked and cannot live with Him. Moreover, he is to be eternally punished in hell. Let us see if this is not what God says in His Word.

He will punish those who do not know God and do not obey the gospel of our Lord Jesus. They will be punished with everlasting destruction and shut out from the presence of the Lord and from the majesty of his power....
(2 Thessalonians 1:8-9)

You are not a God who takes pleasure in evil; with you the wicked cannot dwell. (Psalm 5:4)

If your hand causes you to sin, cut it off. It is better for you to enter life maimed than with two hands to go into hell, where the fire never goes out. And if your foot causes you to sin, cut it off. It is better for you to enter life crippled than to have two feet and be thrown into hell. And if your eye causes you to sin, pluck it out. It is better for you to enter the kingdom of God with one eye than to have two eyes and be thrown into hell, where "their worm does not die, and the fire is not quenched." (Mark 9:43-48)

The Son of Man will send out his angels, and they will weed out of his kingdom everything that causes sin and all who do evil. They will throw them into the fiery furnace, where there will be weeping and gnashing of teeth. (Matthew 13:41-42)

Narrow Road to Heaven

We see how easy it is to go to hell, and that may account for the "many" who will go there. Contrary to much we hear today, getting to heaven is not easy, and that may account for the "few" who will go there.

Enter through the narrow gate. For wide is the gate and broad is the road that leads to destruction, and many enter through it. But small is the gate and narrow the road that leads to life, and only a few find it. (Matthew 7:13-14)

I do not want anyone to be confused and think I am advocating a works salvation—there is no salvation by works taught in the Bible. Being saved, according to the Bible, takes a split second and is easy. However, living the Christian life and enduring in that life to the end takes continued effort. Christ says it involves self-denial.

Then he called the crowd to him along with his disciples, and said: "If anyone would come after me, he must deny himself and take up his cross and follow me." (Mark 8:34)

...and anyone who does not take his cross and follow me is not worthy of me. (Matthew 10:38)

The Apostle Paul, who endured much in his Christian life, exhorts us to endure.

Endure hardship with us like a good soldier of Christ Jesus.
(2 Timothy 2:3)

...if we endure, we will also reign with him.
(2 Timothy 2:12)

We see that Paul, when he knew his death was eminent, could look back at his Christian life and feel confident he had endured and had done those things God had called him to do. The only thing that stood between Paul and heaven was his physical death, and his impending execution would soon remove that barrier.

For I am already being poured out like a drink offering, and
the time has come for my departure. I have fought the good
fight, I have finished the race, I have kept the faith. Now there
is in store for me the crown of righteousness, which the Lord,
the righteous Judge, will award to me on that day—and not
only to me, but also to all who have longed for his appearing.
(2 Timothy 4:6-8)

Paul referred to his Christian life as one of running a race, fighting a good fight, and keeping the faith—all of which speak of effort. Only those who truly belong to Christ are entitled to think of themselves as on the road to heaven. This is a wonderful and a blessed road. It is where Christ's joy is found and His "peace that passes all understanding" is found. Yet it is also a road of struggle with sin and temptation. A road fraught with danger from the lure of complacency and of warfare with the world, the flesh, and Satan. If you find this is not the case with you, that none of this holds true in your Christian walk, then I suggest you check your road map—you may be on the wrong road.

True and False Profession

There are those who deceive themselves and others by their response when they hear the Gospel. Christ points this out in His parable of the sower.

That same day Jesus went out of the house and sat by the lake.
Such large crowds gathered around him that he got into a boat
and sat in it, while all the people stood on the shore. Then he

told them many things in parables, saying: "A farmer went out to sow his seed. As he was scattering the seed, some fell along the path, and the birds came and ate it up. Some fell on rocky places, where it did not have much soil. It sprang up quickly, because the soil was shallow. But when the sun came up, the plants were scorched, and they withered because they had no root. Other seed fell among thorns, which grew up and choked the plants. Still other seed fell on good soil, where it produced a crop—a hundred, sixty or thirty times what was sown." (Matthew 13:1-8)

Listen then to what the parable of the sower means: When anyone hears the message about the kingdom and does not understand it, the evil one comes and snatches away what was sown in his heart. This is the seed sown along the path. The one who received the seed that fell on rocky places is the man who hears the word and at once receives it with joy. But since he has no root, he lasts only a short time. When trouble or persecution comes because of the word, he quickly falls away. The one who received the seed that fell among the thorns is the man who hears the word, but the worries of this life and the deceitfulness of wealth choke it, making it unfruitful. But the one who received the seed that fell on good soil is the man who hears the word and understands it. He produces a crop, yielding a hundred, sixty or thirty times what was sown. (Matthew 13:18-23)

In considering the four situations, we see that only in the case of the fourth does true Christian life take place. In the first case there is no understanding of the Gospel at all, but in the second and third cases there appears to be an understanding and acceptance. However, we see that there is no depth to the understanding and no real commitment in the acceptance. They are not true believers. Although outwardly they appear as any other Christian, in time the condition of their hearts becomes evident. The Bible tells us about people like this.

They went out from us, but they did not really belong to us. For if they had belonged to us, they would have remained with us; but their going showed that none of them belonged to us. (1 John 2:19)

At that time many will turn away from the faith and will betray and hate each other....(Matthew 24:10)

It would have been better for them not to have known the way of righteousness, than to have known it and then to turn their backs on the sacred command that was passed on to them. Of them the proverbs are true: "A dog returns to its vomit," and, "A sow that is washed goes back to her wallowing in the mud." (2 Peter 2:21-22)

This is a good time to ask ourselves the question I referred to at the beginning of this chapter, What must I do to be saved? We know that God's plan of salvation gives us the answer. That answer is in His Son, Jesus Christ. But just what does that mean? How does the plan work? What is involved? What does God do, and what must we do? Let us look at God's Word to see what He says.

Who is Jesus Christ?

First, we need to establish who Jesus Christ is—that will help us to understand why He is the answer to our question. Christ tells us that He came down from heaven.

For I have come down from heaven not to do my will but to do the will of him who sent me. (John 6:38)

Paul, in comparing Adam and Christ, also says Christ came from heaven.

The first man was of the dust of the earth, the second man from heaven. (1 Corinthians 15:47)

Christ was born of a virgin.

In the sixth month, God sent the angel Gabriel to Nazareth, a town in Galilee, to a virgin pledged to be married to a man named Joseph, a descendant of David. The virgin's name was Mary. The angel went to her and said, "Greetings, you who are highly favored! The Lord is with you."

Mary was greatly troubled at his words and wondered what kind of greeting this might be. But the angel said to her, "Do not be afraid, Mary, you have found favor with God. You will be with child and give birth to a son, and you are to give him the name Jesus. He will be great and will be called the Son of the Most High. The Lord God will give him the throne of his father David, and he will reign over the house of Jacob forever; his kingdom will never end."

"How will this be," Mary asked the angel, "since I am a virgin?"

The angel answered, "The Holy Spirit will come upon you, and the power of the Most High will overshadow you. So the holy one to be born will be called the Son of God." (Luke 1:26-35)

This is how the birth of Jesus Christ came about: His mother Mary was pledged to be married to Joseph, but before they came together, she was found to be with child through the Holy Spirit. Because Joseph her husband was a righteous man and did not want to expose her to public disgrace, he had in mind to divorce her quietly.

But after he had considered this, an angel of the Lord appeared to him in a dream and said, "Joseph son of David, do not be afraid to take Mary home as your wife, because what is conceived in her is from the Holy Spirit. She will give birth to a son, and you are to give him the name Jesus, because he will save his people from their sins."

All this took place to fulfill what the Lord had said through the prophet: "The virgin will be with child and will give birth to a son, and they will call him Immanuel"—which means, "God with us."

When Joseph woke up, he did what the angel of the Lord had commanded him and took Mary home as his wife. But he had no union with her until she gave birth to a son. And he gave him the name Jesus. (Matthew 1:18-25)

The Bible tells us that Christ was fully God.

In the beginning was the Word, and the Word was with God, and the Word was God. He was with God in the beginning. (John 1:1-2)

I and the Father are one. (John 10:30)

The Bible also tells us that although Christ was fully God, He lived on earth as fully man.

The Word became flesh and made his dwelling among us. (John 1:14)

For there is one God and one mediator between God and men, the man Christ Jesus.... (1 Timothy 2:5)

Christ, as man, was tempted as we are, but He did not yield to temptation. He was without sin.

Therefore, since we have a great high priest who has gone through the heavens, Jesus the Son of God, let us hold firmly to the faith we profess. For we do not have a high priest who is unable to sympathize with our weaknesses, but we have one who has been tempted in every way, just as we are—yet was without sin. (Hebrews 4:14-15)

He committed no sin, and no deceit was found in his mouth. (1 Peter 2:22)

But you know that he appeared so that he might take away our sins. And in him is no sin. (1 John 3:5)

The Bible teaches that Christ came to live a life of obedience to the law and to fulfill the prophecies about His life, death, and resurrection.

Do not think that I have come to abolish the Law or the Prophets; I have not come to abolish them but to fulfill them. (Matthew 5:17)

We see God prophesying in the Old Testament, hundreds of years before Christ was born, that Christ would come, suffer, and die to atone for our sins. We then see these prophecies being fulfilled in the New Testament.

I am poured out like water, and all my bones are out of joint. My heart has turned to wax; it has melted away within me. My strength is dried up like a potsherd, and my tongue sticks to the roof of my mouth; you lay me in the dust of death. Dogs have surrounded me; a band of evil men has encircled me, they have pierced my hands and my feet. I can count all my bones; people stare and gloat over me. They divide my garments among them and cast lots for my clothing. (Psalm 22:14-18)

Who has believed our message and to whom has the arm of the
Lord been revealed? He grew up before him like a tender
shoot, and like a root out of dry ground. He had no beauty or
majesty to attract us to him, nothing in his appearance that we
should desire him. He was despised and rejected by men, a
man of sorrows, and familiar with suffering. Like one from
whom men hide their faces he was despised, and we esteemed
him not.

Surely he took up our infirmities and carried our sorrows,
yet we considered him stricken by God, smitten by him, and
afflicted. But he was pierced for our transgressions, he was
crushed for our iniquities; the punishment that brought us
peace was upon him, and by his wounds we are healed. We all,
like sheep, have gone astray, each of us has turned to his own
way; and the Lord has laid on him the iniquity of us all.

He was oppressed and afflicted, yet he did not open his
mouth; he was led like a lamb to the slaughter, and as a sheep
before her shearers is silent, so he did not open his mouth. By
oppression and judgment he was taken away. And who can
speak of his descendants? For he was cut off from the land of
the living; for the transgression of my people he was stricken.
He was assigned a grave with the wicked, and with the rich in
his death, though he had done no violence, nor was any deceit
in his mouth.

Yet it was the Lord's will to crush him and cause him to
suffer, and though the Lord makes his life a guilt offering, he
will see his offspring and prolong his days, and the will of the
Lord will prosper in his hand. After the suffering of his soul,
he will see the light of life and be satisfied; by his knowledge
my righteous servant will justify many, and he will bear their
iniquities. Therefore I will give him a portion among the great,
and he will divide the spoils with the strong, because he
poured out his life unto death, and was numbered with the
transgressors. For he bore the sin of many, and made
intercession for the transgressors. (Isaiah Chapter 53)

Jesus took the Twelve aside and told them, "We are going up
to Jerusalem, and everything that is written by the prophets
about the Son of Man will be fulfilled. He will be handed over
to the Gentiles. They will mock him, insult him, spit on him,
flog him and kill him. On the third day he will rise again."
(Luke 18:31-33)

Then the governor's soldiers took Jesus into the Praetorium and gathered the whole company of soldiers around him. They stripped him and put a scarlet robe on him, and then twisted together a crown of thorns and set it on his head. They put a staff in his right hand and knelt in front of him and mocked him. "Hail, king of the Jews!" they said. They spit on him, and took the staff and struck him on the head again and again. After they had mocked him, they took off the robe and put his own clothes on him. Then they led him away to crucify him.

As they were going out, they met a man from Cyrene, named Simon, and they forced him to carry the cross. They came to a place called Golgotha (which means The Place of the Skull). There they offered Jesus wine to drink, mixed with gall; but after tasting it, he refused to drink it. When they had crucified him, they divided up his clothes by casting lots. And sitting down, they kept watch over him there. Above his head they placed the written charge against him: THIS IS JESUS, THE KING OF THE JEWS. Two robbers were crucified with him, one on his right and one on his left. Those who passed by hurled insults at him, shaking their heads and saying, "You who are going to destroy the temple and build it in three days, save yourself! Come down from the cross, if you are the Son of God!" (Matthew 27:27-40)

Very early in the morning, the chief priests, with the elders, the teachers of the law and the whole Sanhedrin, reached a decision. They bound Jesus, led him away and handed him over to Pilate.

"Are you the king of the Jews?" asked Pilate. "Yes, it is as you say," Jesus replied.

The chief priests accused him of many things. So again Pilate asked him, "Aren't you going to answer? See how many things they are accusing you of."

But Jesus still made no reply, and Pilate was amazed. (Mark 15:1-5)

When the soldiers crucified Jesus, they took his clothes, dividing them into four shares, one for each of them, with the undergarment remaining. This garment was seamless, woven in one piece from top to bottom. "Let's not tear it," they said to one another. "Let's decide by lot who will get it." This happened that the Scripture might be fulfilled which said, "They divided my garments among them and cast lots for my clothing." So this is what the soldiers did. (John 19:23-24)

**It is written: "And he was numbered with the transgressors";
and I tell you that this must be fulfilled in me. Yes, what is
written about me is reaching its fulfillment.** (Luke 22:37)

Sinless Christ Suffered for Sinful Man

Let us consider what was required for Christ to pay for our
sins. We see, in the Bible, how awful it is for anyone who goes to
hell. As a result, we cannot begin to imagine how much Christ
suffered to pay for every sin of all those who will be saved
throughout the history of mankind. It is evident from Scripture
that Christ, when He was in the garden of Gethsemane, was aware
that what He was going to go through would be something awful.

**He took Peter and the two sons of Zebedee along with him,
and he began to be sorrowful and troubled. Then he said to
them, "My soul is overwhelmed with sorrow to the point of
death. Stay here and keep watch with me."** (Matthew 26:37-38)

**And being in anguish, he prayed more earnestly, and his sweat
was like drops of blood falling to the ground.** (Luke 22:44)

**Going a little farther, he fell with his face to the ground and
prayed, "My Father, if it is possible, may this cup be taken
from me. Yet not as I will, but as you will."** (Matthew 26:39)

**He went away a second time and prayed, "My Father, if it is
not possible for this cup to be taken away unless I drink it,
may your will be done."** (Matthew 26:42)

Mankind's transgressions of a holy God's perfect and righteous
law called for great punishment. In addition, in order to atone for
these sins, it required the person who would be inflicted with this
punishment to be perfect, righteous, and of great value. Only
Christ could meet these requirements. Christ, as man, lived a
perfect and sinless life, and was obedient to the Law in thought,
word, and deed. He did this as man—not as God. So we see that
Christ met the qualifications of being the perfect and righteous
man.

Throughout history, man has placed great worth on kings and
princes. Great prices have been paid for their safety and
well-being. However, none of them were perfect and righteous as

was the man Christ. Moreover, He was the only begotten Son of the living God. Who is able to imagine the worth of the Son of God? Furthermore, not only was He the Son of God, but He was God Himself in human form. He was of infinite value! This is the Christ who suffered and died so that our sins could be forgiven. Let us always remember: He did not have to die for us, but out of His love and mercy, He chose to do so.

Who, being in very nature God, did not consider equality with God something to be grasped, but made himself nothing, taking the very nature of a servant, being made in human likeness. And being found in appearance as a man, he humbled himself and became obedient to death—even death on a cross! (Philippians 2:6-8)

Jesus replied, "Friend, do what you came for."
Then the men stepped forward, seized Jesus and arrested him. With that, one of Jesus' companions reached for his sword, drew it out and struck the servant of the high priest, cutting off his ear.
"Put your sword back in its place," Jesus said to him, "for all who draw the sword will die by the sword. Do you think I cannot call on my Father, and he will at once put at my disposal more than twelve legions of angels? But how then would the Scriptures be fulfilled that say it must happen in this way?" (Matthew 26:50-54)

I am the good shepherd; I know my sheep and my sheep know me—just as the Father knows me and I know the Father—and I lay down my life for the sheep. I have other sheep that are not of this sheep pen. I must bring them also. They too will listen to my voice, and there shall be one flock and one shepherd. The reason my Father loves me is that I lay down my life—only to take it up again. No one takes it from me, but I lay it down of my own accord. I have authority to lay it down and authority to take it up again. This command I received from my Father. (John 10:14-18)

How much more, then, will the blood of Christ, who through the eternal Spirit offered himself unblemished to God, cleanse our consciences from acts that lead to death, so that we may serve the living God! (Hebrews 9:14)

There had to be punishment for our sins, and Christ took this punishment upon Himself. He was punished just as though He had committed all the sins we have committed or ever will commit. He died for our past, present, and future sins. God's wrath was poured out on Christ. Although the physical suffering He underwent was awful, it was nothing compared to the anguish of His being separated from God. When we think of Christ hanging on the cross, we can think of all our sins hanging there—He was punished for each and every one of them. God says He was made sin for us. He was a sin offering.

> **He himself bore our sins in his body on the tree, so that we might die to sins and live for righteousness; by his wounds you have been healed.** (1 Peter 2:24)

> **Therefore, there is now no condemnation for those who are in Christ Jesus, because through Christ Jesus the law of the Spirit of life set me free from the law of sin and death. For what the law was powerless to do in that it was weakened by the sinful nature, God did by sending his own Son in the likeness of sinful man to be a sin offering. And so he condemned sin in sinful man....** (Romans 8:1-3)

> **God made him who had no sin to be sin for us, so that in him we might become the righteousness of God.**
> (2 Corinthians 5:21)

> **For Christ died for sins once for all, the righteous for the unrighteous, to bring you to God....** (1 Peter 3:18)

The Resurrection of Christ

We move now to the apex of the Christian faith—the resurrection of Jesus Christ. It is the heart of Christianity, around which everything else revolves.

Without the Resurrection nothing else would matter. If Christ was not resurrected then we have believed a lie, and we have no hope of heaven. Moreover, if what the Bible says about Christ is a lie, then we have no reason to believe in the God of the Bible. We are left with no absolutes. Therefore, there is no real purpose or meaning to life and no expectation of anything good on the other side of death—there is only the fear of the unknown. God tells us that if Christ is not risen then we have believed in vain.

> **And if Christ has not been raised, your faith is futile; you are still in your sins.** (1 Corinthians 15:17)

We can thank our God that He has provided so much evidence for, and so many eyewitnesses to, the Resurrection. There are a number of good books attesting to the amount of evidence for the resurrection of Christ. We will not attempt to pursue this here but will look at what God says in His Word. First, we see that Christ said He was the Resurrection.

> **Jesus said to her, "I am the resurrection and the life. He who believes in me will live, even though he dies; and whoever lives and believes in me will never die. Do you believe this?"** (John 11:25-26)

Christ also predicted He would rise on the third day.

> **He then began to teach them that the Son of Man must suffer many things and be rejected by the elders, chief priests and teachers of the law, and that he must be killed and after three days rise again.** (Mark 8:31)

God raised Christ from the dead confirming that His work was complete and successful. It also confirmed that Christ was who He claimed to be.

> **For he has set a day when he will judge the world with justice by the man he has appointed. He has given proof of this to all men by raising him from the dead.** (Acts 17:31)

I believe the eyewitness accounts of the apostles to be overwhelming evidence of Christ's resurrection. These were sensible and practical men who had been with Christ before His death, had been taught by Christ, and had seen Him work many miracles. Yet, they deserted Him when He was arrested. Peter even denied Him in words. However, after seeing the resurrected Christ, they were bold to proclaim the Gospel—even in the face of hardship and a martyr's death. The only explanation for the change in them is the risen Christ. In fact, an essential qualification to be an apostle was that one must have seen the risen Christ.

> Therefore it is necessary to choose one of the men who have been with us the whole time the Lord Jesus went in and out among us, beginning from John's baptism to the time when Jesus was taken up from us. For one of these must become a witness with us of his resurrection. (Acts 1:21-22)

The apostle Paul, though he was not one of the original Twelve, was also an eyewitness of the risen Christ, on the road to Damascus. His conversion from persecutor to disciple, his changed life, and martyr's death are strong testimony for the fact of the Resurrection. Let us look at a few of the verses that confirm the belief of the apostles.

> God has raised this Jesus to life, and we are all witnesses of the fact. (Acts 2:32)

> Now Thomas (called Didymus), one of the Twelve, was not with the disciples when Jesus came. So the other disciples told him, "We have seen the Lord!"
> But he said to them, "Unless I see the nail marks in his hands and put my finger where the nails were, and put my hand into his side, I will not believe it."
> A week later his disciples were in the house again, and Thomas was with them. Though the doors were locked, Jesus came and stood among them and said, "Peace be with you!" Then he said to Thomas, "Put your finger here; see my hands. Reach out your hand and put it into my side. Stop doubting and believe."
> Thomas said to him, "My Lord and my God!"
> Then Jesus told him, "Because you have seen me, you have believed; blessed are those who have not seen and yet have believed." (John 20:24-29)

> You know what has happened throughout Judea, beginning in Galilee after the baptism that John preached—how God anointed Jesus of Nazareth with the Holy Spirit and power, and how he went around doing good and healing all who were under the power of the devil, because God was with him.
> We are witnesses of everything he did in the country of the Jews and in Jerusalem. They killed him by hanging him on

a tree, but God raised him from the dead on the third day and caused him to be seen. He was not seen by all the people, but by witnesses whom God had already chosen—by us who ate and drank with him after he rose from the dead.
(Acts 10:37-41)

He was delivered over to death for our sins and was raised to life for our justification. (Romans 4:25)

By his power God raised the Lord from the dead, and he will raise us also. (1 Corinthians 6:14)

Praise be to the God and Father of our Lord Jesus Christ! In his great mercy he has given us new birth into a living hope through the resurrection of Jesus Christ from the dead....
(1 Peter 1:3)

You killed the author of life, but God raised him from the dead. We are witnesses of this. (Acts 3:15)

There were other followers who saw Christ, such as the women who went to the grave. Paul tells us there were over five hundred people who saw Him at one time, and he indicates that, at the time of his writing, most of those five hundred were still living. If someone doubted Paul they could check with one of them.

The angel said to the women, "Do not be afraid, for I know that you are looking for Jesus, who was crucified. He is not here; he has risen, just as he said. Come and see the place where he lay. Then go quickly and tell his disciples: 'He has risen from the dead and is going ahead of you into Galilee. There you will see him.' Now I have told you."
(Matthew 28:5-7)

Now, brothers, I want to remind you of the gospel I preached to you, which you received and on which you have taken your stand. By this gospel you are saved, if you hold firmly to the word I preached to you. Otherwise, you have believed in vain.
For what I received I passed on to you as of first importance: that Christ died for our sins according to the Scriptures, that he was buried, that he was raised on the third day according to the Scriptures, and that he appeared to Peter,

**and then to the Twelve. After that, he appeared to more than
five hundred of the brothers at the same time, most of whom
are still living, though some have fallen asleep. Then he
appeared to James, then to all the apostles, and last of all he
appeared to me also, as to one abnormally born.**
(1 Corinthians 15:1-8)

At the close of His resurrection appearances, Christ was taken
up to heaven.

**When he had led them out to the vicinity of Bethany, he lifted
up his hands and blessed them. While he was blessing them,
he left them and was taken up into heaven. Then they
worshiped him and returned to Jerusalem with great joy. And
they stayed continually at the temple, praising God.**
(Luke 24:50-53)

By way of review, we see that we are sinners who are lost in
our sins and headed for hell. We also see that Christ came, lived
a sinless life, then suffered and died to pay the penalty for our sins.
Moreover, God has shown His approval and acceptance of Christ's
sacrifice by resurrecting Him and seating Him at His right hand.
In view of these facts, let us turn once again to the question which
was asked earlier: What must I do to be saved?

What Must I Do?—the Question Answered

The question is not what do others do, or what do others say
I should do. It is not even what do I think I should do. The
question is: What must I do? It is apparent that, in the face of the
circumstances, I must do something to be saved from the situation
I am in. To do nothing means I will spend eternity in hell. To do
the wrong thing produces the same result. Therefore, it is
imperative that I discover what I must do to be saved and then do
it. Never again will I face such a crucial question—a question with
such devastating consequences from a wrong response but such
blessed results from a correct one. The question is asked in the
Bible and in the heart of man; the answer is found in the Bible and
in the heart of God. Let us look further.

He then brought them out and asked, "Sirs, what must I do to be saved?"

They replied, "Believe in the Lord Jesus, and you will be saved...." (Acts 16:30-31)

For God so loved the world that he gave his one and only Son, that whoever believes in him shall not perish but have eternal life. For God did not send his Son into the world to condemn the world, but to save the world through him. Whoever believes in him is not condemned, but whoever does not believe stands condemned already because he has not believed in the name of God's one and only Son. (John 3:16-18)

The Father loves the Son and has placed everything in his hands. Whoever believes in the Son has eternal life, but whoever rejects the Son will not see life, for God's wrath remains on him. (John 3:35-36)

But he continued, "You are from below; I am from above. You are of this world; I am not of this world. I told you that you would die in your sins; if you do not believe that I am the one I claim to be, you will indeed die in your sins." (John 8:23-24)

We see that to be saved we must believe in Jesus Christ. But just what does it mean to believe in Christ, and how can we know if we believe or not? According to the Bible, to believe in Christ means to trust in and rely upon Him.

There are many people who say they believe in Christ when in reality they merely believe "about" Him—they are not trusting in Him. They are like a man unable to swim who is holding onto his capsized boat a good distance off an ocean beach. The lifeguard sees the man and swims out to the boat. The man knows who the lifeguard is and that he has an enviable reputation. He has saved many from drowning and has never lost a swimmer. The lifeguard tells the man to let go of the boat, lie back in the water, and he will carry him into shore. "But, I cannot swim," the man says. "I do not want you to swim, just lie still and I will get you to shore safely. Don't you believe I can?" replies the lifeguard. "Yes, I believe you can, but I am afraid," the man says. The lifeguard, seeing it is beginning to get dark and the tide is changing, tells the man to trust him and let him save him. Otherwise, the boat will drift out into the darkness, and he may never be found.

Some people in this situation, though they believe what they have heard about the lifeguard, hesitate to place their lives in his hands. Unable to swim, they realize they will drown if the lifeguard cannot pull them in. Perhaps the water is too rough, the distance too far, or the lifeguard may get a muscle cramp. Putting themselves in his hands, they have no control over whether they live or die. However, as long as they hold onto the boat, they feel secure. At least they have some control over what happens to them. And who knows, maybe they will not drift out. Maybe a boat will come along, or maybe something else will happen. Thinking this way they continue to cling to the boat and drift out into the ocean and the darkness. Others act on their belief, let go of the boat, and trust the lifeguard to take them in to shore.

This is the way it is when people say they believe in Christ. Some believe about Him but are not willing to trust Him to save them. Others, acting on their belief, trust Him for their salvation. Each of us who professes to believe that Christ is our Savior and Lord needs to consider: Is He truly? Do I have only a head knowledge (an intellectual acceptance) of Him, or have I acted on that belief and committed my life to Him?

Some readers may ask, what else must I do in addition to trusting Christ? The answer from Scripture is, Nothing. In fact, any attempt to do anything else (trusting in anyone else or our own deeds) indicates that one is not trusting and relying on Christ alone, and therefore is not saved.

> "You do not want to leave too, do you?" Jesus asked the Twelve. Simon Peter answered him, "Lord, to whom shall we go? You have the words of eternal life. We believe and know that you are the Holy One of God." (John 6:67-69)

> Salvation is found in no one else, for there is no other name under heaven given to men by which we must be saved. (Acts 4:12)

> ...know that a man is not justified by observing the law, but by faith in Jesus Christ. So we, too, have put our faith in Christ Jesus that we may be justified by faith in Christ and not by observing the law, because by observing the law no one will be justified. (Galatians 2:16)

Erroneous Views of Salvation

Many people find God's plan of salvation to be offensive or too simplistic.

...but we preach Christ crucified: a stumbling block to Jews and foolishness to Gentiles.... (1 Corinthians 1:23)

Whether we find the preaching of Christ crucified to be a stumbling block or foolishness, the result is the same. We reject Christ and neglect our salvation. In fleshly wisdom and pride, man turns down the free gift of eternal life and then sets out to work to attain it. He thinks he can merit it through his own efforts. However, the Bible makes it clear that no one can earn salvation through his or her own efforts and deeds. Attempting to do so puts us under the Law, and we must keep the Law to perfection (which none of us can do); otherwise we are accursed and destined for hell.

Therefore no one will be declared righteous in his sight by observing the law; rather, through the law we become conscious of sin. (Romans 3:20)

For we maintain that a man is justified by faith apart from observing the law. (Romans 3:28)

All who rely on observing the law are under a curse, for it is written: "Cursed is everyone who does not continue to do everything written in the Book of the Law." (Galatians 3:10)

You who are trying to be justified by law have been alienated from Christ; you have fallen away from grace. (Galatians 5:4)

For whoever keeps the whole law and yet stumbles at just one point is guilty of breaking all of it. (James 2:10)

Attempting to obtain salvation by being obedient to God's laws, by living a good life, by doing good works was where the Israelites went wrong. Instead of receiving Christ by faith, as their Savior and Lord, they stumbled over Him, rejected Him and sought to earn their salvation by works.

> ...but Israel, who pursued a law of righteousness, has not
> attained it. Why not? Because they pursued it not by faith but
> as if it were by works. They stumbled over the "stumbling
> stone." (Romans 9:31-32)

Even though they were zealous in their efforts, it was to no
avail as man cannot make himself right with God. There is nothing
he can do to merit salvation. He must trust the one who is
righteous (Jesus Christ) and then God will impute Christ's
righteousness to the man. This is what the Israelites who were
saved did, what the Gentiles who were saved did, and what anyone
who would be saved must do, whether Jew or Gentile.

> Is God the God of Jews only? Is he not the God of Gentiles
> too? Yes, of Gentiles too, since there is only one God, who will
> justify the circumcised by faith and the uncircumcised through
> that same faith. (Romans 3:29-30)

> For there is no difference between Jew and Gentile—the same
> Lord is Lord of all and richly blesses all who call on him, for,
> "Everyone who calls on the name of the Lord will be saved."
> (Romans 10:12-13)

Paul tells us that Abraham was not saved by good works but
through faith. He also tells us that David understood salvation is
not by works.

> What then shall we say that Abraham, our forefather,
> discovered in this matter? If, in fact, Abraham was justified by
> works, he had something to boast about—but not before God.
> What does the Scripture say? "Abraham believed God, and it
> was credited to him as righteousness."
> Now when a man works, his wages are not credited to him
> as a gift, but as an obligation. However, to the man who does
> not work but trusts God who justifies the wicked, his faith is
> credited as righteousness. David says the same thing when he
> speaks of the blessedness of the man to whom God credits
> righteousness apart from works:
> "Blessed are they whose transgressions are forgiven, whose
> sins are covered. Blessed is the man whose sin the Lord will
> never count against him." (Romans 4:1-8)

Christ tells us that Abraham looked forward to His coming.

Your father Abraham rejoiced at the thought of seeing my day; he saw it and was glad. (John 8:56)

Some people believe that being born in a Christian country or Christian family makes them a Christian. Others think that being a member of a church qualifies them. However, one does not automatically become a Christian because of one's citizenship, family heritage, or church membership. If that were the case, there would have been no need for Christ to come and die. But if Christ did not come, the penalty for our sins would still be unpaid. Citizenship, family heritage, or church membership cannot pay for sins. Only Christ can do that.

Still others think that if they just acknowledge there is a God and that Jesus Christ is the Son of God, they will go to heaven. Even the devil and his demons acknowledge God and Christ.

Just then a man in their synagogue who was possessed by an evil spirit cried out, "What do you want with us, Jesus of Nazareth? Have you come to destroy us? I know who you are—the Holy One of God!" (Mark 1:23-24)

...and Jesus healed many who had various diseases. He also drove out many demons, but he would not let the demons speak because they knew who he was. (Mark 1:34)

You believe that there is one God. Good! Even the demons believe that—and shudder. (James 2:19)

There are also those people who are so pleased with themselves that they are confident God will be pleased with them too. They concentrate only on their external actions and not the condition of their hearts. They overlook the many things they do or fail to do, that God calls sin. They pride themselves that they do not rob, murder, commit adultery, etc. By comparing themselves with those who do these things, they feel they are doing fine. They seem unaware that the real yardstick by which we should measure ourselves is the life of Christ—His sinless and perfect life. Jesus spoke about this self-righteousness which some people have.

> To some who were confident of their own righteousness and looked down on everybody else, Jesus told this parable: "Two men went up to the temple to pray, one a Pharisee and the other a tax collector. The Pharisee stood up and prayed about himself: 'God, I thank you that I am not like other men—robbers, evildoers, adulterers—or even like this tax collector. I fast twice a week and give a tenth of all I get.'
>
> But the tax collector stood at a distance. He would not even look up to heaven, but beat his breast and said, 'God, have mercy on me, a sinner.'
>
> I tell you that this man, rather than the other, went home justified before God. For everyone who exalts himself will be humbled, and he who humbles himself will be exalted."
> (Luke 18:9-14)

From the human viewpoint, there are some people who are good and others who are bad. However, from God's viewpoint, even the best of men are sinners—all need cleansing from their sins. Only the shed blood of Christ can do that. No matter how good a life (humanly speaking) a person lives, how much they do for their fellow man, what sacrifices they make or how committed and devoted they are to the religion they embrace, they cannot be saved unless they accept Jesus Christ as Savior and Lord—trusting His shed blood to cover their sins.

Some people rely on their faith for their salvation. They are more concerned with how they believe than with what they believe. They think if they have strong enough faith they will get to heaven. But faith never saved anyone. It is Christ who saves. In and of itself, faith has no power. It is not a dynamic force that can impart spiritual life, physical healing or cause much-needed rain. However, faith is essential. Although Christ saves us, it is through our faith that He does so.

> For in the gospel a righteousness from God is revealed, a righteousness that is by faith from first to last, just as it is written: "The righteous will live by faith." (Romans 1:17)

Many people hear the Gospel, but unless they believe it and receive Christ through faith, it does not benefit them.

> Therefore, since the promise of entering his rest still stands, let us be careful that none of you be found to have fallen short

of it. **For we also have had the gospel preached to us, just as they did; but the message they heard was of no value to them, because those who heard did not combine it with faith.** (Hebrews 4:1-2)

The Bible tells us that anything we do that is not by faith is sin.

...and everything that does not come from faith is sin. (Romans 14:23)

We are saved by God's grace, through faith in Christ.

This righteousness from God comes through faith in Jesus Christ to all who believe. (Romans 3:22)

It is also through our faith, and because of our faith, that God blesses us in many ways. However, we must remember that it is God who is blessing us—our faith is only the instrument He uses. Moreover, God only does what He has decreed to do. No matter how much faith we have about a matter, if it is contrary to His decree, it will not come about. (See the chapter on Sovereignty.)

There is a popular misconception of faith being taught and believed by many—"name it and claim it." If you want something you confess it, and by faith you claim it as yours. If you have faith that is strong enough, you will get it—the sky is the limit. However, it is not how much faith we have that counts, but rather the object of our faith. For example: Two men are in an airplane which develops motor trouble and catches on fire. The pilot tells his passenger they will have to jump. The passenger is afraid and wonders if his parachute is in good condition. Hopeful that it is, he jumps, and the chute performs perfectly.

The pilot is very confident his chute is good, and he jumps, unconcerned. However, his chute fails to open and he falls to his death. Now, the pilot had much stronger faith in his chute than the passenger had in his; however, the object of his faith was defective. It was unable to do what he had faith it would do.

There are many people today who are like that pilot. They have strong faith, but the object of their faith is unable to save them. Their faith may be in a person whose teaching they follow. It may be in a god of their imagination, in their church or religion, in the money they give to charity, or in their lifestyle. But any faith, other than faith in Jesus Christ, is a misplaced faith. Like the pilot's chute, the object of that faith will prove to be defective and unable to save them.

There is one other false belief that I think should be mentioned here—Universalism. This is a popular belief and one that many people hold. We see why it is so popular when we understand that Universalism is the belief that everyone will go to heaven. It matters not what religion you embrace or whether you even have a religion. You can be a good person or a very bad person—all go to heaven. This belief is so far from the truth of Scripture that it is difficult to see how anyone could believe it. However, the Bible tells us that there will be those who will turn away from sound doctrine.

> **For the time will come when men will not put up with sound doctrine. Instead, to suit their own desires, they will gather around them a great number of teachers to say what their itching ears want to hear. They will turn their ears away from the truth and turn aside to myths.** (2 Timothy 4:3-4)

There are many verses in the Bible which indicate that not everyone goes to heaven—many go to hell. The following verses attest to this truth:

> **Do you not know that the wicked will not inherit the kingdom of God? Do not be deceived: Neither the sexually immoral nor idolaters nor adulterers nor male prostitutes nor homosexual offenders nor thieves nor the greedy nor drunkards nor slanderers nor swindlers will inherit the kingdom of God.** (1 Corinthians 6:9-10)

> **Whoever believes in the Son has eternal life, but whoever rejects the Son will not see life, for God's wrath remains on him.** (John 3:36)

> **For the message of the cross is foolishness to those who are perishing, but to us who are being saved it is the power of God.** (1 Corinthians 1:18)

> **Do not be amazed at this, for a time is coming when all who are in their graves will hear his voice and come out—those who**

have done good will rise to live, and those who have done evil will rise to be condemned. (John 5:28-29)

Not everyone who says to me, "Lord, Lord," will enter the kingdom of heaven, but only he who does the will of my Father who is in heaven. Many will say to me on that day, "Lord, Lord, did we not prophesy in your name, and in your name drive out demons and perform many miracles?" Then I will tell them plainly, "I never knew you. Away from me, you evildoers!" (Matthew 7:21-23)

Then I saw a great white throne and him who was seated on it. Earth and sky fled from his presence, and there was no place for them. And I saw the dead, great and small, standing before the throne, and books were opened. Another book was opened, which is the book of life. The dead were judged according to what they had done as recorded in the books. The sea gave up the dead that were in it, and death and Hades gave up the dead that were in them, and each person was judged according to what he had done. Then death and Hades were thrown into the lake of fire. The lake of fire is the second death. If anyone's name was not found written in the book of life, he was thrown into the lake of fire. (Revelation 20:11-15)

When the Son of Man comes in his glory, and all the angels with him, he will sit on his throne in heavenly glory. All the nations will be gathered before him, and he will separate the people one from another as a shepherd separates the sheep from the goats. He will put the sheep on his right and the goats on his left.

Then the King will say to those on his right, "Come, you who are blessed by my Father; take your inheritance, the kingdom prepared for you since the creation of the world."

Then he will say to those on his left, "Depart from me, you who are cursed, into the eternal fire prepared for the devil and his angels."

Then they will go away to eternal punishment, but the righteous to eternal life. (Matthew 25:31-34,41,46)

Death and Judgment

Most people, Christian and non-Christian alike, do not want to die. They enjoy life, their families, and their friends. Many feel needed by others, and this gives them a feeling of usefulness and satisfaction. None want the physical pain that often accompanies death. However, each of us must die at our appointed time. Then, after death, comes the judgment.

Just as man is destined to die once, and after that to face judgment.... (Hebrews 9:27)

For we must all appear before the judgment seat of Christ, that each one may receive what is due him for the things done while in the body, whether good or bad. (2 Corinthians 5:10)

Judgment means two different things for the Christian and the non-Christian. The Christian will not be judged for his sins. Christ has already paid the penalty for them, and the Christian accepted the gift of that payment when he accepted Christ as Savior and Lord. Judgment for the Christian will be to determine what rewards, if any, he will receive for his works. Regardless, he goes to heaven.

The non-Christian will be judged for his sins. Because he has not accepted Christ, the penalty for his sins still stands against him; therefore, he will have to pay for them himself. His judgment will be to determine the degree of his punishment. Regardless, he goes to hell.

Knowing that he is going to heaven takes away the fear of dying for the Christian. He does not fear what awaits him on the other side of death. Based on God's Word, he has confidence and faith that his destination is the heavenly city. Moreover, he knows God will be there and it will be a wonderful place.

And I heard a loud voice from the throne saying, "Now the dwelling of God is with men, and he will live with them. They will be his people, and God himself will be with them and be their God. He will wipe every tear from their eyes. There will be no more death or mourning or crying or pain, for the old order of things has passed away." (Revelation 21:3-4)

He can say with Paul, "to die is gain" (Philippians 1:21). The Christian knows that he will only die a physical death because he now has spiritual life. He will live with God forever.

Jesus said to her, "I am the resurrection and the life. He who believes in me will live, even though he dies; and whoever lives and believes in me will never die. Do you believe this?" (John 11:25-26)

Christ defeated Satan and destroyed death when He died on the cross.

...but it has now been revealed through the appearing of our Savior, Christ Jesus, who has destroyed death.... (2 Timothy 1:10)

Since the children have flesh and blood, he too shared in their humanity so that by his death he might destroy him who holds the power of death—that is, the devil—and free those who all their lives were held in slavery by their fear of death. (Hebrews 2:14-15)

The death that Christ destroyed was spiritual death. In destroying it, He also destroyed the fear of physical death. However, this does not do the unbeliever any good because he does not benefit from what Christ did. He does not have salvation. He does not have spiritual life. His sins are not forgiven. He must be punished for them; therefore, he has every reason to fear death. As the Bible teaches, he is held in slavery by his fear of death. He is dying in his sins and will have to suffer the second death.

Once more Jesus said to them, "I am going away, and you will look for me, and you will die in your sin. Where I go, you cannot come."

This made the Jews ask, "Will he kill himself? Is that why he says, 'Where I go, you cannot come?'"

But he continued, "You are from below; I am from above. You are of this world; I am not of this world. I told you that you would die in your sins; if you do not believe that I am the one I claim to be you will indeed die in your sins." (John 8:21-24)

But the cowardly, the unbelieving, the vile, the murderers, the sexually immoral, those who practice magic arts, the idolaters and all liars—their place will be in the fiery lake of burning sulfur. This is the second death. (Revelation 21:8)

Christ—the Only Way

Clinging to a false system of salvation, in the face of all the Scripture we have examined, is much like the little boy who desired greatly to go outside and play. His mother told him it was raining and he would get wet. He looked out the window and saw it was raining. He then said it was not raining, went outside and got soaking wet.

We can all be stubborn at times. However, depending on a false belief to save us has a far greater consequence then getting soaking wet. The Bible says the consequence is eternal damnation. We can consider ourselves blessed that we have God's Bible to guide and direct us. It behooves us to study it with diligence. God makes it clear that there is only one way of salvation, and that way is His Son, Jesus Christ.

> Jesus answered, "I am the way and the truth and the life. No one comes to the Father except through me." (John 14:6)

> "You are Israel's teacher," said Jesus, "and do you not understand these things? I tell you the truth, we speak of what we know, and we testify to what we have seen, but still you people do not accept our testimony. I have spoken to you of earthly things and you do not believe; how then will you believe if I speak of heavenly things? No one has ever gone into heaven except the one who came from heaven—the Son of Man. Just as Moses lifted up the snake in the desert, so the Son of Man must be lifted up, that everyone who believes in him may have eternal life.
>   For God so loved the world that he gave his one and only Son, that whoever believes in him shall not perish but have eternal life. For God did not send his Son into the world to condemn the world, but to save the world through him. Whoever believes in him is not condemned, but whoever does not believe stands condemned already because he has not believed in the name of God's one and only Son."
> (John 3:10-18)

> Whoever believes in the Son has eternal life, but whoever rejects the Son will not see life, for God's wrath remains on him. (John 3:36)

Salvation is found in no one else, for there is no other name under heaven given to men by which we must be saved. (Acts 4:12)

The teaching of Scripture is clear. If we want to be saved we must repent (turn from our way to God's way) and ask Christ, as Savior and Lord, to forgive our sins and to save us. We must do this, believing that He can save us and having faith that He will save us.

Repent, then, and turn to God, so that your sins may be wiped out, that times of refreshing may come from the Lord, and that he may send the Christ, who has been appointed for you—even Jesus. (Acts 3:19-20)

I have declared to both Jews and Greeks that they must turn to God in repentance and have faith in our Lord Jesus. (Acts 20:21)

But what does it say? "The word is near you; it is in your mouth and in your heart," that is, the word of faith we are proclaiming: That if you confess with your mouth, "Jesus is Lord," and believe in your heart that God raised him from the dead, you will be saved. For it is with your heart that you believe and are justified, and it is with your mouth that you confess and are saved. As the Scripture says, "Anyone who trusts in him will never be put to shame." For there is no difference between Jew and Gentile—the same Lord is Lord of all and richly blesses all who call on him, for, "Everyone who calls on the name of the Lord will be saved." (Romans 10:8-13)

And without faith it is impossible to please God, because anyone who comes to him must believe that he exists and that he rewards those who earnestly seek him. (Hebrews 11:6)

For it is by grace you have been saved, through faith—and this not from yourselves, it is the gift of God—not by works, so that no one can boast. (Ephesians 2:8-9)

When we receive Christ we become God's children. All men are God's creatures, but only those who have accepted Christ are God's children.

...because those who are led by the Spirit of God are sons of God. (Romans 8:14)

You are all sons of God through faith in Christ Jesus.... (Galatians 3:26)

Yet to all who received him, to those who believed in his name, he gave the right to become children of God.... (John 1:12)

"I will be a Father to you, and you will be my sons and daughters," says the Lord Almighty. (2 Corinthians 6:18)

Those Who do not Accept Christ

If only those who accept Christ are God's children, then what about the others? Whose children are they? The Bible speaks of those who do not know Christ as being slaves to sin. As a result, they are under the influence of Satan. Jesus, in talking with a group, puts it in strong and plain words when He tells them they are of their father, the devil.

Jesus told them another parable: "The kingdom of heaven is like a man who sowed good seed in his field. But while everyone was sleeping, his enemy came and sowed weeds among the wheat, and went away. When the wheat sprouted and formed heads, then the weeds also appeared.

The owner's servants came to him and said, 'Sir, didn't you sow good seed in your field? Where then did the weeds come from?'

'An enemy did this,' he replied.

The servants asked him, 'Do you want us to go and pull them up?'

'No,' he answered, 'because while you are pulling the weeds, you may root up the wheat with them. Let both grow together until the harvest. At that time I will tell the harvesters: First collect the weeds and tie them in bundles to be burned; then gather the wheat and bring it into my barn.'" (Matthew 13:24-30)

Then he left the crowd and went into the house. His disciples came to him and said, "Explain to us the parable of the weeds in the field."

He answered, "The one who sowed the good seed is the Son of Man. The field is the world, and the good seed stands for the sons of the kingdom. The weeds are the sons of the evil one, and the enemy who sows them is the devil. The harvest is the end of the age, and the harvesters are angels.

As the weeds are pulled up and burned in the fire, so it will be at the end of the age. The Son of Man will send out his angels, and they will weed out of his kingdom everything that causes sin and all who do evil. They will throw them into the fiery furnace, where there will be weeping and gnashing of teeth. Then the righteous will shine like the sun in the kingdom of their Father. He who has ears, let him hear." (Matthew 13:36-43)

Jesus replied, "I tell you the truth, everyone who sins is a slave to sin. Now a slave has no permanent place in the family, but a son belongs to it forever. So if the Son sets you free, you will be free indeed. I know you are Abraham's descendants. Yet you are ready to kill me, because you have no room for my word. I am telling you what I have seen in the Father's presence, and you do what you have heard from your father."

"Abraham is our father," they answered.

"If you were Abraham's children," said Jesus, "then you would do the things Abraham did. As it is, you are determined to kill me, a man who has told you the truth that I heard from God. Abraham did not do such things. You are doing the things your own father does."

"We are not illegitimate children," they protested. "The only Father we have is God himself."

Jesus said to them, "If God were your Father, you would love me, for I came from God and now am here. I have not come on my own; but he sent me. Why is my language not clear to you? Because you are unable to hear what I say. You belong to your father, the devil, and you want to carry out your father's desire. He was a murderer from the beginning, not holding to the truth, for there is no truth in him. When he lies, he speaks his native language, for he is a liar and the father of lies. Yet because I tell you truth, you do not believe me! Can any of you prove me guilty of sin? If I am telling the truth, why don't you believe me? He who belongs to God hears what God says. The reason you do not hear is that you do not belong to God." (John 8:34-47)

I am sure there would be very few who would willingly and knowingly choose to follow Satan, but then that is not what is being taught in these verses. These people do not know they are following Satan. They think of themselves as descendants of Abraham and followers of God. They see themselves as good people. Yet, they want to kill Jesus (verse 40). Christ said the world would hate His disciples and want to kill them also.

> **They will put you out of the synagogue; in fact, a time is coming when anyone who kills you will think he is offering a service to God. They will do such things because they have not known the Father or me.** (John 16:2-3)

Although they think they are offering a service to God, it is not the true God. It is only a god of their imagination for Christ says they hate God.

> **He who hates me hates my Father as well.** (John 15:23)

We see how easy it is to be deceived and think that we are serving God, when we are actually serving Satan. At the time of our death, the one we are serving is the one with whom we will spend eternity.

This teaching of Christ applies not only to the man on the street or the man in the pew, but it also applies to the man in the pulpit. Being a preacher or priest does not automatically ensure a position in heaven. They, like all of mankind, must make a personal appeal to Christ and a personal acceptance of Christ. We must not only know Christ, but He must know us. Again, we see the strong language Christ used—this time to the Pharisees and teachers of the law (the religious leaders of that day).

> **Woe to you, teachers of the law and Pharisees, you hypocrites! You shut the kingdom of heaven in men's faces. You yourselves do not enter, nor will you let those enter who are trying to.**
> **Woe to you, teachers of the law and Pharisees, you hypocrites! You travel over land and sea to win a single convert, and when he becomes one, you make him twice as much a son of hell as you are.** (Matthew 23:13-15)

> **Woe to you, teachers of the law and Pharisees, you hypocrites! You are like whitewashed tombs, which look beautiful on the**

outside but on the inside are full of dead men's bones and
everything unclean. In the same way, on the outside you appear
to people as righteous but on the inside you are full of
hypocrisy and wickedness. (Matthew 23:27-28)

The Indwelling Holy Spirit

When we accept Christ, God's Holy Spirit comes to live within
us—He indwells us. If we do not have the Holy Spirit, we are not
saved.

You, however, are controlled not by the sinful nature but by
the Spirit, if the Spirit of God lives in you. And if anyone does
not have the Spirit of Christ, he does not belong to Christ.
(Romans 8:9)

It is only through the Holy Spirit that we can know and
understand the truth of God's Word. It is amazing how much
better we understand the Bible after we receive Christ.

For who among men knows the thoughts of a man except the
man's spirit within him? In the same way no one knows the
thoughts of God except the Spirit of God. We have not received
the spirit of the world but the Spirit who is from God, that we
may understand what God has freely given us.
(1 Corinthians 2:11-12)

But the Counselor, the Holy Spirit, whom the Father will send
in my name, will teach you all things and will remind you of
everything I have said to you. (John 14:26)

But their minds were made dull, for to this day the same veil
remains when the old covenant is read. It has not been
removed, because only in Christ is it taken away. Even to this
day when Moses is read, a veil covers their hearts. But
whenever anyone turns to the Lord, the veil is taken away.
(2 Corinthians 3:14-16)

In John 3:16 and in other verses, God assures us that if we
trust Christ to save us, we are saved. In addition, His Holy Spirit
testifies to this fact.

The Spirit himself testifies with our spirit that we are God's children. (Romans 8:16)

We know that we live in him and he in us, because he has given us of his Spirit. (1 John 4:13)

As we come to the close of this chapter let us pause for some serious thought. We have looked at what God's Word says is the way of salvation. Now each of us must ask ourselves, Do I believe it? If you believe it, have you acted upon your belief?

Perhaps you are like the man clinging to the capsized boat. You believe, but now you must make a decision—continue clinging to a false way of salvation and drift out into the darkness, or act on your belief and commit your life to Christ. There is only one way of salvation and only one God—turn to Him.

Turn to me and be saved, all you ends of the earth; for I am God, and there is no other. (Isaiah 45:22)

Let go of the false way and trust Christ to save you. The decision is yours. I pray that God will lead you to take that all-important step now.

Prayer for Salvation

Ask Christ to forgive you and save you. In sincerity and faith pray the following prayer:

Dear God, I confess I am a sinner. I am lost in my sins. Please have mercy on me. I thank you that your Son, Jesus Christ, died for my sins. I ask Him to come into my life, to be my Lord and Savior, to forgive my sins, and to do with my life as He pleases. I thank you that, as I pray, this is done. In Jesus' name I pray. Amen.

If you prayed that prayer in sincerity, believing that Christ could and would save you, then let me assure you that you are saved according to God Himself.

And this is the testimony: God has given us eternal life, and this life is in his Son. He who has the Son has life; he who does not have the Son of God does not have life.

I write these things to you who believe in the name of the Son of God so that you may know that you have eternal life. (1 John 5:11-13)

Furthermore, Christ says that once you are saved you can never be lost. It is by God's grace that you are saved, and by God's grace you will remain saved. Christ says He gives His sheep eternal life and that life starts the moment you receive Him. How blessed we are to be His sheep.

All that the Father gives me will come to me, and whoever comes to me I will never drive away. (John 6:37)

My sheep listen to my voice; I know them, and they follow me. I give them eternal life, and they shall never perish; no one can snatch them out of my hand. My Father, who has given them to me, is greater than all; no one can snatch them out of my Father's hand. I and the Father are one. (John 10:27-30)

Let me hasten to add how important it is for you to align yourself with a church where the truth of the Bible is preached and taught. Shop around, test the waters, and do not make a hasty decision. Pray and ask God to direct you to the church He would have you join. Study your Bible and ask God to reveal to you those truths He would have you to know and understand. May you always be blessed with God's peace and joy.

How important is it to be obedient?

What are the consequences of disobedience?

Is tithing relevant for today?

Is the carnal Christian on dangerous ground?

Are there rewards for obedient service?

Whoever has my commands and obeys them, he is the one who loves me. (John 14:21a)

Obedience

Perfect Obedience Our Goal

Perfect obedience to God should be the goal of every Christian. Can you think of any reason why it should not? It is a goal we cannot attain on earth, due to our sinful nature, but the degree to which we strive after it will determine how close we come to reaching it.

Any who think they walk in perfect obedience to God all the time must not understand what obedience to God means. I understand it to at least mean never committing a sin of either commission or omission. Moreover, it means to always do exactly what God wants us to do, in the manner He wants us to do it, and at the time He wants us to do it. We should make perfect obedience our goal; however, it is a goal no one can rightfully claim to have attained.

If we claim to be without sin, we deceive ourselves and the truth is not in us. (1 John 1:8)

...for all have sinned and fall short of the glory of God....
(Romans 3:23)

Reasons for Obedience

1. Commanded

There are a number of reasons why we should be obedient, but we need only one. God commands us to, and that is reason enough.

Keep my commands and follow them. I am the Lord.
(Leviticus 22:31)

The command to obey is not a mere preference or request on God's part. It is a command that we cannot ignore without paying the consequences. It is a directive for a lifestyle, and a charge for a lifetime. Obedience is the heart of the Christian life. It takes place internally, and is evidenced externally. However, this external evidence is not to be confused with the religious acts of the non-Christian or the superficial acts of some Christians. Attending church, serving on a committee, singing in the choir, or leading public prayer, when done in order to appear holy, are not what obedience is about. God does not tell us to appear holy but to be holy.

Be holy because I, the Lord your God, am holy.
(Leviticus 19:2)

The spirit of obedience is more important to God than the letter of obedience. A true spirit of obedience comes from an obedient heart.

My son, do not forget my teaching, but keep my commands in your heart.... (Proverbs 3:1)

...he taught me and said, "Lay hold of my words with all your heart; keep my commands and you will live." (Proverbs 4:4)

The wise in heart accept commands, but a chattering fool comes to ruin. (Proverbs 10:8)

All a man's ways seem right to him, but the Lord weighs the heart. (Proverbs 21:2)

My son, give me your heart and let your eyes keep to my ways.... (Proverbs 23:26)

If you say, "But we knew nothing about this," does not he who weighs the heart perceive it? Does not he who guards your life know it? Will he not repay each person according to what he has done? (Proverbs 24:12)

As water reflects a face, so a man's heart reflects the man. (Proverbs 27:19)

2.   Fear of God

Another reason to obey is because we are afraid not to. Knowing that God is sovereign and all powerful, we should have a reverent fear of Him and dread the consequences of disobeying Him.

The fear of the Lord is the beginning of knowledge, but fools despise wisdom and discipline. (Proverbs 1:7)

"Hear this, you foolish and senseless people,
     who have eyes but do not see,
     who have ears but do not hear:
Should you not fear me?" declares the Lord.
     "Should you not tremble in my presence?
I made the sand a boundary for the sea,
     an everlasting barrier it cannot cross.
The waves may roll, but they cannot prevail;
     they may roar, but they cannot cross it.
But these people have stubborn and rebellious hearts;
     they have turned aside and gone away.
They do not say to themselves,
     'Let us fear the Lord our God....'"
(Jeremiah 5:21-24)

I tell you, my friends, do not be afraid of those who kill the body and after that can do no more. But I will show you whom you should fear: Fear him who, after the killing of the body,

has power to throw you into hell. Yes, I tell you, fear him.
(Luke 12:4-5)

If we deliberately keep on sinning after we have received the
knowledge of the truth, no sacrifice for sins is left, but only a
fearful expectation of judgment and of raging fire that will
consume the enemies of God. Anyone who rejected the law of
Moses died without mercy on the testimony of two or three
witnesses. How much more severely do you think a man
deserves to be punished who has trampled the Son of God
under foot, who has treated as an unholy thing the blood of the
covenant that sanctified him, and who has insulted the Spirit
of grace? For we know him who said, "It is mine to avenge; I
will repay," and again, "The Lord will judge his people." It is
a dreadful thing to fall into the hands of the living God.
(Hebrews 10:26-31)

Therefore, since we are receiving a kingdom that cannot be
shaken, let us be thankful, and so worship God acceptably with
reverence and awe, for our "God is a consuming fire."
(Hebrews 12:28-29)

3. Love for God

A third reason for obedience is because of His love. God loves
us much more than anyone. God, as Jesus Christ, suffered and
died for us; He paid the penalty for our sins and saved us. Our
response to His love for us should be our love for Him shown by
our obedience to Him.

Love for God and gratitude to God should spring forth in our
hearts when we reflect on what Christ saved us from and the
suffering He went through in order to do it. Often, as Christians,
we experience the joy of being saved and the blessings God
bestows on us without really considering the cost. We hear so
much about grace that we think our salvation is free. It is free to
us—a free gift—but the price to the giver was the highest ever
paid. Out of love and mercy God gave His only begotten Son to
suffer and die for us. If this does not cause us to want to be
obedient then we must not understand what took place at the
cross. We must not understand the intense suffering Christ
endured, the eternal damnation from which we are saved, and the

eternal blessing to which we are saved. Our profession of love for God should be exemplified by our obedience to Him.

If you love me, you will obey what I command. (John 14:15)

4. Evidence of salvation

Still another reason for us to be obedient is that we should desire to see evidence in our own lives that we are truly saved. The works we do, the fruit we bear, and the witness of the Holy Spirit with our spirit are important proofs which strengthen our confidence that we are saved. To walk around in doubt as to our salvation would be disheartening, to say the least. However, if we are not walking in obedience, not manifesting the fruit of the Spirit, not performing good works, do we have any reason to believe we are saved? Does this not cause us to doubt our salvation?

We would be much happier if we could look at our lives and see real evidence that God is at work in us. To see God change someone else is to see something wonderful; however, when God changes us personally, we _experience_ something wonderful. When we can shed sins that once had a grip on us, when we can react to difficult situations with a good attitude, when we find God using us, when we see fruit the Holy Spirit has produced in us, when we are hungry to know God better, when we desire to study His Word, when we want His will done—whatever that may bring, then surely we will have increased confidence that we are saved. Surely we will be more sensitive to the witness of the Holy Spirit that we are children of God.

Examples of Obedience

Now that we have discussed reasons to be obedient, let us look at some of the things God says to us about obedience. I think we will discover that, from God's viewpoint, our obedience to Him is vital. Regardless of whether the Scripture is from the Old or the New Testament, directed to Jews or Gentiles, to the Apostles or to others, God makes it clear that He has commanded obedience, expects obedience, and will not tolerate disobedience. He rewards obedience and punishes disobedience.

Throughout the Bible He has given us examples of people who were blessed because of their obedience and people who were punished for their disobedience. It is not important that some of what these people were commanded to do does not apply to us today. What is important is that we learn how strongly God feels about obedience, and that we seek to learn and obey all the things that do apply to us.

Without question, the greatest example of obedience is our Lord Jesus Christ. The Apostle Paul tells us our attitude should be the same as that of Jesus.

> **Your attitude should be the same as that of Christ Jesus: Who, being in very nature God, did not consider equality with God something to be grasped, but made himself nothing, taking the very nature of a servant, being made in human likeness. And being found in appearance as a man, he humbled himself and became obedient to death—even death on a cross!**
> (Philippians 2:5-8)

Of course, the obedience of Jesus was perfect obedience. Christ was the perfect person and the only person to live a sinless life. Although He was fully God, He lived and walked on earth as fully man. As man, He lived His life in obedience to God the Father.

> **For I have come down from heaven not to do my will but to do the will of him who sent me.** (John 6:38)

> **...but the world must learn that I love the Father and that I do exactly what my Father has commanded me.** (John 14:31)

> **I have brought you glory on earth by completing the work you gave me to do. And now, Father, glorify me in your presence with the glory I had with you before the world began.**
> (John 17:4-5)

From the book of Genesis to the book of Revelation we have numerous examples of men and women of God whose trend of life was obedience. None were perfect and none were sinless. However, their examples should inspire and encourage each of us to put forth greater effort to be obedient. When we read about people like Noah and Moses, our faith is strengthened and we are moved to seek a closer walk with God.

> This is the account of Noah. Noah was a righteous man, blameless among the people of his time, and he walked with God. (Genesis 6:9)

> And Noah did all that the Lord commanded him. (Genesis 7:5)

> By faith Moses, when he had grown up, refused to be known as the son of Pharaoh's daughter. He chose to be mistreated along with the people of God rather than to enjoy the pleasures of sin for a short time. He regarded disgrace for the sake of Christ as of greater value than the treasures of Egypt, because he was looking ahead to his reward. (Hebrews 11:24-26)

Although Abraham did not live a sinless life, there came a time when the trend of his life was one of obedience to God. This trend may well have started when he left Haran.

> The Lord had said to Abram, "Leave your country, your people and your father's household and go to the land I will show you. I will make you into a great nation and I will bless you; I will make your name great, and you will be a blessing. I will bless those who bless you, and whoever curses you I will curse; and all peoples on earth will be blessed through you." So Abram left, as the Lord had told him; and Lot went with him. Abram was seventy-five years old when he set out from Haran. (Genesis 12:1-4)

> By faith Abraham, when God tested him, offered Isaac as a sacrifice. He who had received the promises was about to sacrifice his one and only son, even though God had said to him, "It is through Isaac that your offspring will be reckoned." Abraham reasoned that God could raise the dead, and figuratively speaking, he did receive Isaac back from death. (Hebrews 11:17-19)

Joseph is another who walked close to God. He was used by Him and blessed by Him. Most know the story of how Joseph was sold into slavery by his brothers, and ended up in Egypt. He soon was given a position of importance in the household of one of

Pharaoh's officials. Here his obedience to God was tested as the official's wife tempted him to commit sexual sin.

> Now Joseph had been taken down to Egypt. Potiphar, an Egyptian who was one of Pharaoh's officials, the captain of the guard, bought him from the Ishmaelites who had taken him there.
>
> The Lord was with Joseph and he prospered, and he lived in the house of his Egyptian master. When his master saw that the Lord was with him and that the Lord gave him success in everything he did, Joseph found favor in his eyes and became his attendant. Potiphar put him in charge of his household, and he entrusted to his care everything he owned. From the time he put him in charge of his household and of all that he owned, the Lord blessed the household of the Egyptian because of Joseph. The blessing of the Lord was on everything Potiphar had, both in the house and in the field. So he left in Joseph's care everything he had; with Joseph in charge, he did not concern himself with anything except the food he ate.
>
> Now Joseph was well-built and handsome, and after a while his master's wife took notice of Joseph and said, "Come to bed with me!"
>
> But he refused. "With me in charge," he told her, "my master does not concern himself with anything in the house; everything he owns he has entrusted to my care. No one is greater in this house than I am. My master has withheld nothing from me except you, because you are his wife. How then could I do such a wicked thing and sin against God?" And though she spoke to Joseph day after day, he refused to go to bed with her or even be with her. (Genesis 39:1-10)

God's Sovereignty and Our Obedience

We know that Joseph was falsely accused by his master's wife, and put in prison. He was later released, and put in charge of all Egypt, under Pharaoh. Joseph understood that God is sovereign, and that He has a purpose for either bringing about or allowing everything that takes place. He saw that God had a purpose in his being sold into slavery, put into prison, and then put in charge of all Egypt.

His brothers then came and threw themselves down before
him. "We are your slaves," they said.
But Joseph said to them, "Don't be afraid. Am I in the
place of God? You intended to harm me, but God intended it
for good to accomplish what is now being done, the saving of
many lives. So then, don't be afraid. I will provide for you and
your children." And he reassured them and spoke kindly to
them. (Genesis 50:18-21)

We need to be mindful of the relationship between God's
sovereign will and our obedience. We need to seek not just to do
good things but, in His sovereignty, to do those particular things
that God has planned for us to do. If we are Christians, each of us
is in a unique situation because God has certain work cut out for
us that is ours alone to do.

For we are God's workmanship, created in Christ Jesus to do
good works, which God prepared in advance for us to do.
(Ephesians 2:10)

Therefore, since we are surrounded by such a great cloud of
witnesses, let us throw off everything that hinders and the sin
that so easily entangles, and let us run with perseverance the
race marked out for us. (Hebrews 12:1)

...for it is God who works in you to will and to act according to
his good purpose. (Philippians 2:13)

God has ordained where each of us is to fit in the Body of
Christ, and the particular work each of us is to do as a member of
the Body. What God has for you to do is to be done by no one but
you. Others may be used to do the same type work, but no one will
be used to do your work. The work done by the Body of Christ is
the collective work of its members. The more faithful each member
is to do his or her work, the more effective the Body will be in
carrying out the Lord's work.

Instead, speaking the truth in love, we will in all things grow
up into him who is the Head, that is, Christ. From him the
whole body, joined and held together by every supporting
ligament, grows and builds itself up in love, as each part does
its work. (Ephesians 4:15-16)

Each of us must be concerned about doing our own part and less concerned about what the other person is doing. Christ made this clear to Peter when He told him that he would one day be put to death in a manner that would glorify God. Peter did not shrink back from this thought, but he quickly asked Christ what would happen to John. Christ let Peter know that how He used John was not Peter's concern. Peter's concern was to follow Christ.

> **When they had finished eating, Jesus said to Simon Peter, "Simon son of John, do you truly love me more than these?" "Yes, Lord," he said, "you know that I love you." Jesus said, "Feed my lambs." Again Jesus said, "Simon son of John, do you truly love me?" He answered, "Yes, Lord, you know that I love you." Jesus said, "Take care of my sheep." The third time he said to him, "Simon son of John, do you love me?"**
>
> **Peter was hurt because Jesus asked him the third time, "Do you love me?" He said, "Lord, you know all things; you know that I love you."**
>
> **Jesus said, "Feed my sheep. I tell you the truth, when you were younger you dressed yourself and went where you wanted; but when you are old you will stretch out your hands, and someone else will dress you and lead you where you do not want to go." Jesus said this to indicate the kind of death by which Peter would glorify God. Then he said to him, "Follow me!"**
>
> **Peter turned and saw that the disciple whom Jesus loved was following them. (This was the one who had leaned back against Jesus at the supper and had said, "Lord, who is going to betray you?") When Peter saw him, he asked, "Lord, what about him?"**
>
> **Jesus answered, "If I want him to remain alive until I return, what is that to you? You must follow me." Because of this, the rumor spread among the brothers that this disciple would not die. But Jesus did not say that he would not die; he only said, "If I want him to remain alive until I return, what is that to you?"**
>
> **This is the disciple who testifies to these things and who wrote them down. We know that his testimony is true.**
> **(John 21:15-24)**

Each of us should have one concern that is the driving force of our life—to be obedient in following Christ. If, as best we can discern, we are walking in obedience and doing that which God would have us do, then we need not feel less spiritual if others appear to be doing and accomplishing more than we are. On the other hand, we must not feel spiritually superior if we are doing and accomplishing more than others. God may use any of us at different times in our lives in different ways. He may have us busier at sometimes and less busy at others. However, He is always looking to us to be obedient and to let Him work in us to use us as He pleases.

God is Glorified in Our Obedience

As Christians, we should guard against forgetting why we are here. We need to remember that our purpose in being on this earth is not to live for ourselves, but it is to glorify God.

This is to my Father's glory that you bear much fruit, showing yourselves to be my disciples. (John 15:8)

May the God who gives endurance and encouragement give you a spirit of unity among yourselves as you follow Christ Jesus, so that with one heart and mouth you may glorify the God and Father of our Lord Jesus Christ. (Romans 15:5-6)

We glorify God in the type of lives we lead, by what we are and what we do. The ways in which we glorify Him are as varied as our lives. One way to glorify God is to praise Him in word and song.

I will extol the Lord at all times;
    his praise will always be on my lips.
My soul will boast in the Lord;
    let the afflicted hear and rejoice.
Glorify the Lord with me;
    let us exalt his name together.
(Psalm 34:1-3)

O God, you are my God,
    earnestly I seek you;
my soul thirsts for you,
    my body longs for you,
in a dry and weary land
    where there is no water.

I have seen you in the sanctuary
    and beheld your power and your glory.
Because your love is better than life,
    my lips will glorify you.
I will praise you as long as I live,
    and in your name I will lift up my hands.
My soul will be satisfied as with the richest of foods;
    with singing lips my mouth will praise you.
(Psalm 63:1-5)

I will praise God's name in song
    and glorify him with thanksgiving.
(Psalm 69:30)

Sing to the Lord, for he has done glorious things;
let this be known to all the world. (Isaiah 12:5)

Another way to glorify God is to tell others how wonderful He is and what He has done for you.

Come and listen, all you who fear God; let me tell you what he has done for me. (Psalm 66:16)

But as for me, I will always have hope;
    I will praise you more and more.
My mouth will tell of your righteousness,
    of your salvation all day long,
    though I know not its measure.
I will come and proclaim your mighty acts,
    O Sovereign Lord;
    I will proclaim your righteousness, yours alone.
Since my youth, O God, you have taught me,
    and to this day I declare your marvelous deeds.
Even when I am old and gray,
    do not forsake me, O God,
    till I declare your power to the next generation,
    your might to all who are to come.
(Psalm 71:14-18)

But in your hearts set apart Christ as Lord. Always be prepared to give an answer to everyone who asks you to give the reason for the hope that you have. But do this with gentleness and respect.... (1 Peter 3:15)

Actually, to glorify God means to give Him honor, to worship Him, to praise Him, and to acknowledge who He is (the one and only true God, the living God, the Sovereign Lord of all). It also means to acknowledge what He is (a God of love, mercy, justice, wrath and compassion), and what He does (He showers His creatures with His love, mercy, justice, wrath and compassion). Acknowledging, worshiping, and praising God are all part of the fruit of a Christian life.

There is also the fruit of souls that are saved through our witness, Bible classes taught, money given for God's work, widows helped, the poor helped, prisoners and the sick visited.

There are numerous other ways that the Christian bears fruit; however, there is one common denominator in all of it—obedience. Our obedience is of the utmost importance to God.

> Jesus replied, "If anyone loves me, he will obey my teaching. My Father will love him, and we will come to him and make our home with him." (John 14:23)

> If you obey my commands, you will remain in my love, just as I have obeyed my Father's commands and remain in his love. (John 15:10)

> You did not choose me, but I chose you and appointed you to go and bear fruit—fruit that will last. Then the Father will give you whatever you ask in my name. (John 15:16)

Folly to Rationalize Obedience and Become Comfortable with Disobedience

Being obedient needs to be taken very seriously. It is folly to rationalize obedience and become comfortable with disobedience. Too often Christians are complacent about their sin on the basis that God knows that they are sinners. They know that if they confess their sins, He is faithful to forgive them. They twist this reality for their own convenience. In other words, their attitude is that God knows they will sin, and He has promised to forgive them when they do—so it is no big deal. They have not yet learned to hate sin, particularly that sin in their own hearts. They accept its presence instead of trying to eradicate it from their lives.

At other times there is the swap-out of sin. A Christian rationalizes that he or she is unable to give up a certain sin. So, consciously or unconsciously, another sin is discarded to justify retaining that one.

Also, as our human nature is prone to do, there are those Christians who revert back to a works-oriented approach toward sin. They allow themselves a certain amount of sin if they feel they are doing enough good works to offset it. For example: If a man and woman are having an adulterous affair, the man may justify it on the grounds that he is a deacon, Sunday-school teacher, and serves on two church committees. She may justify it because she is active in the church women's work, does volunteer work with the underprivileged, and sings in the choir. They might see themselves as two very good people who are contributing to society and furthering the work of the church. Therefore, though what they are doing is wrong, in light of all the good they do, it is really not too bad—in fact, it is okay. However, no matter how sincere or intense our rationalizing may be, it does not change the truth. Sin is sin. God does not make allowances for it or accept excuses about it. He hates it. The wages of sin is still death.

Warning Against Disobedience

Paul warns us against disobedience, using as one example the Israelites wandering in the desert.

> For I do not want you to be ignorant of the fact, brothers, that our forefathers were all under the cloud and that they all passed through the sea. They were all baptized into Moses in the cloud and in the sea. They all ate the same spiritual food and drank the same spiritual drink; for they drank from the spiritual rock that accompanied them, and that rock was Christ. Nevertheless, God was not pleased with most of them; their bodies were scattered over the desert.
> Now these things occurred as examples to keep us from setting our hearts on evil things as they did. Do not be idolaters, as some of them were; as it is written: "The people sat down to eat and drink and got up to indulge in pagan revelry." We should not commit sexual immorality, as some of them did—and in one day twenty-three thousand of them died. We should not test the Lord, as some of them did—and were

killed by snakes. And do not grumble, as some of them did—and were killed by the destroying angel.

These things happened to them as examples and were written down as warnings for us, on whom the fulfillment of the ages has come. So, if you think you are standing firm, be careful that you don't fall! (1 Corinthians 10:1-12)

Disobedience Disguised as Obedience

We must remember that disobedience often takes on a subtle disguise and appears to us as obedience. For example: A father leaving for work in the morning tells his son to be sure and clean out the garage that day. Upon his arrival home that evening, the father sees that the garage has not been cleaned. When he asks the son why, the son tells him that the grass needed cutting and he thought his father would rather he cut the grass. It may be true that the grass needed cutting, but the garage also needed cleaning. The son should have assumed his father knew the grass needed cutting but preferred the son clean the garage. The son may have hated to clean out the garage, or he may have actually thought it more important to cut the grass. However, that was not his decision to make. Although to him it might appear as obedience, it was actually disobedience in disguise.

Those professing to be Christians are sometimes guilty of this type of disobedience. They feel that God wants them to do one thing, but they choose to do another and expect God to be pleased with their action. Something of this nature may have taken place when Cain and Abel made their offerings to God.

In the course of time Cain brought some of the fruits of the soil as an offering to the Lord. But Abel brought fat portions from some of the firstborn of his flock. The Lord looked with favor on Abel and his offering, but on Cain and his offering he did not look with favor. So Cain was very angry, and his face was downcast. (Genesis 4:3-5)

God was pleased with Abel and his offering but not with Cain or his offering. What was the difference? It could have been the quality of the offerings. The Bible does not tell us that Cain offered just any fruit of the ground, but it does not tell us that he brought the best and firstfruits either. It does say that Abel brought the fat from his firstborn.

The difference could be the type of offering. Cain's was not a sin offering for "without the shedding of blood there is no forgiveness" (Hebrews 9:22b), possibly indicating that he did not feel the need to make an atonement offering. Abel's was a sin offering.

It may be that the difference in the offerings was how they were offered. Cain made his offering in the flesh, seeking to win God's approval, to earn and merit a "well done" from God. Abel, the Word tells us, made his offering in faith—faith in God, dependent upon God for the forgiveness of his sins through the Redeemer.

> **By faith Abel offered God a better sacrifice than Cain did. By faith he was commended as a righteous man, when God spoke well of his offerings. And by faith he still speaks, even though he is dead.** (Hebrews 11:4)

We see that Abel did it God's way—he was obedient. He acted in faith, and it pleased God. Cain did not act in faith but rather according to his own will, and God was displeased. Anything not done in faith is sin.

> **And without faith it is impossible to please God, because anyone who comes to him must believe that he exists and that he rewards those who earnestly seek him.** (Hebrews 11:6)

> **...and everything that does not come from faith is sin.** (Romans 14:23b)

We must seek to always act in faith, and stay constantly on guard against those things that would weaken our faith. It behooves us to ask God to strengthen our faith.

> **Immediately the boy's father exclaimed, "I do believe; help me overcome my unbelief!"** (Mark 9:24)

> **The apostles said to the Lord, "Increase our faith!"** (Luke 17:5)

Cain, in his disobedience, did it his own way, just as many people have done throughout the history of mankind and are still doing today. God speaks of this type of worship in Isaiah.

> **The Lord says: "These people come near to me with their mouth and honor me with their lips, but their hearts are far from me. Their worship of me is made up only of rules taught by men."** (Isaiah 29:13)

Hopefully, we are beginning to understand more fully that it is not the appearance of obedience that counts, but it is the obedience that comes from an obedient heart that God wants. We see that being disobedient does not mean that we must outwardly rebel against God. We are being disobedient when we go through the motions of obedience—even those acts of worshiping God, when they are not from a humble and obedient heart.

Partial Obedience is Disobedience

Another way we are often disobedient is when we are not totally obedient but are only partially obedient.

> **For whoever keeps the whole law and yet stumbles at just one point is guilty of breaking all of it.** (James 2:10)

Think what would have happened to Naaman if he had dipped in the Jordan river only four, five, or six times. I feel sure he would still have had his leprosy.

> **Elisha sent a messenger to say to him, "Go, wash yourself seven times in the Jordan, and your flesh will be restored and you will be cleansed." So he went down and dipped himself in the Jordan seven times, as the man of God had told him, and his flesh was restored and became clean like that of a young boy.** (2 Kings 5:10,14)

I once heard a sermon preached on 1 Samuel 15; the title of the sermon was "Partial Obedience." I would like to look with you at some of the verses in this chapter and see the partial obedience of Saul.

Samuel said to Saul, "I am the one the Lord sent to anoint you king over his people Israel; so listen now to the message from the Lord. This is what the Lord Almighty says: 'I will punish the Amalekites for what they did to Israel when they waylaid them as they came up from Egypt. Now go, attack the Amalekites and totally destroy everything that belongs to them. Do not spare them; put to death men and women, children and infants, cattle and sheep, camels and donkeys.'"
(1 Samuel 15:1-3)

Then Saul attacked the Amalekites all the way from Havilah to Shur, to the east of Egypt. He took Agag king of the Amalekites alive, and all his people he totally destroyed with the sword. But Saul and the army spared Agag and the best of the sheep and cattle, the fat calves and lambs—everything that was good. These they were unwilling to destroy completely, but everything that was despised and weak they totally destroyed.

Then the word of the Lord came to Samuel: "I am grieved that I have made Saul king, because he has turned away from me and has not carried out my instructions." Samuel was troubled, and he cried out to the Lord all that night.

Early in the morning Samuel got up and went to meet Saul, but he was told, "Saul has gone to Carmel. There he has set up a monument in his own honor and has turned and gone on down to Gilgal."

When Samuel reached him, Saul said, "The Lord bless you! I have carried out the Lord's instructions."

But Samuel said, "What then is this bleating of sheep in my ears? What is this lowing of cattle that I hear?"

Saul answered, "The soldiers brought them from the Amalekites; they spared the best of the sheep and cattle to sacrifice to the Lord your God, but we totally destroyed the rest."

"Stop!" Samuel said to Saul. "Let me tell you what the Lord said to me last night."

"Tell me," Saul replied.

Samuel said, "Although you were once small in your own eyes, did you not become the head of the tribes of Israel? The Lord anointed you king over Israel. And he sent you on a mission, saying, 'Go and completely destroy those wicked people, the Amalekites; make war on them until you have wiped them out.' Why did you not obey the Lord? Why did you pounce on the plunder and do evil in the eyes of the Lord?"

"But I did obey the Lord," Saul said. "I went on the mission the Lord assigned me. I completely destroyed the Amalekites and brought back Agag their king. The soldiers took sheep and cattle from the plunder, the best of what was devoted to God, in order to sacrifice them to the Lord your God at Gilgal."

But Samuel replied: "Does the Lord delight in burnt offerings and sacrifices as much as in obeying the voice of the Lord? To obey is better than sacrifice, and to heed is better than the fat of rams. For rebellion is like the sin of divination, and arrogance like the evil of idolatry. Because you have rejected the word of the Lord, he has rejected you as king."

Then Saul said to Samuel, "I have sinned. I violated the Lord's command and your instructions. I was afraid of the people and so I gave in to them. Now I beg you, forgive my sin and come back with me, so that I may worship the Lord."

But Samuel said to him, "I will not go back with you. You have rejected the word of the Lord, and the Lord has rejected you as king over Israel!" (1 Samuel 15:7-26)

Saul did most of that which God had commanded. He put to death all the Amalekite men, women, children and infants he encountered except King Agag. He destroyed all the cattle, sheep, camels, and donkeys except the best of the sheep and cattle, the fat calves and lambs. Saul was certainly obedient up to a point, but that was not good enough. God considered Saul's partial obedience to be disobedience, and punished him. It was true in the case of Saul, and it will hold true with us; when obedience ends, disobedience begins, and partial obedience is disobedience. In this 15th chapter of 1 Samuel, verse 22, is a "word to the wise":

Does the Lord delight in burnt offerings and sacrifices as much as in obeying the voice of the Lord? To obey is better than sacrifice, and to heed is better than the fat of rams. (1 Samuel 15:22)

Well-Intended Disobedience

There is another kind of disobedience which, for lack of a better title, I will call well-intended disobedience. The Apostle Paul, who was called Saul before his conversion, would be a prime example. He persecuted the Christians in a severe and relentless

fashion, thinking he was doing the right thing before God. He had
a number of Christians imprisoned and was present at the stoning
of Stephen.

> When they heard this, they were furious and gnashed their
> teeth at him. But Stephen, full of the Holy Spirit, looked up to
> heaven and saw the glory of God, and Jesus standing at the
> right hand of God.
>
> "Look," he said, "I see heaven open and the Son of Man
> standing at the right hand of God."
>
> At this they covered their ears and, yelling at the top of
> their voices, they all rushed at him, dragged him out of the city
> and began to stone him. Meanwhile, the witnesses laid their
> clothes at the feet of a young man named Saul.
>
> While they were stoning him, Stephen prayed, "Lord
> Jesus, receive my spirit." Then he fell on his knees and cried
> out, "Lord, do not hold this sin against them." When he had
> said this, he fell asleep.
>
> And Saul was there, giving approval to his death.
> (Acts 7:54-60)

We must remember that most of the early Christians were
Jews, as was Paul. But, before his conversion, he was like those
Jews he wrote about in Romans.

> Brothers, my heart's desire and prayer to God for the
> Israelites is that they may be saved. For I can testify about
> them that they are zealous for God, but their zeal is not based
> on knowledge. Since they did not know the righteousness that
> comes from God and sought to establish their own, they did
> not submit to God's righteousness. (Romans 10:1-3)

Throughout history, much bad has been done by people who
claimed to be "God's people." During the Reformation, the burning
of Christians at the stake would be an example. This type of
"well-intended disobedience" is spoken of in God's Word.

> They will put you out of the synagogue; in fact, a time is
> coming when anyone who kills you will think he is offering a
> service to God. They will do such things because they have not
> known the Father or me. (John 16:2-3)

These verses speak of those who do not know Christ, but does any reader doubt that during the Crusades there were atrocities (well-intended disobedience) committed by Christians?

Obedience is Not Automatic for Christians

Being a Christian does not ensure automatic obedience. On the contrary, once we become Christians we often begin to realize what sinful creatures we really are, and how far short we fall of living up to what God expects and requires.

> We know that the law is spiritual; but I am unspiritual, sold as a slave to sin. I do not understand what I do. For what I want to do I do not do, but what I hate I do. And if I do what I do not want to do, I agree that the law is good. As it is, it is no longer I myself who do it, but it is sin living in me. I know that nothing good lives in me, that is, in my sinful nature. For I have the desire to do what is good, but I cannot carry it out. For what I do is not the good I want to do; no, the evil I do not want to do—this I keep on doing. Now if I do what I do not want to do, it is no longer I who do it, but it is sin living in me that does it. (Romans 7:14-20)

If we are to be obedient to God, we must put aside our wills (the desires of the flesh), and let God's will have its way in our lives. We must give ourselves totally to God and seek with all we are and all we have to serve Him, to please Him, and to glorify Him. We must let God's Holy Spirit control and direct our thoughts, words, and actions.

> Then he said to them all: "If anyone would come after me, he must deny himself and take up his cross daily and follow me." (Luke 9:23)

> Therefore, I urge you, brothers, in view of God's mercy, to offer your bodies as living sacrifices, holy and pleasing to God—this is your spiritual act of worship. (Romans 12:1)

> Do not get drunk on wine, which leads to debauchery. Instead, be filled with the Spirit. (Ephesians 5:18)

These last three verses give us important instructions which we must understand and heed if we are to live obedient and fruitful Christian lives. Luke 9:23 tells us we must put aside our wills in preference to God's will. We are not to pursue what we want to do to further our own happiness, comfort, or ambition. Instead we are to do that which, to the best of our knowledge and discernment, is what God would have us to do.

Problems and sickness are not what is meant by crosses we bear. These are common to all people, both Christians and non-Christians. Our cross is denying our sinful nature, putting aside our will and making every effort to do the will of God, regardless of the consequences—even if it leads to persecution or death. The teaching of Scripture is that a lessor commitment is not sufficient to be a disciple of Christ.

In Romans 12:1, Paul urges us to present our bodies as living sacrifices to God. This is a voluntary act by us—just as Christ voluntarily died for us. His death was payment in full for our sins, and no further atonement can be made. Becoming living sacrifices should be our response to His supreme sacrifice. It is because of His death that we live. God's mercies toward us should elicit devotion from us. We should cease to live for self, and seek to live for God. Doing this involves giving our bodies, minds, and hearts to the service of God, and placing them under the direction of God. This is not a momentary thing or something done for a specific period of time. It is something we do for the rest of our lives.

> **Through Jesus, therefore, let us continually offer to God a sacrifice of praise—the fruit of lips that confess his name. And do not forget to do good and to share with others, for with such sacrifices God is pleased.** (Hebrews 13:15-16)

Properly carried out, this will result in not only being a way of life, but it will find its ultimate fruition in being the whole of life. As this becomes a reality, the Christian can rest assured that his or her life will produce much fruit, and thereby glorify God.

When we come to God to present our bodies, to give ourselves, we need to be mindful of the fact that He will only receive those who are consecrated to Him, and who are pleasing and acceptable to Him. Our offering will not be accepted if it is mixed with deeds of willful sin or stained with lingering thoughts of sin. We know that we are not free of sin, but we know that we are free from the power of sin; therefore, we have no reason to tolerate willful sin. God does not tolerate it; furthermore, He has promised us a way out. Therefore, we are without excuse.

> **No temptation has seized you except what is common to man. And God is faithful; he will not let you be tempted beyond what you can bear. But when you are tempted, he will also provide a way out so that you can stand up under it.** (1 Corinthians 10:13)

To offer ourselves to God while living with willful sin would be mockery. It not only would be hypocritical, but it could be dangerous—it might bring God's wrath down on the offender.

> **The priest is to make atonement before the Lord for the one who erred by sinning unintentionally, and when atonement has been made for him, he will be forgiven. One and the same law applies to everyone who sins unintentionally, whether he is a native-born Israelite or an alien.**
> **But anyone who sins defiantly, whether native-born or alien, blasphemes the Lord, and that person must be cut off from his people. Because he has despised the Lord's word and broken his commands, that person must surely be cut off; his guilt remains on him.** (Numbers 15:28-31)

We should pray to be kept from willful sin.

> **Keep your servant also from willful sins;**
> **may they not rule over me.**
> **Then will I be blameless,**
> **innocent of great transgression.**
> (Psalm 19:13)

One final thought Paul gives us in Romans 12:1 is that to become a living sacrifice is our spiritual act of worship, which means our reasonable act. It is not something that is exceptional, but rather it is something reasonable. It is something that reason tells us should be done in view of the situation—not something to be expected only of spiritual giants, but to be expected of all Christians.

Obedience in God's Strength

How does the Christian fulfill what is called for in Luke 9:23 and Romans 12:1? Before we were saved we could not do it. In fact, we could not do anything to please God and were totally dependent on God for our salvation. Our dependency on God has not changed. Now that God has brought about our justification, He is bringing about our sanctification. It is all His work from beginning to end.

Then back to our question: As Christians, how do we fulfill Luke 9:23 and Romans 12:1? The answer is found in Scripture. We must acknowledge our dependency on God, yield our lives to God, seek to walk with God, and ask for the power of God to accomplish what is required of us. We must remember that without Christ we can do nothing, but through Christ we can do all things. God's strength is shown in our weakness. Paul acknowledged this by telling the Corinthians that when he was weak then he was strong. We must look to God for strength and direction—in short, the only way we can fulfill this is to turn the control of our lives over to God's Holy Spirit. This is what is commanded in Ephesians 5:18. (See chapter on the Ministry of the Holy Spirit.)

Actually, living our lives under the control of the Holy Spirit is the bottom line of obedience. It is the sum and substance of the Christian life as it should be lived. God has given many commands which tell us what to do and what not to do. As the Holy Spirit leads us, we should study the Bible to learn what these commands are—looking to Him to teach us, to open our understanding, and to show us how to apply these truths in our lives. One thing we can be sure of: The Holy Spirit will always lead us to do what God's Word says, and never to do anything that is not in accordance with the Word. Remember, the Holy Spirit is God; the Bible is God's written Word, and God never changes.

> God is not a man, that he should lie, nor a son of man, that he should change his mind. Does he speak and then not act? Does he promise and not fulfill? (Numbers 23:19)

> I the Lord do not change. (Malachi 3:6a)

Do We Measure Up to What Is Required?

Most of us know the greatest commandment is to love God, and the second to love our neighbor.

> Hearing that Jesus had silenced the Sadducees, the Pharisees got together. One of them, an expert in the law, tested him with this question: "Teacher, which is the greatest commandment in the Law?"
>
> Jesus replied: "'Love the Lord your God with all your heart and with all your soul and with all your mind.' This is the first and greatest commandment. And the second is like it: 'Love your neighbor as yourself.' All the Law and the Prophets hang on these two commandments." (Matthew 22:34-40)

We do not have to look long to see how far short we fall in keeping these two commandments. In addition, I wonder what our lives reflect about our obedience to Christ in regard to the following:

> You have heard that it was said, "Do not commit adultery." But I tell you that anyone who looks at a woman lustfully has already committed adultery with her in his heart. (Matthew 5:27-28)

> For if you forgive men when they sin against you, your heavenly Father will also forgive you. But if you do not forgive men their sins, your Father will not forgive your sins. (Matthew 6:14-15)

> Do to others as you would have them do to you. (Luke 6:31)

> It has been said, "Anyone who divorces his wife must give her a certificate of divorce." But I tell you that anyone who divorces his wife, except for marital unfaithfulness, causes her to become an adulteress, and anyone who marries the divorced woman commits adultery. (Matthew 5:31-32)

> ...bless those who curse you, pray for those who mistreat you. If someone strikes you on one cheek, turn to him the other also. If someone takes your cloak, do not stop him from taking your tunic. Give to everyone who asks you, and if anyone takes what belongs to you, do not demand it back. (Luke 6:28-30)

Honor your father and your mother, so that you may live long
in the land the Lord your God is giving you. (Exodus 20:12)

You shall not covet your neighbor's house. You shall not covet
your neighbor's wife, or his manservant or maidservant, his ox
or donkey, or anything that belongs to your neighbor.
(Exodus 20:17)

And he has given us this command: Whoever loves God must
also love his brother. (1 John 4:21)

And what about the Great Commission? What are we doing
to see that it is carried out? Remember, it involves not only telling
others about Christ, but it includes teaching them to obey Christ.
The command is to not only evangelize but to teach the new
believers to obey all that Christ taught. The way of evangelism and
discipleship is to be passed on from one person to another and
from one generation to another. The command of the Great
Commission applies to us today just as much as if Christ were
standing before us and speaking the words.

Then Jesus came to them and said, "All authority in heaven
and on earth has been given to me. Therefore go and make
disciples of all nations, baptizing them in the name of the
Father and of the Son and of the Holy Spirit, and teaching
them to obey everything I have commanded you. And surely I
am with you always, to the very end of the age."
(Matthew 28:18-20)

Are we being obedient to this command? Are we wise? Will
we shine bright as stars?

The fruit of the righteous is a tree of life, and he who wins
souls is wise. (Proverbs 11:30)

Those who are wise will shine like the brightness of the
heavens, and those who lead many to righteousness, like the
stars for ever and ever. (Daniel 12:3)

Are We in the Faith?

All of us can profit from reading this last series of verses again, giving thought to how we measure up to what is required of us. Pondering these verses will not only cause us to weigh our obedience, but it will cause us to consider the reality of our belief: Do we truly believe what we profess, or is ours a shallow profession backed up by a double-minded belief and a half-hearted faith? It will cause us to do as Paul said do: examine ourselves to see if we are in the faith.

Examine yourselves to see whether you are in the faith; test yourselves. Do you not realize that Christ Jesus is in you—unless, of course, you fail the test? (2 Corinthians 13:5)

How do we examine and test ourselves to determine if we are in the faith? Remembering when we received the Gospel with joy, and professed to receive Christ is certainly helpful, but not sufficient for a thorough examination. Many people make a profession of Christ which is later shown to be superficial when they fall by the wayside. No, our self-examination must go much deeper than our profession. We must look closely at our internal workings and our external works. There should be internal evidence that God is at work in us and external evidence that He is working through us. If we see evidence for external work but none for internal work, something is wrong. We may not be in the faith; we may well be in the flesh. We need not concern ourselves with finding internal work without the external—that is never the case. The internal work of God will always produce external fruit for God. A good tree produces good fruit.

There is another fruit that should be in evidence if we are in the faith—the fruit of the Holy Spirit. We know that all Christians are indwelt by the Holy Spirit (Romans 8:9) and that the Holy Spirit produces fruit in the Christian. We should know what this fruit is and check to see if it is manifested in our lives. A life rooted in the Spirit will manifest the fruit of the Spirit.

But the fruit of the Spirit is love, joy, peace, patience, kindness, goodness, faithfulness, gentleness and self-control.
(Galatians 5:22-23a)

An important step in our self-examination is to take a rational but critical look at our obedience. It is through obedience that the degree of our commitment to God and the depth of our love for God are confirmed.

This is love for God: to obey his commands. (1 John 5:3a)

Whoever has my commands and obeys them, he is the one who loves me. (John 14:21a)

It is only because we are known and loved by God that we are able to show love for God. If by a lack of obedience we imply a lack of love for God, then it follows that we may not be known and loved by God—hence we may not be in the faith. We can see that we need to take this admonition to examine ourselves seriously. We can ill afford to treat it lightly. It is a matter involving life-changing and life-threatening results in this world and in the world to come.

Essential to Study the Bible

We can see the importance of not just reading the Bible, but of studying it in depth. If our lives are to please God, we must know the truth and correctly apply it.

Do your best to present yourself to God as one approved, a workman who does not need to be ashamed and who correctly handles the word of truth. (2 Timothy 2:15)

It becomes obvious that the Word of God is as essential to our spiritual life as blood is to our physical life. We cannot pick and choose the Scriptures we will obey, but rather, we are to bow before God and seek to know and obey His every word. All Scripture is beneficial to us.

All Scripture is God-breathed and is useful for teaching, rebuking, correcting and training in righteousness, so that the man of God may be thoroughly equipped for every good work. (2 Timothy 3:16-17)

Imagine for a moment that God was coming to your town to make a talk. He would speak in the town auditorium which holds a limited number of people; admission would be free. Once word got out that God was going to speak, I think we can safely assume that people would begin to line up at the auditorium much ahead of time. Many would come from surrounding towns and neighboring states. Think how anxious you would be to hear God. The day of His talk would be bedlam, with traffic jams, pushing and shoving, and people doing most anything in an effort to hear God.

Now, let go of our imaginative scene and return to reality. We have God's Word, the Bible. It is His Word for us and to us, but how many people put forth the effort to find out what He says? How much time do we spend in Bible study seeking to know what God is saying to us? It all boils down to this: We have the Bible; God is speaking to us. Are we paying attention—are we listening? After all, the Bible is God's Word to us just as though He were speaking it audibly. It is a wonder that more of us do not spend more time studying God's Word and listening to God speak with our spiritual ears. Christ tells us we will be blessed if we hear and obey.

He replied, "Blessed rather are those who hear the word of God and obey it." (Luke 11:28)

He also quotes Deuteronomy 8:3 when tempted by the devil.

Jesus answered, "It is written: 'Man does not live on bread alone, but on every word that comes from the mouth of God.'" (Matthew 4:4)

If we choose not to read and study God's Word, we are guilty of a self-inflicted spiritual blindness because it is the Written Word that the Holy Spirit uses to teach us about the Living Word and our life in Him. When we do study, if we read only with our natural eyes instead of our spiritual eyes, it is like trying to read in the dark. However, if we read under the guidance of the Holy Spirit, He casts light on the Scriptures in order that we may see.

Flawed Teaching and False Teaching

I would like to caution you about something that seems to be rather commonplace these days: people depending on someone else to tell them what the Word says. Whether it is your preacher, your Sunday-school teacher, a good friend, or a book, you cannot afford to take it at face value without knowing for yourself that it is the truth. Not that any of these people are not telling you the truth, but someone could be in error and mislead you. And, of course, there are the false teachers about whom we are warned—the cults, and the so-called Christian religions that use the name of Christ but do not belong to Christ. We see then two basic types of false teaching. First, we see teaching that, although it is Christian, it is laced with flaws and errors; and second, we see teaching that is non-Christian or anti-Christian.

The first Satan can use to render ineffective those who are already in God's kingdom. The second he can use to keep souls out of God's kingdom. False teaching from without and within the church has always been a problem, and it is no less so today. The Bible contains a number of references to false teachers, several of which I will list here:

> As I urged you when I went into Macedonia, stay there in Ephesus so that you may command certain men not to teach false doctrines any longer.... (1 Timothy 1:3)

> Nevertheless, I have a few things against you: You have people there who hold to the teaching of Balaam, who taught Balak to entice the Israelites to sin by eating food sacrificed to idols and by committing sexual immorality. Likewise you also have those who hold to the teaching of the Nicolaitans. Repent therefore! Otherwise, I will soon come to you and will fight against them with the sword of my mouth. (Revelation 2:14-16)

> Anyone who runs ahead and does not continue in the teaching of Christ does not have God; whoever continues in the teaching has both the Father and the Son. If anyone comes to you and does not bring this teaching, do not take him into your house or welcome him. Anyone who welcomes him shares in his wicked work. (2 John 9-11)

> For there are many rebellious people, mere talkers and deceivers, especially those of the circumcision group. They

must be silenced, because they are ruining whole households by teaching things they ought not to teach—and that for the sake of dishonest gain. (Titus 1:10-11)

Avoid godless chatter, because those who indulge in it will become more and more ungodly. Their teaching will spread like gangrene. Among them are Hymenaeus and Philetus, who have wandered away from the truth. They say that the resurrection has already taken place, and they destroy the faith of some. (2 Timothy 2:16-18)

Nevertheless, I have this against you: You tolerate that woman Jezebel, who calls herself a prophetess. By her teaching she misleads my servants into sexual immorality and the eating of food sacrificed to idols. (Revelation 2:20)

I urge you, brothers, to watch out for those who cause divisions and put obstacles in your way that are contrary to the teaching you have learned. Keep away from them. For such people are not serving our Lord Christ, but their own appetites. By smooth talk and flattery they deceive the minds of naive people. (Romans 16:17-18)

Peter points out that false teachers will be a problem and many will be led into disobedience by them.

But there were also false prophets among the people, just as there will be false teachers among you. They will secretly introduce destructive heresies, even denying the sovereign Lord who bought them—bringing swift destruction on themselves. Many will follow their shameful ways and will bring the way of truth into disrepute. In their greed these teachers will exploit you with stories they have made up. Their condemnation has long been hanging over them, and their destruction has not been sleeping. (2 Peter 2:1-3)

Today, we see many who fit Peter's description of the false teachers of his day. There are those who teach that if you profess Christ as Savior, you are set free to do anything and live anyway you please.

> With eyes full of adultery, they never stop sinning; they seduce
> the unstable; they are experts in greed—an accursed brood!
> (2 Peter 2:14)

> For they mouth empty, boastful words and, by appealing to the
> lustful desires of sinful human nature, they entice people who
> are just escaping from those who live in error. They promise
> them freedom, while they themselves are slaves of
> depravity—for a man is a slave to whatever has mastered him.
> (2 Peter 2:18-19)

Opposite to these teachers would be those who teach salvation by works. There are a number of teachers today who teach that salvation is obtained by doing works. Paul warned the Galatians about teachers like these. He told them it was foolish to try to earn salvation by human effort.

> I am astonished that you are so quickly deserting the one who
> called you by the grace of Christ and are turning to a different
> gospel—which is really no gospel at all. Evidently some people
> are throwing you into confusion and are trying to pervert the
> gospel of Christ. But even if we or an angel from heaven
> should preach a gospel other than the one we preached to you,
> let him be eternally condemned! (Galatians 1:6-8)

> Are you so foolish? After beginning with the Spirit, are you
> now trying to attain your goal by human effort? (Galatians 3:3)

Check the Message and the Messenger

John's warning to the early church about testing and discerning the spirits certainly applies to us today.

> Dear friends, do not believe every spirit, but test the spirits to
> see whether they are from God, because many false prophets
> have gone out into the world. (1 John 4:1)

Christ commended the church at Ephesus for testing those who claimed to be apostles.

> I know your deeds, your hard work and your perseverance. I
> know that you cannot tolerate wicked men, that you have tested

those who claim to be apostles but are not, and have found them false. (Revelation 2:2)

Paul says the false apostles are servants of Satan.

For such men are false apostles, deceitful workmen, masquerading as apostles of Christ. And no wonder, for Satan himself masquerades as an angel of light. It is not surprising, then, if his servants masquerade as servants of righteousness. Their end will be what their actions deserve. (2 Corinthians 11:13-15)

We should always be careful of any person or group who claims to be the only one who has the truth. We should carefully check out the message and the messenger. If we are obedient, we will study the Bible to see if what is being taught is true—whether in Bible class, in a sermon at church, in a book, by radio, or on TV. The Bereans even checked the Apostle Paul against the Scriptures to see if he was teaching truth.

As soon as it was night, the brothers sent Paul and Silas away to Berea. On arriving there, they went to the Jewish synagogue. Now the Bereans were of more noble character than the Thessalonians, for they received the message with great eagerness and examined the Scriptures every day to see if what Paul said was true. Many of the Jews believed, as did also a number of prominent Greek women and many Greek men. (Acts 17:10-12)

Sound Doctrine is Essential

Sound doctrine is essential to Christian living. Paul certainly believed this as evidenced by the vast amount of doctrine contained in his letters. He knew that obedience to sound doctrine produced sound living.

You must teach what is in accord with sound doctrine. (Titus 2:1)

Watch your life and doctrine closely. Persevere in them, because if you do, you will save both yourself and your hearers. (1 Timothy 4:16)

In light of what we have just read, does it not behoove us to
do as the psalmist said and not neglect God's Word?

How can a young man keep his way pure?
   By living according to your word.
I delight in your decrees;
   I will not neglect your word.
(Psalm 119:9,16)

New Life Produces New Lives

The Bible teaches that there are two kinds of people—the
believer and the unbeliever. The believer of today was the
unbeliever of yesterday. Now that he is a believer, he is not only
expected to act differently but to be different.

In reality, he is different. God has done a work in him in
order that He may work through him. He has been born again,
born from above, born of God. Although he is still a sinner with
a sinful nature, things have changed. Although the old nature is
not destroyed, it is weakened. Although it is still dangerous, it is
restrained. Although it is still operative, it is rendered ineffective.
The believer has been declared righteous and has been given a new
nature. He has been given a heart of flesh. He is a new man—a
new creation. Now that he is a new man, he is to live a new life.

**I will give them an undivided heart and put a new spirit in
them; I will remove from them their heart of stone and give
them a heart of flesh.** (Ezekiel 11:19)

**You were taught, with regard to your former way of life, to put
off your old self, which is being corrupted by its deceitful
desires; to be made new in the attitude of your minds; and to
put on the new self, created to be like God in true
righteousness and holiness.** (Ephesians 4:22-24)

**We were therefore buried with him through baptism into death
in order that, just as Christ was raised from the dead through
the glory of the Father, we too may live a new life.**
(Romans 6:4)

**Therefore, if anyone is in Christ, he is a new creation; the old
has gone, the new has come!** (2 Corinthians 5:17)

A Christian should continually praise and thank God for the change in his situation when he compares what it once was to what it is now: once a lost sinner, now a found saint; once powerless over sin, now enabled to resist sin; once dead in transgressions, now alive in Christ; once condemned by law, now pardoned by grace; once without any hope, now with a living hope; once without any faith, now walk by faith; once headed to hell, now headed to heaven; once without God, now indwelt by God.

We hear the world talk of success. We see the world seek after success, but the world does not know what real success is. True success is spiritual success—the only success that continues beyond the grave. Think of the success story of Christians. We come into this world as spiritual paupers, condemned sinners headed to hell, but we leave this world spiritually rich, with a full pardon and a home in heaven.

Considering how pathetic our situation once was and how wonderful it is now, we should be like a boxer who eagerly answers the bell and comes out fighting—determined to do his best. We should eagerly begin each day determined to do our best and, in God's power, to fight the fight of faith. And in so doing show the world, particularly those around us, that we are children of God. We can begin by putting into practice some instructions that Paul gave to the Colossians.

> **Since, then, you have been raised with Christ, set your hearts on things above, where Christ is seated at the right hand of God. Set your minds on things above, not on earthly things. For you died, and your life is now hidden with Christ in God. When Christ, who is your life, appears, then you also will appear with him in glory.**
>
> **Put to death, therefore, whatever belongs to your earthly nature: sexual immorality, impurity, lust, evil desires and greed, which is idolatry. Because of these, the wrath of God is coming. You used to walk in these ways, in the life you once lived. But now you must rid yourselves of all such things as these: anger, rage, malice, slander, and filthy language from your lips. Do not lie to each other, since you have taken off your old self with its practices and have put on the new self, which is being renewed in knowledge in the image of its Creator. Here there is no Greek or Jew, circumcised or uncircumcised, barbarian, Scythian, slave or free, but Christ is all, and is in all.**

> Therefore, as God's chosen people, holy and dearly loved, clothe yourselves with compassion, kindness, humility, gentleness and patience. Bear with each other and forgive whatever grievances you may have against one another. Forgive as the Lord forgave you. And over all these virtues put on love, which binds them all together in perfect unity.
> Let the peace of Christ rule in your hearts, since as members of one body you were called to peace. And be thankful. Let the word of Christ dwell in you richly as you teach and admonish one another with all wisdom, and as you sing psalms, hymns and spiritual songs with gratitude in your hearts to God. And whatever you do, whether in word or deed, do it all in the name of the Lord Jesus, giving thanks to God the Father through him. (Colossians 3:1-17)

In our attempt to live above sin and the world, it will be helpful to us to keep reminding ourselves that we are new creatures. When Christ died to sin, we died to sin—our old self was crucified with Him.

> For we know that our old self was crucified with him so that the body of sin might be done away with, that we should no longer be slaves to sin.... In the same way, count yourselves dead to sin but alive to God in Christ Jesus. (Romans 6:6,11)

As new men living new lives, we are to break with the ways of the world.

> Do not love the world or anything in the world. If anyone loves the world, the love of the Father is not in him. For everything in the world—the cravings of sinful man, the lust of his eyes and the boasting of what he has and does—comes not from the Father but from the world. The world and its desires pass away, but the man who does the will of God lives forever. (1 John 2:15-17)

The world is the enemy of our Lord, and His enemy is our enemy.

> If the world hates you, keep in mind that it hated me first. If you belonged to the world, it would love you as its own. As it is, you do not belong to the world, but I have chosen you out of the world. That is why the world hates you. (John 15:18-19)

We must keep in mind that, through the Crucifixion of Christ, we have been freed from the power of sin in our lives. We have also been freed from the pull of the world on our lives.

Those who belong to Christ Jesus have crucified the sinful nature with its passions and desires. (Galatians 5:24)

May I never boast except in the cross of our Lord Jesus Christ, through which the world has been crucified to me, and I to the world. (Galatians 6:14)

Christ has freed us from the legal penalty of sin, the moral guilt of sin, the strong bondage of sin, and the active power of sin. Therefore, we are to walk as men who are dead to sin. As new men with new freedom, we are being disobedient if we do not live a new life.

Sanctification Produces Obedient and Fruitful Service

Sometimes we make it seem too easy to be a Christian. Many people get the impression that an external profession of faith and external works are sufficient. In reality, it is the internal profession and the internal work in the believer that counts. If we are not right on the inside, nothing we do on the outside is of any value. God looks at the inside. He looks at our hearts.

Woe to you, teachers of the law and Pharisees, you hypocrites! You clean the outside of the cup and dish, but inside they are full of greed and self-indulgence. Blind Pharisee! First clean the inside of the cup and dish, and then the outside also will be clean. (Matthew 23:25-26)

As for you, son of man, your countrymen are talking together about you by the walls and at the doors of the houses, saying to each other, "Come and hear the message that has come from the Lord." My people come to you, as they usually do, and sit before you to listen to your words, but they do not put them into practice. With their mouths they express devotion, but their hearts are greedy for unjust gain. (Ezekiel 33:30-31)

The crucible for silver and the furnace for gold, but the Lord tests the heart. (Proverbs 17:3)

All a man's ways seem right to him, but the Lord weighs the heart. (Proverbs 21:2)

When we were saved our hearts were made right, and through the process of sanctification our hearts are kept right. It is the process wherein we have been set apart and are being conformed to the image of Christ and thereby glorify God. Sanctification in the Christian's life begins at the time of spiritual birth. The word sanctify means to set apart, and those who are set apart by God are set apart for God. They are consecrated to God. When we were justified by Christ, we were sanctified by Christ. We were set apart to live our lives in God, to serve and work for God.

And by that will, we have been made holy through the sacrifice of the body of Jesus Christ once for all. (Hebrews 10:10)

The act of sanctification was a one-time thing as was the act of justification. However, just as we are to work out our salvation, we are to undergo the process of sanctification. We have been declared sanctified—now we are being sanctified. We have been declared clean—now we are being made clean.

...because by one sacrifice he has made perfect forever those who are being made holy. (Hebrews 10:14)

The immediate purpose of our sanctification is to conform us to the image of Christ; the resultant purpose is to glorify God. God uses all that happens in the Christian's life as a means to work this process of sanctification. He uses discipline, persecution, suffering, and trials, along with the joys and pleasures in our lives, causing them all to work together for our sanctification.

And we know that in all things God works for the good of those who love him, who have been called according to his purpose. For those God foreknew he also predestined to be conformed to the likeness of his Son, that he might be the first born among many brothers. (Romans 8:28-29)

As God works sanctification in our lives, our faith and knowledge are increased and we become more fruitful in His service. This process is a purging of the Christian life of those things that retard spiritual growth, hinder godly work, and tarnish

Christian witness. It is a process that cleanses from the inside out. It goes beyond discipline for sin; it weakens the desire to sin, and it removes things that occasion sin. It turns a life budding with fruit into a life ripe with fruit.

> I am the true vine, and my Father is the gardener. He cuts off every branch in me that bears no fruit, while every branch that does bear fruit he prunes so that it will be even more fruitful. (John 15:1-2)

Being Made Holy

We should rejoice in sanctification as it is the process by which we are made holy—it is a process of holiness. God declares us holy, commands us to be holy, and works to make us holy.

> Both the one who makes men holy and those who are made holy are of the same family. So Jesus is not ashamed to call them brothers. (Hebrews 2:11)

> Make every effort to live in peace with all men and to be holy; without holiness no one will see the Lord. (Hebrews 12:14)

> But now that you have been set free from sin and have become slaves to God, the benefit you reap leads to holiness, and the result is eternal life. (Romans 6:22)

Holiness is God's work. There is nothing we can do to make ourselves holy, but there is something we must do if we would be made holy. We must yield our hearts and minds (our wills) to God. We must not only be willing to be made holy but we must will to be made holy. We must petition God for the enabling power to not only do better, but to be better. The Christian life is a work of God; however, the Christian is to be active and is to put forth effort in living that life for God. If we are to be holy, we must live under the control of the One who is holy—God the Holy Spirit.

Continue Spiritual Growth

It is important to realize that where we are today is not good enough for tomorrow. We know we are to persevere in the faith and endure to the end. However, that does not mean we are to reach a certain level of spiritual maturity and then stop there, going into a holding pattern and persevering at that level for the remainder of our lives.

No, the process of sanctification is just that, a process—an ongoing process. We are not only to continue and persevere in the Christian life, but we are to continue and persevere in Christian growth. There is no room for complacency in the Christian life; there is no "having arrived." We should always be growing spiritually, growing in the grace and knowledge of Jesus Christ.

> **Finally, brothers, we instructed you how to live in order to please God, as in fact you are living. Now we ask you and urge you in the Lord Jesus to do this more and more.**
> (1 Thessalonians 4:1)

> **But grow in the grace and knowledge of our Lord and Savior Jesus Christ.** (2 Peter 3:18a)

Where there is spiritual life, there should be spiritual growth—where there is no growth, there may be no life. At best it is a stunted life, a life lived on the brink of spiritual death. The possibility of spiritual death should be enough to cause us to heed the admonition of Scripture, and by our lives and our deeds prove that we are saved.

> **...continue to work out your salvation with fear and trembling....** (Philippians 2:12)

We have reason to fear and tremble because this has to do with our salvation. Whether we spend eternity in hell or in heaven depends on whether or not we are saved. This is serious business. We better be serious now, or we will be sorry later. If we lose our soul, we have lost it all.

> **What good will it be for a man if he gains the whole world, yet forfeits his soul? Or what can a man give in exchange for his soul?** (Matthew 16:26)

Salvation is not something to be toyed with or played around with. It is something to be worked out. It is true that salvation is a gift and, as such, cannot be earned; however, it is a gift that always evokes a response from the recipient. The response is one of obedience to Christ. If there is no response, we have never received the gift. We have only deceived ourselves.

> **Why do you call me, "Lord, Lord," and do not do what I say?** (Luke 6:46)

There are other Scriptures that express a thought similar to "work out your salvation with fear and trembling."

> **And, "If it is hard for the righteous to be saved, what will become of the ungodly and the sinner?"** (1 Peter 4:18)

> **Watch out that you do not lose what you have worked for, but that you may be rewarded fully.** (2 John 8)

> **Therefore, since the promise of entering his rest still stands, let us be careful that none of you be found to have fallen short of it.** (Hebrews 4:1)

Working out our salvation is not only our working for God, but it includes our being changed by the work of God. It is all part of the process of sanctification—God's sanctifying work in us. Through it, we gain confidence that we are His.

> **Therefore, my brothers, be all the more eager to make your calling and election sure. For if you do these things, you will never fall, and you will receive a rich welcome into the eternal kingdom of our Lord and Savior Jesus Christ.** (2 Peter 1:10-11)

If we will get busy working out our salvation with fear and trembling, seeking to do the will of God, in the power of the Holy Spirit, we will find sanctification seeping through our souls.

Rewards for Obedient Service

Rewards for our Christian works are something that many Christians do not give thought to. It is a subject that some Christians feel should not be discussed. They think it is contrary to Christian thought and behavior. However, that is not what the Bible teaches.

In Scripture, the subject of rewards is taught as a concept, and it is held forth as a reality. Christ spoke of punishment, but He also spoke of rewards. The Bible threatens the ultimate punishment of hell, but it offers the ultimate reward of heaven. If something is taught in the Bible, we should accept the fact of it, believe the truth of it, and seek to benefit from the knowledge of it.

Let us look into the subject of rewards, with the hope of gaining a better understanding of where they fit into our lives here on earth and in heaven. We find in the Old Testament, God promised a reward of special affection to Israel for obedience.

Now if you obey me fully and keep my covenant, then out of all nations you will be my treasured possession. (Exodus 19:5)

We also find that what He commanded them to do was for their own good.

And now, O Israel, what does the Lord your God ask of you but to fear the Lord your God, to walk in all his ways, to love him, to serve the Lord your God with all your heart and with all your soul, and to observe the Lord's commands and decrees that I am giving you today for your own good? (Deuteronomy 10:12-13)

Obedience Rewarded—Disobedience Punished

God's ways are above man's ways. His ways lead to a lifestyle that we could never find if left to ourselves; therefore, we would miss all the benefits such a lifestyle produces. Foremost is the fact that the ways of sinful man lead to death, but the ways of our righteous God lead to life. Obedience to God's commands was for Israel's own good then, and it is for our own good now. As was the case with Israel, we will either reap the rewards of obedience or suffer the punishment of disobedience.

Observe therefore all the commands I am giving you today, so that you may have the strength to go in and take over the land that you are crossing the Jordan to possess, and so that you may live long in the land that the Lord swore to your

forefathers to give to them and their descendants, a land
flowing with milk and honey. (Deuteronomy 11:8-9)

So if you faithfully obey the commands I am giving you
today—to love the Lord your God and to serve him with all
your heart and with all your soul—then I will send rain on
your land in its season, both autumn and spring rains, so that
you may gather in your grain, new wine and oil. I will provide
grass in the fields for your cattle, and you will eat and be
satisfied.
    Be careful, or you will be enticed to turn away and
worship other gods and bow down to them. Then the Lord's
anger will burn against you, and he will shut the heavens so
that it will not rain and the ground will yield no produce, and
you will soon perish from the good land the Lord is giving you.
(Deuteronomy 11:13-17)

See, I am setting before you today a blessing and a curse—the
blessing if you obey the commands of the Lord your God that
I am giving you today; the curse if you disobey the commands
of the Lord your God and turn from the way that I command
you today by following other gods, which you have not known.
(Deuteronomy 11:26-28)

Too often, we take God's words of blessings for obedience,
and curses for disobedience much too lightly. It seems we do not
believe all that God says, or we think we are an exception to what
He says. It behooves us to look at what He told Israel, and then
see how it has all unfolded in the history of Israel. When we see
what happened to them because of their disobedience, we may well
wonder what will happen to America because of ours.

If you fully obey the Lord your God and carefully follow all his
commands I give you today, the Lord your God will set you
high above all the nations on earth. All these blessings will
come upon you and accompany you if you obey the Lord your
God:
    You will be blessed in the city and blessed in the country.
    The fruit of your womb will be blessed, and the crops of
your land and the young of your livestock—the calves of your
herds and the lambs of your flocks.
    Your basket and your kneading trough will be blessed.

You will be blessed when you come in and blessed when you go out.

The Lord will grant that the enemies who rise up against you will be defeated before you. They will come at you from one direction but flee from you in seven.

The Lord will send a blessing on your barns and on everything you put your hand to. The Lord your God will bless you in the land he is giving you.

The Lord will establish you as his holy people, as he promised you on oath, if you keep the commands of the Lord your God and walk in his ways. Then all the peoples on earth will see that you are called by the name of the Lord, and they will fear you. The Lord will grant you abundant prosperity—in the fruit of your womb, the young of your livestock and the crops of your ground—in the land he swore to your forefathers to give you.

The Lord will open the heavens, the storehouse of his bounty, to send rain on your land in season and to bless all the work of your hands. You will lend to many nations but will borrow from none. The Lord will make you the head, not the tail. If you pay attention to the commands of the Lord your God that I give you this day and carefully follow them, you will always be at the top, never at the bottom. Do not turn aside from any of the commands I give you today, to the right or to the left, following other gods and serving them.

However, if you do not obey the Lord your God and do not carefully follow all his commands and decrees I am giving you today, all these curses will come upon you and overtake you:

You will be cursed in the city and cursed in the country.

Your basket and your kneading trough will be cursed.

The fruit of your womb will be cursed, and the crops of your land, and the calves of your herds and the lambs of your flocks.

You will be cursed when you come in and cursed when you go out.

The Lord will send on you curses, confusion and rebuke in everything you put your hand to, until you are destroyed and come to sudden ruin because of the evil you have done in forsaking him. The Lord will plague you with diseases until he has destroyed you from the land you are entering to possess. The Lord will strike you with wasting disease, with fever and inflammation, with scorching heat and drought, with blight and mildew, which will plague you until you perish. The sky over your head will be bronze, the ground beneath you iron.

The Lord will turn the rain of your country into dust and powder; it will come down from the skies until you are destroyed.

The Lord will cause you to be defeated before your enemies. You will come at them from one direction but flee from them in seven, and you will become a thing of horror to all the kingdoms on earth. Your carcasses will be food for all the birds of the air and the beasts of the earth, and there will be no one to frighten them away. The Lord will afflict you with the boils of Egypt and with tumors, festering sores and the itch, from which you cannot be cured. The Lord will afflict you with madness, blindness and confusion of mind. At midday you will grope about like a blind man in the dark. You will be unsuccessful in everything you do; day after day you will be oppressed and robbed, with no one to rescue you.

You will be pledged to be married to a woman, but another will take her and ravish her. You will build a house, but you will not live in it. You will plant a vineyard, but you will not even begin to enjoy its fruit. Your ox will be slaughtered before your eyes, but you will eat none of it. Your donkey will be forcibly taken from you and will not be returned. Your sheep will be given to your enemies, and no one will rescue them. Your sons and daughters will be given to another nation, and you will wear out your eyes watching for them day after day, powerless to lift a hand. A people that you do not know will eat what your land and labor produce, and you will have nothing but cruel oppression all your days. The sights you see will drive you mad. The Lord will afflict your knees and legs with painful boils that cannot be cured, spreading from the soles of your feet to the top of your head.

The Lord will drive you and the king you set over you to a nation unknown to you or your fathers. There you will worship other gods, gods of wood and stone. You will become a thing of horror and an object of scorn and ridicule to all the nations where the Lord will drive you.

You will sow much seed in the field but you will harvest little, because locusts will devour it. You will plant vineyards and cultivate them but you will not drink the wine or gather the grapes, because worms will eat them. You will have olive trees throughout your country but you will not use the oil, because the olives will drop off. You will have sons and daughters but you will not keep them, because they will go into captivity. Swarms of locusts will take over all your trees and the crops of your land.

The alien who lives among you will rise above you higher and higher, but you will sink lower and lower. He will lend to you, but you will not lend to him. He will be the head, but you will be the tail.

All these curses will come upon you. They will pursue you and overtake you until you are destroyed, because you did not obey the Lord your God and observe the commands and decrees he gave you. They will be a sign and a wonder to you and your descendants forever. Because you did not serve the Lord your God joyfully and gladly in the time of prosperity, therefore in hunger and thirst, in nakedness and dire poverty, you will serve the enemies the Lord sends against you. He will put an iron yoke on your neck until he has destroyed you.

The Lord will bring a nation against you from far away, from the ends of the earth, like an eagle swooping down, a nation whose language you will not understand, a fierce-looking nation without respect for the old or pity for the young. They will devour the young of your livestock and the crops of your land until you are destroyed. They will leave you no grain, new wine or oil, nor any calves of your herds or lambs of your flocks until you are ruined. They will lay siege to all the cities throughout your land until the high fortified walls in which you trust fall down. They will besiege all the cities throughout the land the Lord your God is giving you.

Because of the suffering that your enemy will inflict on you during the siege, you will eat the fruit of the womb, the flesh of the sons and daughters the Lord your God has given you. Even the most gentle and sensitive man among you will have no compassion on his own brother or the wife he loves or his surviving children, and he will not give to one of them any of the flesh of his children that he is eating. It will be all he has left because of the suffering your enemy will inflict on you during the siege of all your cities. The most gentle and sensitive woman among you—so sensitive and gentle that she would not venture to touch the ground with the sole of her foot—will begrudge the husband she loves and her own son or daughter the afterbirth from her womb and the children she bears. For she intends to eat them secretly during the siege and in the distress that your enemy will inflict on you in your cities.

If you do not carefully follow all the words of this law, which are written in this book, and do not revere this glorious and awesome name—the Lord your God—the Lord will send fearful plagues on you and your descendants, harsh and prolonged disasters, and severe and lingering illnesses. He will bring upon you all the diseases of Egypt that you dreaded, and they will cling to you. The Lord will also bring on you every kind of sickness and disaster not recorded in this Book of the Law, until you are destroyed. You who were as numerous as the stars in the sky will be left but few in number, because you did not obey the Lord your God. Just as it pleased the Lord to make you prosper and increase in number, so it will please him to ruin and destroy you. You will be uprooted from the land you are entering to possess.

Then the Lord will scatter you among all nations, from one end of the earth to the other. There you will worship other gods—gods of wood and stone, which neither you nor your fathers have known. Among those nations you will find no repose, no resting place for the sole of your foot. There the Lord will give you an anxious mind, eyes weary with longing, and a despairing heart. You will live in constant suspense, filled with dread both night and day, never sure of your life. In the morning you will say, "If only it were evening!" and in the evening, "If only it were morning!"—because of the terror that will fill your hearts and the sights that your eyes will see. The Lord will send you back in ships to Egypt on a journey I said you should never make again. There you will offer yourselves for sale to your enemies as male and female slaves, but no one will buy you. (Deuteronomy Chapter 28)

When we look at what Israel did and then look at what America is doing, we see that the only hope the Israelites had is the only hope we have—to repent and turn to God. Not just the church in America, but the nation of America must repent and be obedient. If we would avoid the punishment of God, we must stop sinning against God.

This is the word that came to Jeremiah from the Lord: "Go down to the potter's house, and there I will give you my message." So I went down to the potter's house, and I saw him working at the wheel. But the pot he was shaping from the clay was marred in his hands; so the potter formed it into another pot, shaping it as seemed best to him.

Then the word of the Lord came to me: "O house of Israel, can I not do with you as this potter does?" declares the Lord. "Like clay in the hand of the potter, so are you in my hand, O house of Israel. If at any time I announce that a

nation or kingdom is to be uprooted, torn down and destroyed,
and if that nation I warned repents of its evil, then I will relent
and not inflict on it the disaster I had planned. And if at
another time I announce that a nation or kingdom is to be
built up and planted, and if it does evil in my sight and does
not obey me, then I will reconsider the good I had intended to
do for it." (Jeremiah 18:1-10)

Obedient Giving

Regardless of promised reward or threatened punishment, one
area where the Israelites had a problem of obedience was in the
area of giving. This continues to be a problem with Christians
today. Few things cause such a tug-of-war in the hearts of so many
as the question of giving.

The question is not whether to give or not, for all true
believers would say the Bible teaches giving. There is a question of
what the Bible teaches about how much to give; however, that is
not the question that causes the war. And it is not the question of
where to give, or to whom to give, because most Christians reach
this answer without great difficulty. The question that causes the
tug-of-war is one that each of us must find the answer to within
our own heart. It is: Am I willing to give what I truly feel God
would have me give, regardless of the amount?

The tug-of-war is that age-old war between God's will and our
will. For some, the war is in its infancy. Whereas before, there was
no thought to giving—just a mechanical reaction to the passing of
the offering plate, dropping in a token amount for the sake of
appearances—now there is concern. As God works in the heart,
questions begin to pop into the mind. Should I give more? Do
others in my income bracket give more? If they do, does that mean
I should?

Thinking this way, the Christian sees this only as a conflict
between his giving and the giving of others. Later, when he
becomes aware that he is contending with God, not man, the
tug-of-war begins in earnest. His love for God and the desire to do
God's will pull in one direction, and his love of money and the
desire to do his own will pull in the opposite direction. The love of
money is the way of the world; it is the motivating factor in life for
many, reaching a point of obsession for some. The Christian is not

immune to this, and must constantly be on guard to prevent it from happening. The Bible warns against the love of money.

> Now the overseer must be above reproach, the husband of but one wife, temperate, self-controlled, respectable, hospitable, able to teach, not given to drunkenness, not violent but gentle, not quarrelsome, not a lover of money. (1 Timothy 3:2-3)

> For the love of money is a root of all kinds of evil. Some people, eager for money, have wandered from the faith and pierced themselves with many griefs. (1 Timothy 6:10)

Tithing—is it Required Today?

As the war grows in duration, it grows in intensity. The Christian often finds himself wrestling with the proposition of tithing—is it required? He is now faced with the thought of giving a larger amount of his income than ever before. The desire to keep money can be as strong as the desire to get money and, for some people, parting with it is even more difficult than earning it.

There are Christians who contend the Bible does not teach tithing in the New Testament; therefore, it does not apply to us today. Most who believe this are sincere in their belief. However, there are those who do not want to give as much as the tithe, and who use this as their reason not to give it. Others believe the New Testament teaches giving more than the tithe. So often, both those who believe more than the tithe and those who believe less than the tithe is taught, use verses from the 16th chapter of 1 Corinthians in an attempt to support their view.

> Now about the collection for God's people. Do what I told the Galatian churches to do. On the first day of every week, each one of you should set aside a sum of money in keeping with his income, saving it up, so that when I come no collections will have to be made. Then, when I arrive, I will give letters of introduction to the men you approve and send them with your gift to Jerusalem. If it seems advisable for me to go also, they will accompany me. (1 Corinthians 16:1-4)

They point to the fact that these verses indicate giving in proportion to your income—if you have a large income you should give more than someone with a smaller income. However, the only way it could be assured that this would happen would be for everyone to give the same percentage of their income—whether it is a tenth, more than a tenth, or less than a tenth. Otherwise, one with a small income could give more than one with a larger income. In this instance, the members of the Corinthian church may have given as each felt led, or they could have agreed on a percentage of income that all would abide by. However, as far as having a bearing on whether or not tithing is in effect today, I think it matters not. This was not direction from Paul to the church in general concerning Christian giving. This was direction to the Corinthian church concerning a special gift and involving special giving for the Christians at Jerusalem.

> **The disciples, each according to his ability, decided to provide help for the brothers living in Judea. This they did, sending their gift to the elders by Barnabas and Saul.** (Acts 11:29)

> **Now, however, I am on my way to Jerusalem in the service of the saints there. For Macedonia and Achaia were pleased to make a contribution for the poor among the saints in Jerusalem.** (Romans 15:25-26)

> **There is no need for me to write to you about this service to the saints. For I know your eagerness to help, and I have been boasting about it to the Macedonians, telling them that since last year you in Achaia were ready to give; and your enthusiasm has stirred most of them to action. But I am sending the brothers in order that our boasting about you in this matter should not prove hollow, but that you may be ready, as I said you would be. For if any Macedonians come with me and find you unprepared, we—not to say anything about you—would be ashamed of having been so confident. So I thought it necessary to urge the brothers to visit you in advance and finish the arrangements for the generous gift you had promised. Then it will be ready as a generous gift, not as one grudgingly given.** (2 Corinthians 9:1-5)

The Macedonian church had asked Paul if they too could contribute to help the saints at Jerusalem.

> **And now, brothers, we want you to know about the grace that God has given the Macedonian churches. Out of the most**

severe trial, their overflowing joy and their extreme poverty welled up in rich generosity. For I testify that they gave as much as they were able, and even beyond their ability. Entirely on their own, they urgently pleaded with us for the privilege of sharing in this service to the saints. (2 Corinthians 8:1-4)

Tithing Before the Law

This then, being for a special gift, neither supports nor denies tithing as a principle for regular giving. However, it certainly sets an example for generous giving. But let us look further at what the Word has to say. Tithing was commanded in the Law of Moses. However, before the Law of Moses was given, we see that Abraham (Abram) tithed to Melchizedek.

Then Melchizedek king of Salem brought out bread and wine. He was priest of God Most High, and he blessed Abram, saying, "Blessed be Abram by God Most High, Creator of heaven and earth. And blessed be God Most High, who delivered your enemies into your hand." Then Abram gave him a tenth of everything. (Genesis 14:18-20)

Also, before the Law, Jacob vowed to give God a tenth.

Then Jacob made a vow, saying, "If God will be with me and will watch over me on this journey I am taking and will give me food to eat and clothes to wear so that I return safely to my father's house, then the Lord will be my God and this stone that I have set up as a pillar will be God's house, and of all that you give me I will give you a tenth." (Genesis 28:20-22)

Tithing Under the Law

When Moses' Law was given, the tithe was looked upon as belonging to the Lord; it was holy, set aside for God.

A tithe of everything from the land, whether grain from the soil or fruit from the trees, belongs to the Lord; it is holy to the Lord. (Leviticus 27:30)

They were required to tithe, but some Israelites went beyond the tithe by giving offerings and special gifts.

...there bring your burnt offerings and sacrifices, your tithes and special gifts, what you have vowed to give and your freewill offerings, and the firstborn of your herds and flocks. (Deuteronomy 12:6)

The tithe was law. However, there were some who kept the letter but not the spirit of the law.

"When you bring injured, crippled or diseased animals and offer them as sacrifices, should I accept them from your hands?" says the Lord. "Cursed is the cheat who has an acceptable male in his flock and vows to give it, but then sacrifices a blemished animal to the Lord. For I am a great king," says the Lord Almighty, "and my name is to be feared among the nations." (Malachi 1:13b-14)

There were others who kept neither the letter or the spirit of the law.

"Ever since the time of your forefathers you have turned away from my decrees and have not kept them. Return to me, and I will return to you," says the Lord Almighty. "But you ask, 'How are we to return?' Will a man rob God? Yet you rob me. But you ask, 'How do we rob you?' In tithes and offerings. You are under a curse —the whole nation of you—because you are robbing me." (Malachi 3:7-9)

It is clear that tithing is taught in the Old Testament. In the New Testament we do not find a verse that states tithing is required or suggested. However, it is equally true that we do not find a verse that states tithing is no longer the rule or guide for Christian giving. To the contrary, we find that Jesus, while rebuking the Pharisees for their neglect of justice and love, gives his approval to the fact that they tithed. However, consideration must be given to the fact that the Law had not been abolished at that time.

Woe to you Pharisees, because you give God a tenth of your mint, rue and all other kinds of garden herbs, but you neglect

justice and the love of God. You should have practiced the latter without leaving the former undone. (Luke 11:42)

We saw Abraham tithing before the Law. We know tithing is called for in the Law, and we have no indication that tithing has been rescinded due to the fact that we are not under the Law. Therefore, although I cannot point to a verse that proves it, I believe tithing is the guideline for the Christian today.

Personal Experience with Tithing

Not long after my wife and I became Christians, we were faced with the question of whether or not to tithe. Our pastor preached a sermon on stewardship, which God used in both of our lives. Pledge time at our church was coming up and each of us, unknown to the other, began to consider whether or not we should tithe. We had never tithed and had not considered tithing before; however, both of us felt led to tithe. We discussed it between ourselves and then with our pastor. We questioned whether one should tithe on his gross or net income. As our feeling that God wanted us to tithe grew stronger, we looked closer at our financial situation.

We had recently moved into a new home, owed money on furniture, a car, and braces for both children's teeth. On paper, there was no way we could tithe. We were already much in debt and would have to go to the bank for a loan to make ends meet. However, after much prayer and serious consideration, we came to the conclusion that we were supposed to tithe our gross income. We made an agreement with each other that, if it were necessary in order to pay our tithe, we would sell the car. If things got really bad, we would sell the house, but the tithe would be paid.

We made this decision acting in obedience to what we felt God would have us do. Knowing that all things work together for our good (Romans 8:28), any type of response from Him would have been for our good—even having to sell the house. However, God gave me an increase in pay that year that was very close to the amount of the tithe. He did the same thing the next year. Our decision to tithe was reached more than twenty years ago, and for us it has been a settled fact of life ever since.

Blessing for Tithing—does it Apply Today?

I suggest that if you are wondering whether or not to tithe, give the verses about tithing further consideration and look to God to lead you in your decision. One more Scripture that might be helpful is found in the third chapter of Malachi.

> **"Bring the whole tithe into the storehouse, that there may be food in my house. Test me in this," says the Lord Almighty, "and see if I will not throw open the floodgates of heaven and pour out so much blessing that you will not have room enough for it."** (Malachi 3:10)

Although this was addressed to the nation of Israel, it is for our example. Whether you believe it teaches tithing for our day or not, you will have to agree that faithful obedience in giving is being taught; moreover, it is rewarded. We are not to begin tithing from a motivation of rewards but rather because we believe it is what God wants. If rewards come—whether material, spiritual, or both—we can rejoice in them. I am convinced that most people who tithe can tell of some incidence of increased income, or reduced expenses, or spiritual blessing that they connect to their tithing. However, I must add that, although I do not know of anyone personally who experienced a financial set back, I have heard of a few. In some of these cases there may be extenuating circumstances of disobedience in other areas.

Scholars disagree as to whether or not the promise in Malachi of blessing for tithing applies to us today. Although we may assume that there were blessings other than those mentioned, Scripture says the blessing was that the crops would be protected.

> **"I will prevent pests from devouring your crops, and the vines in your fields will not cast their fruit," says the Lord Almighty. "Then all the nations will call you blessed, for yours will be a delightful land," says the Lord Almighty.** (Malachi 3:11-12)

The promise was made to the nation of Israel and, though the nation was made up of individuals, it was to the individuals collectively. I doubt that there is anyone who would think that every single Israelite had to tithe before God would bless the nation. I also doubt that there is anyone who would think that not a single Israelite was tithing while the land was under a curse.

> **You are under a curse—the whole nation of you—because you are robbing me.** (Malachi 3:9)

Would we think that every individual was under a curse—even all of those who were living in obedience and tithing? There are a number of verses in the Old Testament that are specific in their application to the nation of Israel; however, they are the general rule in their application to the individual Israelite. Whether or not some of these verses apply to us today is one thing but, if they do, how we apply them is still another thing. We must be careful in their application.

If this promise of blessing in Malachi does apply to us today, it should be viewed as a general promise—a promise of what usually happens and of what is generally the rule, not a promise without exception. We are all familiar with statements or promises in Scripture concerning health, long life, wealth, and other things that are given as the general rule rather than as a rule without exception. For example:

> **The fear of the Lord adds length to life, but the years of the wicked are cut short.** (Proverbs 10:27)

That would be the general rule, but we know that some Christians are taken early in life while some of the wicked live to an old age.

> **The glory of young men is their strength, gray hair the splendor of the old.** (Proverbs 20:29)

Again, the general rule is that men tend to have more strength in their younger years. However, this is not always the case. All young men do not have strength—some are weakly and sick. Some have more strength later in life than they had when they were young.

We know that man is destined to die once and then face the judgment.

> **Just as man is destined to die once, and after that to face judgment....** (Hebrews 9:27)

The fact that Elijah and Enoch did not die but were translated to heaven in no way nullifies the fact that all men are to physically die.

As they were walking along and talking together, suddenly a chariot of fire and horses of fire appeared and separated the two of them, and Elijah went up to heaven in a whirlwind. (2 Kings 2:11)

By faith Enoch was taken from this life, so that he did not experience death; he could not be found, because God had taken him away. For before he was taken, he was commended as one who pleased God. (Hebrews 11:5)

Lazarus died once, and then Christ raised him from the dead (Luke 11:43); therefore, he died twice. This does not negate the fact that men are to die once. These exceptions in no way make the statements or promises untrue. We are to take them as they are given in the light of Scripture. They are the normal thing and are what will usually happen—the general rule.

Whether we see it as suggested or required, I believe tithing is the minimum amount Christians should give to God's work. There is certainly no reason, if led by God, not to give more than the tithe. There are a number of Christians who do. Giving to God is one way of worshiping Him. Although all Christians are to give, some are especially equipped to give—they have a gift of giving.

We have different gifts, according to the grace given us. If a man's gift is prophesying, let him use it in proportion to his faith. If it is serving, let him serve; if it is teaching, let him teach; if it is encouraging, let him encourage; if it is contributing to the needs of others, let him give generously; if it is leadership, let him govern diligently; if it is showing mercy, let him do it cheerfully. (Romans 12:6-8)

God Provides for Us

There is much said in the Bible about giving. We are encouraged to be generous, always remembering that everything we have is given to us by God. It is God who gives the ability to earn money and God who sovereignly brings in the money.

Honor the Lord with your wealth, with the firstfruits of all your crops; then your barns will be filled to overflowing, and your vats will brim over with new wine. (Proverbs 3:9-10)

One man gives freely, yet gains even more; another withholds unduly, but comes to poverty. (Proverbs 11:24)

Every good and perfect gift is from above, coming down from the Father of the heavenly lights, who does not change like shifting shadows. (James 1:17)

For who makes you different from anyone else? What do you have that you did not receive? And if you did receive it, why do you boast as though you did not? (1 Corinthians 4:7)

You may say to yourself, "My power and the strength of my hands have produced this wealth for me." But remember the Lord your God, for it is he who gives you the ability to produce wealth, and so confirms his covenant, which he swore to your forefathers, as it is today. (Deuteronomy 8:17-18)

Abraham was a wealthy man. However, he and those of his household knew that God had given him his wealth. His chief servant certainly understood Abraham's wealth came from God.

So he said, "I am Abraham's servant. The Lord has blessed my master abundantly, and he has become wealthy. He has given him sheep and cattle, silver and gold, menservants and maidservants, and camels and donkeys." (Genesis 24:34-35)

Rewards for Generous Giving

Scripture says much about ill-gotten wealth—the abuse and the sinful use of it. However, it does not criticize wealth itself. There are a number of Christians who are wealthy who use their wealth for God's glory. A God-fearing man, using God-given wealth, in a God-directed manner, can accomplish much good. The Bible teaches that God rewards generous giving.

Remember this: Whoever sows sparingly will also reap sparingly, and whoever sows generously will also reap

generously. Each man should give what he has decided in his heart to give, not reluctantly or under compulsion, for God loves a cheerful giver. And God is able to make all grace abound to you, so that in all things at all times, having all that you need, you will abound in every good work.
(2 Corinthians 9:6-8)

Good will come to him who is generous and lends freely....
(Psalm 112:5)

Give, and it will be given to you. A good measure, pressed down, shaken together and running over, will be poured into your lap. For with the measure you use, it will be measured to you. (Luke 6:38)

As important as obedient giving is, it must not be thought of as an end in itself. Obedient giving in no way lessens the necessity for obedience in every other area of life. The wealthy in particular must be on guard against this temptation. They are able to give much. In giving much, they may be tempted to think they have done much and slip into disobedience in other areas. We must remember that it is not how much we give that counts with God—some give much from much, many give less from less—but it is the motivation for our giving that God judges.

Jesus sat down opposite the place where the offerings were put and watched the crowd putting their money into the temple treasury. Many rich people threw in large amounts. But a poor widow came and put in two very small copper coins, worth only a fraction of a penny.
Calling his disciples to him, Jesus said, "I tell you the truth, this poor widow has put more into the treasury than all the others. They all gave out of their wealth; but she, out of her poverty, put in everything—all she had to live on."
(Mark 12:41-44)

For if the willingness is there, the gift is acceptable according to what one has, not according to what he does not have.
(2 Corinthians 8:12)

God knows that man often seeks riches merely for the sake of being rich and having the power that riches can buy. This leads to man being dependent on his riches instead of God. Even though wealth is honestly come by, if it is put to selfish use it is not pleasing to God. And, sooner or later, it will prove to be unprofitable to the selfish user.

Then he said to them, "Watch out! Be on your guard against all kinds of greed; a man's life does not consist in the abundance of his possessions."
And he told them this parable: "The ground of a certain rich man produced a good crop. He thought to himself, 'What shall I do? I have no place to store my crops.'
Then he said, 'This is what I'll do. I will tear down my barns and build bigger ones, and there I will store all my grain and my goods. And I'll say to myself, "You have plenty of good things laid up for many years. Take life easy; eat, drink and be merry."'
But God said to him, 'You fool! This very night your life will be demanded from you. Then who will get what you have prepared for yourself?'
This is how it will be with anyone who stores up things for himself but is not rich toward God." (Luke 12:15-21)

Wealth is worthless in the day of wrath, but righteousness delivers from death. (Proverbs 11:4)

They will throw their silver into the streets, and their gold will be an unclean thing. Their silver and gold will not be able to save them in the day of the Lord's wrath. They will not satisfy their hunger or fill their stomachs with it, for it has made them stumble into sin. (Ezekiel 7:19)

No servant can serve two masters. Either he will hate the one and love the other, or he will be devoted to the one and despise the other. You cannot serve both God and Money. (Luke 16:13)

Store Up Treasure in Heaven

Scripture warns us against storing up treasure here on earth because it will take first place in our hearts. Nothing is to come between us and God. The treasures we accumulate on earth are temporal and do not provide the security we place in them. We can enjoy them for only a short period of time. And, even during that brief period, our earthly treasures are subject to loss in many ways.

> Command those who are rich in this present world not to be arrogant nor to put their hope in wealth, which is so uncertain, but to put their hope in God, who richly provides us with everything for our enjoyment. Command them to do good, to be rich in good deeds, and to be generous and willing to share. In this way they will lay up treasure for themselves as a firm foundation for the coming age, so that they may take hold of the life that is truly life. (1 Timothy 6:17-19)

> Do not store up for yourselves treasures on earth, where moth and rust destroy, and where thieves break in and steal. But store up for yourselves treasures in heaven, where moth and rust do not destroy, and where thieves do not break in and steal. For where your treasure is, there your heart will be also. (Matthew 6:19-21)

If we store up treasure in heaven, our hearts will be there with God. There is not a safer place for our treasure or a more satisfying place for our hearts. There are some Christians who, feeling led of God and out of faithfulness to God, have lived lives that afforded little time or opportunity to accumulate earthly treasure. But, oh, how they have piled up treasure in heaven. They may not be counted among the affluent of this earth, but they will be found among the rich in heaven. The treasure we store up in heaven is based on the service we render on earth. The amount we accumulate there depends on our faithfulness here.

A life lived in faithful obedience consists of more than what we do or how much we do. It involves why we do it and how we do it. Our motivation for doing and our attitude in doing must be right in God's eyes. Our giving to God's work is no exception. We should seek God's will and, as best we can discern, give the amount we feel led to give. In addition, we should give to the work that we feel He would have us give. As we close this discussion on giving, let us remember that our giving to God is one way we honor and glorify Him.

Obedient Service Expected

In continuing our study of rewards, we must not forget that none of us deserve a reward. God has never been indebted to us, but we are eternally indebted to Him. He has freed us from what we were (servants of sin) and He has made us what we are (servants to Him). It is by His grace that we are privileged to serve Him, and by His grace that we are enabled to serve Him. However, we are imperfect; therefore, our service is imperfect. But, even if we did everything that God commanded, we would only be doing our duty as His servants, and would not deserve a reward. This is made clear by Christ as He speaks to His disciples.

> Suppose one of you had a servant plowing or looking after the sheep. Would he say to the servant when he comes in from the field, 'Come along now and sit down to eat?' Would he not rather say, 'Prepare my supper, get yourself ready and wait on me while I eat and drink; after that you may eat and drink?' Would he thank the servant because he did what he was told to do? So you also, when you have done everything you were told to do, should say, 'We are unworthy servants; we have only done our duty.' (Luke 17:7-10)

We should take note of the fact that, although the servant had been out in the field working, when he came in he did not sit down to rest or eat. He prepared his master's meal and served it to him. As Christians, we must realize that because we have been used of God to accomplish something worthwhile, that does not mean that our work is over. Regardless of what we have done for God, we do not rest from serving God. Our rewards for service are undeserved, but our punishment for lack of service is deserved. We see this in the parable of the talents, and we should let it be an admonishment to us to be faithful in our service.

> Again, it will be like a man going on a journey, who called his servants and entrusted his property to them. To one he gave five talents of money, to another two talents, and to another one talent, each according to his ability. Then he went on his journey. The man who had received the five talents went at once and put his money to work and gained five more. So also, the one with the two talents gained two more. But the man who had received the one talent went off, dug a hole in the ground and hid his master's money.

After a long time the master of those servants returned
and settled accounts with them. The man who had received the
five talents brought the other five. 'Master,' he said, 'you
entrusted me with five talents. See, I have gained five more.'

His master replied, 'Well done, good and faithful servant!
You have been faithful with a few things; I will put you in
charge of many things. Come and share your master's
happiness!'

The man with the two talents also came. 'Master,' he said,
'you entrusted me with two talents; see, I have gained two
more.'

His master replied, 'Well done, good and faithful servant!
You have been faithful with a few things; I will put you in
charge of many things. Come and share your master's
happiness!'

Then the man who had received the one talent came.
'Master,' he said, 'I knew that you are a hard man, harvesting
where you have not sown and gathering where you have not
scattered seed. So I was afraid and went out and hid your
talent in the ground. See, here is what belongs to you.'

His master replied, 'You wicked, lazy servant! So you
knew that I harvest where I have not sown and gather where
I have not scattered seed? Well then, you should have put my
money on deposit with the bankers, so that when I returned I
would have received it back with interest.

Take the talent from him and give it to the one who has
the ten talents. For everyone who has will be given more, and
he will have an abundance. Whoever does not have, even what
he has will be taken from him. And throw that worthless
servant outside, into the darkness, where there will be weeping
and gnashing of teeth.' (Matthew 25:14-30)

Comparison of Faithful and Unfaithful Servants

As servants of God, we are stewards of God. All we have
comes from Him. It belongs to Him, and we are to use it for His
glory. We find in the parable that the faithful servants put to work
what their master had entrusted to them, and they gained an
increase. The unfaithful servant was lazy. He saw the other two
working, but he took the easy way out. Can we be comfortable
doing nothing while others are doing so much? Spiritually
speaking, a lazy soul tends to sleep, and a soul that is spiritually
asleep is in danger of waking up in hell.

The unfaithful servant had an unrealistic opinion of, and an unwarranted attitude toward, his master. Consequently, he was unprofitable to the master. He was lazy and unwilling to work, but he excused himself with the false claim that his master was a hard man. He made it appear that he was afraid because his master was so demanding. Although this was not true, his master pointed out that, even if all the servant had said was true, he at least could have placed the money with the bankers so it could have drawn interest. It is evident that the servant is uncaring about his master's cause, and uncommitted to his master's work. He had only been asked to do that which his master felt he was capable of doing. The master had asked more of the other two servants, each in line with their abilities. Too often it is true among those who claim to know Christ that those who are asked to do the least for God do even less than that which is asked.

There are Christians who seldom, if ever, exercise their spiritual gifts. A gift unused is like a gift undelivered; it is of no benefit to those for whom it is intended. We find that the worthless servant is thrown into the outer darkness. If we are not working for God, we are not producing for God; therefore, we become of no use to God and are in danger of being cast away.

I am the vine; you are the branches. If a man remains in me and I in him, he will bear much fruit; apart from me you can do nothing. If anyone does not remain in me, he is like a branch that is thrown away and withers; such branches are picked up, thrown into the fire and burned. (John 15:5-6)

Some who profess Christ seem to think that a profession is all that is required of them. However, a profession that exists alone is a profession that is alone—it is one without faith and trust. We were not saved to sit idle as did the unfaithful servant, but we are to work and produce as the two faithful servants did. We see that as soon as the master left, the two faithful servants went to work at once. They could have procrastinated. They could have put their personal business before the master's business. Their master was gone a long time, but during his absence their enthusiasm did not wane. They appeared glad to be able to report what they had accomplished.

Because they had been obedient, when they settled accounts with their master, they were confident and unashamed of their report.

And now, dear children, continue in him, so that when he appears we may be confident and unashamed before him at his coming. (1 John 2:28)

The two faithful servants had done more than intend to be obedient—they had been obedient. Many Christians intend to be obedient—but are not. Good intentions produce nothing unless they are forced to work by an act of the will.

Being used of God is both a privilege and a pleasure. All Christians have the potential to enjoy both. However, many neglect to act on the privilege; therefore, they do not experience the pleasure. Not only do they miss the pleasure of working for God, but they will miss the joy of reward from God—the joy of a "well done, good and faithful servant!" When we are finished working here for God, we will be rewarded in heaven by God. If we are faithful over our little here, we will be put over more there. Heaven will be wonderful for all, but all will not have equal status. Faithfulness in our position here will affect the rank of our position there. We make many preparations for our short stay here on earth. Considering that we will spend eternity in heaven, should we not prepare well for our stay there?

No Neutrality in the Christian Life

There is no neutral position in the Christian life. We are always being either obedient or disobedient. We are either doing God's will or we are not doing it. Those who would know His will must first be willing to do His will. Those choosing to go their own way deprive themselves of knowing His way. If we are not seeking His will, we are not doing His will.

Too many Christians think of sin only as a sin of commission and seem unaware of the sin of omission. The Christian life is not just a life of don'ts, but it is very much a life of dos. We will be held accountable not only for the wrong we do but also for the right we fail to do.

> Anyone, then, who knows the good he ought to do and doesn't do it, sins. (James 4:17)

Christ lives in us. He wants to use us and do His work through us—this calls for action. We must be doers of the Word. If we are, He will bless us in what we do.

> Do not merely listen to the word, and so deceive yourselves. Do what it says. Anyone who listens to the word but does not do what it says is like a man who looks at his face in a mirror and, after looking at himself, goes away and immediately forgets what he looks like. But the man who looks intently into the perfect law that gives freedom, and continues to do this, not forgetting what he has heard, but doing it—he will be blessed in what he does. (James 1:22-25)

We learn the Word not just to know it but in order to do it. Being a doer of the Word is to be our way of life. We deceive ourselves if we hear the Word but do not act upon it. Salvation is neglected when, having heard about Christ, the hearer thinks he possesses Christ. Having heard and believed about Christ, he fails to do anything in response to what he has heard—he does not act on his belief. He does not commit his life to Christ.

There are those who seem to think that if they have heard how to live the Christian life, they are indeed living it. They deceive themselves. They go to one seminar after another, attend Bible classes, and listen to tapes. However, they are like a person looking into a mirror; they see their flaws and their sins, but instead of doing something about them, they go on as usual. They are always hearing but never doing what the Word says. In their self-deception, they are pretending to live the Christian life instead of purposing to live it. The Scriptures tell us that claiming we have faith when we do not back it up by deeds, is worthless. That faith is a dead faith. It is a claim made by one who professes to know God but who does not serve God.

> What good is it, my brothers, if a man claims to have faith but has no deeds? Can such faith save him? Suppose a brother or sister is without clothes and daily food. If one of you says to him, "Go, I wish you well; keep warm and well fed," but does nothing about his physical needs, what good is it? In the same

way, faith by itself, if it is not accompanied by action, is dead.
(James 2:14-17)

We know that we cannot be saved by our works, but it would appear that if we have no works, God has not saved us. A live faith is a productive faith. Taking root in the heart, it produces work of the hand. Labor that is done for God, according to the will of God, will always prove fruitful—it is never done in vain.

Therefore, my dear brothers, stand firm. Let nothing move you. Always give yourselves fully to the work of the Lord, because you know that your labor in the Lord is not in vain.
(1 Corinthians 15:58)

Faithful Labor Rewarded

Faithful labor will be rewarded labor, and it will be added to our treasure in heaven.

Then I heard a voice from heaven say, "Write: Blessed are the dead who die in the Lord from now on."
"Yes," says the Spirit, "they will rest from their labor, for their deeds will follow them." (Revelation 14:13)

The above verse is spoken about Christian martyrs, but it applies to all Christians. Having lived and died in the Lord, they will spend eternity with the Lord.

Some Christians are called upon to work more than others, some to suffer more than others, and some to give more than others. One thing we can be sure of—whatever God has called us to do, He will equip us to do. And we will be rewarded for our labor.

Many missionaries have labored in a foreign land for years with little or no visible success. God had to equip them in a special way to be patient and steadfast under such trying circumstances. He alone knows the purpose for their work, and He will bring to pass His purpose through their work—their job is to be faithful to do the work. It is not the success of our labor for which we are rewarded but the faithful labor itself.

The man who plants and the man who waters have one purpose, and each will be rewarded according to his own labor. (1 Corinthians 3:8)

At this point in our discussion, it should be evident to all that God delights in rewarding His people for their obedience. This should be an encouragement to us as we strive to be obedient to those commands that most of us find very difficult to obey—commands that tell us to love our enemies and pray for those who persecute us.

You have heard that it was said, 'Eye for eye, and tooth for tooth.' But I tell you: Do not resist an evil person. If someone strikes you on the right cheek, turn to him the other also. And if someone wants to sue you and take your tunic, let him have your cloak as well. If someone forces you to go one mile, go with him two miles. Give to the one who asks you, and do not turn away from the one who wants to borrow from you.

You have heard that it was said, 'Love your neighbor and hate your enemy.' But I tell you: Love your enemies and pray for those who persecute you, that you may be sons of your Father in heaven. He causes his sun to rise on the evil and the good, and sends rain on the righteous and the unrighteous. If you love those who love you, what reward will you get? Are not even the tax collectors doing that? And if you greet only your brothers, what are you doing more than others? Do not even pagans do that? Be perfect, therefore, as your heavenly Father is perfect. (Matthew 5:38-48)

Loss of Reward for Disobedience

Just as there is a reward for obedience, there is a loss of reward for disobedience.

By the grace God has given me, I laid a foundation as an expert builder, and someone else is building on it. But each one should be careful how he builds. For no one can lay any foundation other than the one already laid, which is Jesus Christ. If any man builds on this foundation using gold, silver, costly stones, wood, hay or straw, his work will be shown for what it is, because the Day will bring it to light. It will be revealed with fire, and the fire will test the quality of each

man's work. If what he has built survives, he will receive his reward. If it is burned up, he will suffer loss; he himself will be saved, but only as one escaping through the flames.
(1 Corinthians 3:10-15)

We find in these last verses that if we truly know Christ as Savior and Lord, He is the foundation upon which we build our Christian life. However, while acknowledging that Christ is our foundation, we may fail to realize that how we build and what we build on that foundation is most important. Obedient service to God, under the direction of the Holy Spirit, will result in work that will stand the test of fire. It is work that will be rewarded. Disobedience, work done in the flesh, will result in work that will be burned up. The Christian producing this work will be saved, but will lose his reward.

Suffering the loss of rewards in heaven is one thing, but suffering the loss of the reward of heaven is still another. There are those who are religious but who have not built their house on the Rock. They have heard the words of Christ, but they do not know Christ. They build their religious life on something other than Christ—they build on sand. They will think everything is fine until that day when the rain comes and the wind blows. Then they will find that they have built on the wrong foundation.

Therefore everyone who hears these words of mine and puts them into practice is like a wise man who built his house on the rock. The rain came down, the streams rose, and the winds blew and beat against that house; yet it did not fall, because it had its foundation on the rock. But everyone who hears these words of mine and does not put them into practice is like a foolish man who built his house on sand. The rain came down, the streams rose, and the winds blew and beat against that house, and it fell with a great crash. (Matthew 7:24-27)

Knowing the final destination of all who are not saved, we should be careful not to become complacent about our salvation.

We must pay more careful attention, therefore, to what we have heard, so that we do not drift away. For if the message spoken by angels was binding, and every violation and disobedience received its just punishment, how shall we escape if we ignore such a great salvation? This salvation, which was first

announced by the Lord, was confirmed to us by those who heard him. (Hebrews 2:1-3)

There are many who follow Christ while the following is easy, but when they encounter difficulties they turn back and no longer follow Him.

Jesus said to them, "I tell you the truth, unless you eat the flesh of the Son of Man and drink his blood, you have no life in you. Whoever eats my flesh and drinks my blood has eternal life, and I will raise him up at the last day. For my flesh is real food and my blood is real drink. Whoever eats my flesh and drinks my blood remains in me, and I in him. Just as the living Father sent me and I live because of the Father, so the one who feeds on me will live because of me. This is the bread that came down from heaven. Your forefathers ate manna and died, but he who feeds on this bread will live forever." He said this while teaching in the synagogue in Capernaum.

On hearing it, many of his disciples said, "This is a hard teaching. Who can accept it?"

Aware that his disciples were grumbling about this, Jesus said to them, "Does this offend you? What if you see the Son of Man ascend to where he was before! The Spirit gives life; the flesh counts for nothing. The words I have spoken to you are spirit and they are life. Yet there are some of you who do not believe." For Jesus had known from the beginning which of them did not believe and who would betray him. He went on to say, "This is why I told you that no one can come to me unless the Father has enabled him."

From this time many of his disciples turned back and no longer followed him. (John 6:53-66)

There are those people who turn back because of their love for the world. It appears that Demas, who worked with Paul, was one of these. We see that he was with Paul at the time Paul wrote to the Colossians and to Philemon. Later, in a letter to Timothy, we see that Demas deserted Paul and returned to the world.

Our dear friend Luke, the doctor, and Demas send greetings. (Colossians 4:14)

> Epaphras, my fellow prisoner in Christ Jesus, sends you
> greetings. And so do Mark, Aristarchus, Demas and Luke, my
> fellow workers. (Philemon 23-24)

> Do your best to come to me quickly, for Demas, because he
> loved this world, has deserted me and has gone to
> Thessalonica. (2 Timothy 4:9-10a)

Judas, who betrayed Christ, would be a notable example of someone who appeared to follow Christ but was not a true disciple.

In 2 Peter we have words that should stand as a warning to us not to turn back to the ways of the world. It is not how we start but how we finish that counts. There are some people who become weary of running the race. Their endurance wanes and they choose to drop out. They feel happier and more comfortable with their old lifestyle, so they return to it. They would be better off if they had never left it—there would be less condemnation upon them.

> If they have escaped the corruption of the world by knowing
> our Lord and Savior Jesus Christ and are again entangled in
> it and overcome, they are worse off at the end than they were
> at the beginning. It would have been better for them not to
> have known the way of righteousness, than to have known it
> and then to turn their backs on the sacred command that was
> passed on to them. Of them the proverbs are true: "A dog
> returns to its vomit," and, "A sow that is washed goes back to
> her wallowing in the mud." (2 Peter 2:20-22)

These are people who have been exposed to the Gospel. They have an unstable belief about Christ, but they have never truly committed their lives to Him. They are not and never were Christians. They twist the Scriptures to their own destruction. Although they know about the truth, they turn their backs on it and do not practice the truth. They would have been better off if they had remained ignorant. There is a penalty for disobedience, but the disobedience done in knowledge carries a greater penalty than that done in ignorance. The more we know about God, the more accountable we are to God.

> That servant who knows his master's will and does not get
> ready or does not do what his master wants will be beaten with
> many blows. But the one who does not know and does things

deserving punishment will be beaten with few blows. From everyone who has been given much, much will be demanded; and from the one who has been entrusted with much, much more will be asked. (Luke 12:47-48)

Scripture teaches that it is not even necessary to go back to the world to show that you are not a true disciple. All you need to do is look back to it. In looking back, you show that, in your heart, you have never really broken with the world. Memories of the pleasure of sin still bind you to it. Just as one who plows must look straight ahead if he is to plow a straight furrow, one who follows Christ must keep his eyes on Christ—he must not look back.

Jesus replied, "No one who puts his hand to the plow and looks back is fit for service in the kingdom of God." (Luke 9:62)

But Lot's wife looked back, and she became a pillar of salt. (Genesis 19:26)

Wise is the professor of Christ who makes certain he abides, and continues to abide, in Christ. We do well for ourselves when we take time to hear the Word and then carry through by obeying the Word.

Now that you know these things, you will be blessed if you do them. (John 13:17)

As we bring our discussion of rewards to a close, let us each remember that, although we enjoy our rewards, our purpose is to glorify the One who does the rewarding. To this effect, our lives should be lived by the measure of grace given to each of us.

We have looked at rewards for obedience, and punishment for disobedience. For most of us, it is probably easier to understand the teaching of Scripture on rewards than the teaching on punishment. We do not have a problem with what happens after physical death. We know that the Christian's sins are all forgiven, and that he goes to heaven. The non-Christian is condemned to hell to suffer punishment for his sins.

It is what takes place while we are on earth that can sometimes be confusing and cause us a problem. Often we see Christians suffering problems of health, finances, personal tragedy, and persecution while, in contrast, we see non-Christians flourishing in good health, much wealth, and a very carefree life.

This is certainly not the case all the time or even most of the time, but it is the case enough of the time to cause some Christians concern—even more so when the non-Christian who seems to have it so good is a very immoral person. This can be difficult for the Christian to reconcile. It certainly was difficult for the writer of the 73rd Psalm. We need to do as the psalmist did: Seek understanding from God, and look into the Word of God. Then we will be as the psalmist was—more aware of the non-Christian's final end.

> But as for me, my feet had almost slipped;
>   I had nearly lost my foothold.
> For I envied the arrogant
>   when I saw the prosperity of the wicked.
> They have no struggles;
>   their bodies are healthy and strong.
> They are free from the burdens common to man;
>   they are not plagued by human ills.
> Therefore pride is their necklace;
>   they clothe themselves with violence.
> From their callous hearts comes iniquity;
>   the evil conceits of their minds know no limits.
> They scoff, and speak with malice;
>   in their arrogance they threaten oppression.
> (Psalm 73:2-8)

> When I tried to understand all this,
>   it was oppressive to me
> till I entered the sanctuary of God;
>   then I understood their final destiny.
> Surely you place them on slippery ground;
>   you cast them down to ruin.
> How suddenly are they destroyed,
>   completely swept away by terrors!
> (Psalm 73:16-19)

The non-Christian may prosper in this life, but it is only for a short time. He is riding for a fall, and it will be a hard fall. His destruction is sure. He will spend his next life without Christ, because in this life he refused Christ. Let not a child of God envy the life of the non-Christian for his feet are on slippery ground.

Discipline of the Christian

Let us now turn our attention to the person who is truly a Christian—the person who does not just profess Christ but who possesses Christ—the person who is "in Christ" and "Christ is in him." Is he punished for his sins while here on earth? The answer from Scripture is yes; there is some degree of punishment for all Christians while on earth. Actually, the punishment of the Christian is for the purpose of discipline. There is punishment that is nothing but payment for breaking the law. It is purely the payment demanded by the law. However, God's punishment of the Christian is discipline or chastisement to correct him. It is to correct his character as well as his behavior.

My son, do not despise the Lord's discipline and do not resent his rebuke, because the Lord disciplines those he loves, as a father the son he delights in. (Proverbs 3:11-12)

He who ignores discipline despises himself, but whoever heeds correction gains understanding. (Proverbs 15:32)

Those whom I love I rebuke and discipline. So be earnest, and repent. (Revelation 3:19)

Discipline is for our benefit—to keep us from going astray, to teach us the way of godly living, to make us more like Christ, and to keep us from being lost. Think of what it would be like if parents were to let a child grow up from infancy to adulthood without ever saying no, and without ever punishing or correcting the child. We would feel the parents had harmed the child, been unfair, and done the child an injustice. Surely we see the need for God to say no to us and to punish and correct us as we grow from baby Christians to mature Christians. God's chastisement is a blessing to us.

Blessed is the man whom God corrects; so do not despise the discipline of the Almighty. (Job 5:17)

Scripture teaches that, if strong discipline is called for, God may even use sickness or take Christians in death to keep us from going to hell.

Then Jesus said to him, "Get up! Pick up your mat and walk."
... Later Jesus found him at the temple and said to him, "See,
you are well again. Stop sinning or something worse may
happen to you." (John 5:8,14)

For I received from the Lord what I also passed on to you: The
Lord Jesus, on the night he was betrayed, took bread, and
when he had given thanks, he broke it and said, "This is my
body, which is for you; do this in remembrance of me." In the
same way, after supper he took the cup, saying, "This cup is
the new covenant in my blood; do this, whenever you drink it,
in remembrance of me." For whenever you eat this bread and
drink this cup, you proclaim the Lord's death until he comes.
    Therefore, whoever eats the bread or drinks the cup of the
Lord in an unworthy manner will be guilty of sinning against
the body and blood of the Lord. A man ought to examine
himself before he eats of the bread and drinks of the cup. For
anyone who eats and drinks without recognizing the body of
the Lord eats and drinks judgment on himself. That is why
many among you are weak and sick, and a number of you have
fallen asleep. But if we judged ourselves, we would not come
under judgment. When we are judged by the Lord, we are
being disciplined so that we will not be condemned with the
world. (1 Corinthians 11:23-32)

God's discipline is an act of love and mercy. It is much better
that we undergo chastening here and now if it will prevent us from
suffering in hell later. We know that a Christian will not go to
hell—God will not let that happen. However, we see that in certain
cases one way He prevents this from happening is to take the
Christian in death. This prevents him from going deeper into sin
and disgracing God's name.

Notice that in 1 Corinthians 11:28, we were told to examine
ourselves. This should be a critical examination—a searching of our
souls, to see if we are walking right before God. We are then told
in verse 31 to judge ourselves so that God will not have to judge us.
If we examine ourselves, pass judgment, and then discipline
ourselves, God will not have to discipline us. Refraining from sin
prevents chastisement for sin. We learn from the example of
Ananias and Sapphira that sometimes God's discipline of
individuals can have a strong effect on the rest of the church, and
even those outside the church.

Now a man named Ananias, together with his wife Sapphira, also sold a piece of property. With his wife's full knowledge he kept back part of the money for himself, but brought the rest and put it at the apostles' feet.

Then Peter said, "Ananias, how is it that Satan has so filled your heart that you have lied to the Holy Spirit and have kept for yourself some of the money you received for the land? Didn't it belong to you before it was sold? And after it was sold, wasn't the money at your disposal? What made you think of doing such a thing? You have not lied to men but to God."

When Ananias heard this, he fell down and died. And great fear seized all who heard what had happened. Then the young men came forward, wrapped up his body, and carried him out and buried him.

About three hours later his wife came in, not knowing what had happened. Peter asked her, "Tell me, is this the price you and Ananias got for the land?"

"Yes," she said, "that is the price."

Peter said to her, "How could you agree to test the Spirit of the Lord? Look! The feet of the men who buried your husband are at the door, and they will carry you out also."

At that moment she fell down at his feet and died. Then the young men came in and, finding her dead, carried her out and buried her beside her husband. Great fear seized the whole church and all who heard about these events. (Acts 5:1-11)

Delayed Discipline

There should be a word of caution as well as admonition to us in the account of David and Bathsheba concerning discipline. Because we do not receive immediate discipline for a sin does not mean God has passed over that sin. If we sin and God disciplines us for that sin, the discipline may be delayed. David committed adultery with Bathsheba and she became pregnant. He then had her husband killed in battle (see 2 Samuel, chapters 11 and 12). This displeased God; He disciplined David by having the son that Bathsheba bore him die. We do not know what the exact time-frame was from the time of the sins to the discipline, but there was a definite lapse of time. Other discipline was also imposed on David—discipline that continued over the years. We should strive to live our lives so that there will be no reason for

God to discipline us. However, when He does have to, we should acknowledge the need for it, see the value in it, and attempt to benefit from it. It is for our good.

No discipline seems pleasant at the time, but painful. Later on, however, it produces a harvest of righteousness and peace for those who have been trained by it. (Hebrews 12:11)

We have talked about discipline of the Christian and have seen that although we are not condemned to hell for our sins, we can suffer much on earth as discipline for them.

Not All Trials are Discipline

However, discipline is not the reason for all our trials. So many of our problems and sufferings are the results of our lifestyles and the choices we make that violate the natural laws God has set in motion in His universe. Also, many are due to living on an earth that has been cursed by God because of Adam's sin, and is inhabited by sinful man. The sinful nature of man produces the sinful acts of man, and these acts in turn produce untold hardships.

To Adam he said, "Because you listened to your wife and ate from the tree about which I commanded you, 'You must not eat of it,' Cursed is the ground because of you; through painful toil you will eat of it all the days of your life." (Genesis 3:17)

We know that the whole creation has been groaning as in the pains of childbirth right up to the present time. (Romans 8:22)

Therefore, just as sin entered the world through one man, and death through sin, and in this way death came to all men, because all sinned.... (Romans 5:12)

All men go through the common trials and hardships of mankind. However, as Christians, we can expect to go through persecution also.

> If the world hates you, keep in mind that it hated me first. If you belonged to the world, it would love you as its own. As it is, you do not belong to the world, but I have chosen you out of the world. That is why the world hates you. Remember the words I spoke to you: 'No servant is greater than his master.' If they persecuted me, they will persecute you also. (John 15:18-20a)

> In fact, everyone who wants to live a godly life in Christ Jesus will be persecuted.... (2 Timothy 3:12)

We can also expect to go through trials or testing by God. This is not so God can see how we do in them, but it is so we can see how we do. God uses them to strengthen our faith.

> Remember how the Lord your God led you all the way in the desert these forty years, to humble you and to test you in order to know what was in your heart, whether or not you would keep his commands. (Deuteronomy 8:2)

We are told that we should accept trials with joy, and that how we go through them can prove our faith is genuine.

> Consider it pure joy, my brothers, whenever you face trials of many kinds, because you know that the testing of your faith develops perseverance. Perseverance must finish its work so that you may be mature and complete, not lacking anything. (James 1:2-4)

> In this you greatly rejoice, though now for a little while you may have had to suffer grief in all kinds of trials. These have come so that your faith—of greater worth than gold, which perishes even though refined by fire—may be proved genuine and may result in praise, glory and honor when Jesus Christ is revealed. (1 Peter 1:6-7)

How do we get through these trials? There is only one way. It is the same way and the only way we can live the Christian life. It must be done under the control and in the power of the Holy Spirit.

As we attempt to live the Christian life in a manner that is pleasing to God, knowing what God has said becomes very important. Therefore, it behooves us to study the Scriptures. The

Holy Spirit is the one who teaches us by opening our understanding of what we read and study.

> **But the Counselor, the Holy Spirit, whom the Father will send in my name, will teach you all things and will remind you of everything I have said to you.** (John 14:26)

> **Fix these words of mine in your hearts and minds; tie them as symbols on your hands and bind them on your foreheads. Teach them to your children, talking about them when you sit at home and when you walk along the road, when you lie down and when you get up.** (Deuteronomy 11:18-19)

> **You are my refuge and my shield;**
>   **I have put my hope in your word.**
> **Direct my footsteps according to your word;**
>   **let no sin rule over me.**
> (Psalm 119:114, 133)

> **For everything that was written in the past was written to teach us, so that through endurance and the encouragement of the Scriptures we might have hope.** (Romans 15:4)

The Backslider and Carnal Christian

Any discussion of obedience should include a look at the backslider and the carnal Christian. They are common in our Christian society.

What is a backslider? Most of us picture a backslider as a person who, having advanced to a certain level of spiritual maturity and a corresponding level of behavior, then regresses to a lower level of each. Generally we would think of that person as having regressed to a state of carnality. I believe this would be a reasonable description of a true backslider.

I use the term true backslider because there are some who consider themselves to be backsliders when in reality they may not even be Christians. They are like the person who says he is a Christian but who lives like the world and seeks the pleasures of the world. They want to have their cake and eat it too. They want the blessing without the Blesser, the gift without the Giver, and sin without its wages. They will voluntarily admit that they fall far short of living the Christian life as they should.

At best these people are carnal Christians, but the question remains—are they Christians? There is a true carnal Christian just as there is a true backslider; however, they are basically the same, both are carnal with the apparent difference being: The carnal Christian has never moved out of the carnal state; while the blackslider has attained a degree of growth before sliding back into the carnal state. However, to lump into these two categories all those who claim to know Christ but live as if they do not is a deceptive practice. For a person to risk his or her eternal destination by being content to think of themselves as belonging to either of these groups is both foolish and dangerous.

The carnal Christian is not to be thought of as living a life that is representative of the worst man of this world, but rather living a life that is representative of the average man of this world. We find that Paul speaks of the Corinthians as being carnal. The word translated "carnal" in the King James Version is translated "worldly", "natural", "unspiritual", and "fleshly" in some other translations.

> **Brothers, I could not address you as spiritual but as worldly—mere infants in Christ. I gave you milk, not solid food, for you were not yet ready for it. Indeed, you are still not ready. You are still worldly. For since there is jealousy and quarreling among you, are you not worldly? Are you not acting like mere men?** (1 Corinthians 3:1-3)

Being carnal or worldly is opposite to being spiritual. Paul tells the Corinthians that they are behaving like the non-Christian people around them. They are behaving like they behaved before they were saved. Paul saw little or no change in their attitudes and actions. Although they had been Christians long enough to have grown spiritually, they were still as though they had just become Christians. They were like babies who had never grown up.

All who are born into the kingdom come in as babes in Christ. And it takes time for most of us to grow spiritually, some growing faster than others. However, with time, there should be growth. If there is no growth, there either is an unspiritual attitude that has retarded growth or there is no life.

If we would grow spiritually, we must live up to the light we have been given. We must seek to obey as much of the Word as we understand. Until we have understood and obeyed the "milk" of the Word, we will not be able to receive or benefit from the "meat" of the Word.

> Anyone who lives on milk, being still an infant, is not acquainted with the teaching about righteousness. But solid food is for the mature, who by constant use have trained themselves to distinguish good from evil. (Hebrews 5:13-14)

You may be a backslider or a carnal Christian, but one thing is certain, the longer you remain in that condition the more likely it is that you will find you are not even a Christian—that you have never been born again. There is a warning from Scripture against falling away when you have tasted the goodness of God.

> It is impossible for those who have once been enlightened, who have tasted the heavenly gift, who have shared in the Holy Spirit, who have tasted the goodness of the word of God and the powers of the coming age, if they fall away, to be brought back to repentance, because to their loss they are crucifying the Son of God all over again and subjecting him to public disgrace.
> Land that drinks in the rain often falling on it and that produces a crop useful to those for whom it is farmed receives the blessing of God. But land that produces thorns and thistles is worthless and is in danger of being cursed. In the end it will be burned. (Hebrews 6:4-8)

You may even find yourself under God's wrath.

> "You have rejected me," declares the Lord.
> "You keep on backsliding.
> So I will lay hands on you and destroy you;
>   I can no longer show compassion."
> (Jeremiah 15:6)

The backslider and the carnal Christian would both do well to heed Christ's admonition to the church at Sardis.

> To the angel of the church in Sardis write:
> These are the words of him who holds the seven spirits of God and the seven stars. I know your deeds; you have a reputation of being alive, but you are dead. Wake up! Strengthen what remains and is about to die, for I have not

found your deeds complete in the sight of my God. Remember, therefore, what you have received and heard; obey it, and repent. But if you do not wake up, I will come like a thief, and you will not know at what time I will come to you. (Revelation 3:1-3)

The Spiritual Christian

Our discussion thus far may cause some readers to ask how they may know if they are spiritual Christians. The answer from Scripture is that those who, by faith, are living in obedience to the Word of God and are under the control of the Spirit of God, are spiritual Christians. All else falls short of the mark.

Because we are spiritually alive does not mean that we are living the spiritual life called for in Scripture. This can only be done as, in the power of the Holy Spirit, we submit our wills to His will. None of us do this all the time, and some do it more than others. However, if we are to think of ourselves as living the spiritual life, then this must be the trend of our lives. The more effort we make to be sure the Holy Spirit is controlling our lives, the more we will find we are living the spiritual life (see chapter on the Holy Spirit).

With that in mind, let each of us look at his or her own life and ask ourselves these questions: Do I start every day seeking His will and His control of my life for that day? If not, why not? If not every day, most days, some days, any days? I know Christians should not just read the Bible; they should study the Bible. Do I study the Bible, often, some, occasionally? Do I pray throughout the day, several times a day, twice, once? Do I love my brothers and sisters in Christ? Do I attend church on a regular basis, to worship God and to be encouraged? Do I encourage others in love and devotion to Him, and to each other? God saved me for a purpose. Am I fulfilling that purpose? Is doing what He wants me to do the main desire of my life? If not, why not? Am I living for Him or for myself? Do I think going to Sunday school and church on Sunday is all that God requires of me? If not, do I try to find out what He does want me to do? Would the cause of Christ be helped or hurt if all Christians were as obedient as I am in studying the Bible, praying, and witnessing to others about Christ? Do I want my children and other loved ones to live the Christian life as I live it? Am I satisfied with the Christian life I live—my obedience to God? By God's grace, what am I going to do to live a more obedient life? Am I going to start right now? If not, why not?

Thoughts Indicate the Condition of the Heart

There are many things most of us need to learn and do to improve the spiritual quality of our lives. One thing that is a strong hindrance of spirituality for most of us is our thoughts. Our thoughts reflect what we are because they come from our hearts; they indicate the condition of our hearts.

> **For out of the heart come evil thoughts, murder, adultery, sexual immorality, theft, false testimony, slander.** (Matthew 15:19)

The thought of the heart leads to the deed of the hand.

> **...but each one is tempted when, by his own evil desire, he is dragged away and enticed. Then, after desire has conceived, it gives birth to sin; and sin, when it is full-grown, gives birth to death.** (James 1:14-15)

We cannot separate our thoughts from our deeds. Whether deeds are good or bad, they are the result of our thoughts.

> **The good man brings good things out of the good stored up in his heart, and the evil man brings evil things out of the evil stored up in his heart. For out of the overflow of his heart his mouth speaks.** (Luke 6:45)

However, we must not think of sin as being limited to those thoughts that result in a sinful deed. The thought by itself can be sin.

> **You have heard that it was said to the people long ago, 'Do not murder, and anyone who murders will be subject to judgment.' But I tell you that anyone who is angry with his brother will be subject to judgment.** (Matthew 5:21-22a)

> **Anyone who hates his brother is a murderer, and you know that no murderer has eternal life in him.** (1 John 3:15)

Christians may not be able to keep wrong thoughts from entering their minds, but they can prevent them from remaining there. Unfortunately, there are times when some Christians not only let them stay but ask them to stay. Sometimes they even invite them to visit again and look forward to their return. Often Christians feel secure in their sinful thoughts knowing that no one knows what they are thinking. They forget that God knows. They seem unaware that there is a battle for the control of their minds between their old natures and their new natures.

> So I find this law at work: When I want to do good, evil is right there with me. For in my inner being I delight in God's law; but I see another law at work in the members of my body, waging war against the law of my mind and making me a prisoner of the law of sin at work within my members. (Romans 7:21-23)

> What causes fights and quarrels among you? Don't they come from your desires that battle within you? (James 4:1)

> For the sinful nature desires what is contrary to the Spirit, and the Spirit what is contrary to the sinful nature. They are in conflict with each other, so that you do not do what you want. (Galatians 5:17)

It is important that our new natures, which are now our true natures, win this battle. It will have a great effect on the course of the war, and it is truly a war that we are in—a spiritual war.

> Finally, be strong in the Lord and in his mighty power. Put on the full armor of God so that you can take your stand against the devil's schemes. For our struggle is not against flesh and blood, but against the rulers, against the authorities, against the powers of this dark world and against the spiritual forces of evil in the heavenly realms. (Ephesians 6:10-12)

In this battle for the control of our minds we must constantly be on guard, stay alert, and keep control of our thought patterns.

> Be self-controlled and alert. Your enemy the devil prowls around like a roaring lion looking for someone to devour. (1 Peter 5:8)

A word of caution to all of us: Just because we are not thinking thoughts of sin does not mean that our thoughts are not sinful. We know that we sin when we make idols of neutral things like money, sports, music, and people—when anything or anyone becomes more important to us than God. In the same way, if something or someone other than God takes a disproportionate amount of our thoughts, then we know where our heart is, and we should correct the problem.

If we are to live spiritual lives, we must think spiritual thoughts. We must make our thoughts obedient to Christ.

> **We demolish arguments and every pretension that sets itself up against the knowledge of God, and we take captive every thought to make it obedient to Christ.** (2 Corinthians 10:5)

We must seek to not only not think about wrong things but to think about right things.

> **Brothers, stop thinking like children. In regard to evil be infants, but in your thinking be adults.** (1 Corinthians 14:20)

> **Finally, brothers, whatever is true, whatever is noble, whatever is right, whatever is pure, whatever is lovely, whatever is admirable—if anything is excellent or praiseworthy—think about such things.** (Philippians 4:8)

> **Dear friends, this is now my second letter to you. I have written both of them as reminders to stimulate you to wholesome thinking.** (2 Peter 3:1)

One way to be sure we are thinking right thoughts is to meditate on God's Word.

> **I have hidden your word in my heart**
> **that I might not sin against you.**
> **I meditate on your precepts**
> **and consider your ways.**
> **Let me understand the teaching of your precepts;**
> **then I will meditate on your wonders.**
> **I lift up my hands to your commands, which I love,**
> **and I meditate on your decrees.**
> **My eyes stay open through the watches of the**
> **night,**

that I may meditate on your promises.
(Psalm 119:11,15,27,48,148)

However, if we are to meditate on the Word, we must know
the Word. We must study the Bible, not just read it. We need to
not only know what the words say, we need to know what the
Word says; therefore, we must look to God. Man can teach man
what the words say, but only God can teach man what the Word
says.

If asked which book is the most important book in the world,
most Christians would quickly answer, the Bible. Yet, for many,
their reading habits do not confirm this. Some will read magazines
and novels to the exclusion of the Bible, while others will watch a
worthless TV program when they could benefit from the worth of
the Word. How can anyone expect to live a spiritual life if they
value other things above spiritual things?

Those who do not study the Bible but think of themselves as
spiritual because they live moral lives, should bear in mind that
there is a difference in living a moral life and living a spiritual life.
There are a number of non-Christians who live moral lives, but as
non-Christians they do not have spiritual life. Living a moral life
is at the heart of many non-Christian religions, and the morals are
determined by man. Living a spiritual life includes living a moral
life, but the morals are those exemplified in the life of the Living
Word and commanded by God in the written Word.

Having received spiritual life from the Living Word, we are to
live in obedience to the written Word. We are blessed to have the
Bible. It is up to us to read it and to heed it.

Be Serious about Service

If we Christians are to have an impact on this world, we must
get deadly serious about the lives we live, the works we do, and
those we fail to do. We cannot be content with doing things
halfway; a job half-done is a job undone. We must get off the
fence and start living for God. We must evidence a life that is holy
before Him, if we hope to evidence His life in us before men. If we
would be instruments through whom God speaks, we must first be
ones to whom God speaks. To be ones to whom God speaks, we
must be willing listeners.

If we would teach others, we must first learn—we cannot teach what we do not know. We must learn to share the Gospel with those who are lost, and offer words of encouragement to those who are saved. Being used of God to save one soul is worth more than all the treasures of this earth. It is even more precious if it is one of your loved ones.

Telling others about Christ, that salvation is found only in Christ, is one of the most important things a Christian can do. The Bible tells us that faith comes by hearing the Word of God, hearing about Christ (Romans 10:17). Each of us who knows Christ had to hear or read the truth about Him. We have been commanded by God to tell others (Matthew 28:18-20). Christ came to bring salvation—to seek and save the lost.

> She will give birth to a son, and you are to give him the name Jesus, because he will save his people from their sins. (Matthew 1:21)

> Jesus said to him, "Today salvation has come to this house, because this man, too, is a son of Abraham. For the Son of Man came to seek and to save what was lost." (Luke 19:9-10)

God says He does not want any to perish.

> The Lord is not slow in keeping his promise, as some understand slowness. He is patient with you, not wanting anyone to perish, but everyone to come to repentance. (2 Peter 3:9)

> I urge, then, first of all, that requests, prayers, intercession and thanksgiving be made for everyone—for kings and all those in authority, that we may live peaceful and quiet lives in all godliness and holiness. This is good, and pleases God our Savior, who wants all men to be saved and to come to a knowledge of the truth. (1 Timothy 2:1-4)

Christ now lives in us and, by His Holy Spirit, He wants to continue His saving work through us. Are we helping or hindering His work? We should seek to be used by God to win souls for His kingdom.

All this is from God, who reconciled us to himself through Christ and gave us the ministry of reconciliation: that God was reconciling the world to himself in Christ, not counting men's sins against them. And he has committed to us the message of reconciliation. We are therefore Christ's ambassadors, as though God were making his appeal through us. We implore you on Christ's behalf: Be reconciled to God. (2 Corinthians 5:18-20)

Those who had been scattered preached the word wherever they went. (Acts 8:4)

But you will receive power when the Holy Spirit comes on you; and you will be my witnesses in Jerusalem, and in all Judea and Samaria, and to the ends of the earth. (Acts 1:8)

Spiritual Warfare

The unseen world is as real as the one we see, and it is every bit as important. There is a war raging with principalities and powers, and souls are being won or lost daily. Some Christians spend most of their lives on the front lines of this war. There are others who are in support of those on the front lines, and still others who have yet to report for duty—though they signed up when they accepted Christ. Lastly, there are those who object to saying or doing anything that would be embarrassing to them. For them this appears to cover all that is involved in spiritual warfare, so they become conscientious objectors. They enjoy their salvation but somehow do not seem to truly understand the awful plight of the unsaved.

Each of us must remember that we may be the only witness for Christ in our sphere of influence. We may be the only opportunity someone has to hear the Gospel. Are you telling others about Christ? If not, why not?

Some people speak of their religion as a private matter; however, in true Christianity, although we may accept Christ privately, we are to acknowledge Him publicly.

...That if you confess with your mouth, "Jesus is Lord," and believe in your heart that God raised him from the dead, you will be saved. For it is with your heart that you believe and are

justified, and it is with your mouth that you confess and are saved. (Romans 10:9-10)

Whoever acknowledges me before men, I will also acknowledge him before my Father in heaven. But whoever disowns me before men, I will disown him before my Father in heaven. (Matthew 10:32-33)

If anyone is ashamed of me and my words in this adulterous and sinful generation, the Son of Man will be ashamed of him when he comes in his Father's glory with the holy angels. (Mark 8:38)

Here is a trustworthy saying: If we died with him, we will also live with him; if we endure, we will also reign with him. If we disown him, he will also disown us.... (2 Timothy 2:11-12)

If we will not talk about Christ to others, are we disowning Him? Most people are happy to tell others about their spouse, children, and grandchildren—why not tell them about the One who saved you and who loves you with a love beyond understanding. I suspect that most people who will not talk about Christ are people who cannot talk about Christ—because they do not know Him. We must not only be willing to talk about Him, but we must also be willing to go for Him.

Then I heard the voice of the Lord saying, "Whom shall I send? And who will go for us?"
And I said, "Here am I. Send me!" (Isaiah 6:8)

Count the Cost

Actually, we must be willing to do anything and everything He asks. This is something that should be considered at the time we accept Christ. We should count the cost of following Him.

Large crowds were traveling with Jesus, and turning to them he said: "If anyone comes to me and does not hate his father and mother, his wife and children, his brothers and sisters—yes, even his own life—he cannot be my disciple. And anyone who does not carry his cross and follow me cannot be my disciple.

Suppose one of you wants to build a tower. Will he not first sit down and estimate the cost to see if he has enough money to complete it? For if he lays the foundation and is not able to finish it, everyone who sees it will ridicule him, saying, 'This fellow began to build and was not able to finish.'

Or suppose a king is about to go to war against another king. Will he not first sit down and consider whether he is able with ten thousand men to oppose the one coming against him with twenty thousand? If he is not able, he will send a delegation while the other is still a long way off and will ask for terms of peace. In the same way, any of you who does not give up everything he has cannot be my disciple.

Salt is good, but if it loses its saltiness, how can it be made salty again? It is fit neither for the soil nor for the manure pile; it is thrown out.

He who has ears to hear, let him hear. (Luke 14:25-35)

Christ gave up all for us. If we would be His disciples, we must be willing to give up all for Him. We are not to actually hate our family but love our family. However, by comparison to the love we have for Christ, it might seem like hate because of the great degree of difference. It actually means we love our family and ourselves less than we love Christ.

We must not only be willing to suffer the trials and persecutions that will come our way, but we must be willing to die for Christ if necessary. If called to do so, we must be prepared to give up our dreams and ambitions, to forsake our wealth, and to jeopardize our health for His cause.

We must be ready to do spiritual battle. Although we are saved by grace, the time span from the point of our salvation until we arrive at the gates of heaven is a battlefield—across which we must fight every inch of the way. It is a battle that cannot be won by the weak and complacent; we must be alert and strong. If we lose the battle, we lose our saltiness and are not fit to be used but are thrown away. If we are to win, we must continue in faith moment by moment. We cannot afford to rest on our laurels and look back at the faith we once had. The faith we had last year, during an emergency or sickness, does not count for the present moment. It is not a question of, Have we had faith; but one of, Do we have faith? God is the Giver of faith, but we must exercise it or it will wilt and wither. We must not only have faith, but we must stand firm in our faith.

Be on your guard; stand firm in the faith; be men of courage; be strong. (1 Corinthians 16:13)

If you do not stand firm in your faith, you will not stand at all. (Isaiah 7:9b)

If we have never before counted the cost of following Christ, now is the time to do it. If we find we cannot finish the course, it is better to quit now than to quit later. However, we should compare the cost of going on with the cost of quitting. If we go on, we lose our lives (our lower nature and its enjoyment of sin and the world) to gain life (spiritual life—eternal life). If we turn back, we will enjoy the pleasure of sin for a season, and then spend eternity in hell. There are those people who have quit and those who will quit, but let us not be counted among them. Let us follow the example of the apostle Paul and "fight the good fight." Let us be among those forceful people who take the kingdom by force.

From the days of John the Baptist until now, the kingdom of heaven has been forcefully advancing, and forceful men lay hold of it. (Matthew 11:12)

Be Forceful

These forceful men are those who are determined to be counted among the faithful—to enter into heaven. Forceful men and women press on in their Christian lives; they strive to get to heaven. They run the race and fight the fight. They do battle with the sin inside them and the sin that is around them. They give up what is necessary, and they take on what is required. They never let up. They keep pushing forward! They are determined to prove to themselves that they are totally surrendered to God and to show the world that they faithfully serve their God. They have set their faces like flint toward heaven, and their gaze will remain fixed until they have achieved their goal.

...the good news of the kingdom of God is being preached, and everyone is forcing his way into it. (Luke 16:16b)

Those who are saved by grace and kept by grace must make every effort to enter the kingdom by the means of grace. We can be confident that as Christ has achieved victory for us, we will achieve victory through Him.

I can do everything through him who gives me strength. (Philippians 4:13)

Blessed in Christ

In view of all that we have discussed in this chapter, it becomes evident that living the Christian life is not easy. And I do not see anywhere in the Word that God says it will be easy. However, we are blessed in Christ—we can and should be joyful. We have the peace that Christ gives. We have the privilege of praying to God.

Praise be to the God and Father of our Lord Jesus Christ, who has blessed us in the heavenly realms with every spiritual blessing in Christ. For he chose us in him before the creation of the world to be holy and blameless in his sight. (Ephesians 1:3-4)

Peace I leave with you; my peace I give you. I do not give to you as the world gives. Do not let your hearts be troubled and do not be afraid. (John 14:27)

And the peace of God, which transcends all understanding, will guard your hearts and your minds in Christ Jesus. (Philippians 4:7)

Be joyful in hope, patient in affliction, faithful in prayer. (Romans 12:12)

All that happens in our lives is working to conform us more and more to the image of Christ. We could have no higher calling. When God saved us, He blessed us. And in conforming us more to the image of His Son, He continues to bless us. The more like Christ we are, the more blessed we are, and the greater blessing we will be to others.

Persevere

If we understand and agree with all that has been said, then the question arises, What do we do now? The answer from Scripture is: Continue on, persevere, endure, do not quit, and do not give up.

> Let us not become weary in doing good, for at the proper time we will reap a harvest if we do not give up. (Galatians 6:9)

> Brothers, I do not consider myself yet to have taken hold of it. But one thing I do: Forgetting what is behind and straining toward what is ahead, I press on toward the goal to win the prize for which God has called me heavenward in Christ Jesus. (Philippians 3:13-14)

> See to it, brothers, that none of you has a sinful, unbelieving heart that turns away from the living God. But encourage one another daily, as long as it is called Today, so that none of you may be hardened by sin's deceitfulness. We have come to share in Christ if we hold firmly till the end the confidence we had at first. (Hebrews 3:12-14)

> We want each of you to show this same diligence to the very end, in order to make your hope sure. We do not want you to become lazy, but to imitate those who through faith and patience inherit what has been promised. (Hebrews 6:11-12)

> You need to persevere so that when you have done the will of God, you will receive what he has promised. (Hebrews 10:36)

We must continue to be obedient to the light we have been given—knowing that as we are, we will be given more light, until one day we stand in light where there is no darkness. Then we can glory in Him who is the source of all light—our God.

As we persevere we have much to overcome: the world, the flesh, and Satan. But the prize is there for those who do. And the wonderful thing is that we are in Christ, and He has already overcome the world. He has overcome the prince of the world, the people of the world, and the sin in the world. His victory has made us victors. All we have to do is persevere, and we do this in faith.

> To him who overcomes and does my will to the end, I will give
> authority over the nations.... (Revelation 2:26)

> ...for everyone born of God overcomes the world. This is the
> victory that has overcome the world, even our faith.
> (1 John 5:4)

Confidence in God

If we pass the test we will receive the Crown of Life. And as
Christians, we <u>will</u> pass (1 John 5:4). Many other verses assure us
that we will make it (see chapter on Election). As it is God's plan
and God's purpose, He will make sure we do not fail.

> ...being confident of this, that he who began a good work in you
> will carry it on to completion until the day of Christ Jesus.
> (Philippians 1:6)

This being the case, let us resolve to serve and obey our God.

> And the people said to Joshua, "We will serve the Lord our
> God and obey him." (Joshua 24:24)

On the day we stand before Christ, if we have lived in
obedience, we can have the hope of hearing Him say:

> "Well done, good and faithful servant." (Matthew 25:21)

Who is the Holy Spirit?

What does He do?

What is the fruit of the Spirit?

How is one filled with the Spirit?

"Not by might nor by power, but by my Spirit," says the Lord Almighty. (Zechariah 4:6b)

The Holy Spirit

For the Christian, the ministry of the Holy Spirit is probably the most important doctrine taught in the Bible. In order to live the Christian life that is called for in Scripture, it is essential to not only understand the doctrine but to apply it in our lives.

We know that it is God who enables the unbeliever to understand the Gospel and accept Christ.

He went on to say, "This is why I told you that no one can come to me unless the Father has enabled him." (John 6:65)

When Jesus came to the region of Caesarea Philippi, he asked his disciples, "Who do people say the Son of Man is?"

They replied, "Some say John the Baptist; others say Elijah; and still others, Jeremiah or one of the prophets."

But what about you?" he asked. "Who do you say I am?"

Simon Peter answered, "You are the Christ, the Son of the living God."

Jesus replied, "Blessed are you, Simon son of Jonah, for this was not revealed to you by man, but by my Father in heaven." (Matthew 16:13-17)

It is also God who opens the believer's understanding of the work of the Holy Spirit in his life and enables him to turn the control of his life over to the Holy Spirit.

...for it is God who works in you to will and to act according to his good purpose. (Philippians 2:13).

God does this in His time. He does this when it pleases Him to do so, and to the degree that it pleases Him to do it. Yet, it is our responsibility to accept Christ as Savior and Lord. Once we do, it is our responsibility as Christians to let the Holy Spirit control and empower our lives. It is only in the power of the Holy Spirit that we can do anything that pleases God. Only in the power of the Holy Spirit can we live the Christian life as God intends us to, and only in the power of the Holy Spirit can we know God's peace and joy. With this in view, it certainly behooves us to diligently seek to understand the ministry of the Holy Spirit and to turn the control of our lives over to Him.

Names and Symbols of the Holy Spirit

To better understand all of this, let us look at what the Bible says about the Holy Spirit. The Holy Spirit is referred to as the Holy Ghost, Spirit of the Lord, Spirit of Christ, Spirit of God, Spirit of Truth, etc. Symbols such as wind, oil, fire, water, breath, and the finger of God are also used to indicate the Spirit. An example of water being used as a symbol of the Spirit is found in the book of John.

On the last and greatest day of the Feast, Jesus stood and said in a loud voice, "If anyone is thirsty, let him come to me and drink. Whoever believes in me, as the Scripture has said, streams of living water will flow from within him." By this he meant the Spirit, whom those who believed in him were later to receive. Up to that time the Spirit had not been given, since Jesus had not yet been glorified. (John 7:37-39)

A dove was the symbol used when Jesus was baptized.

As soon as Jesus was baptized, he went up out of the water. At that moment heaven was opened, and he saw the Spirit of God descending like a dove and lighting on him. (Matthew 3:16)

Holy Spirit—Third Person of Trinity

As we seek to understand who the Holy Spirit is, we do not want to be confused by our lack of understanding of the Trinity. The Bible teaches that there is one God who is three persons. No one can explain it, but God's Word teaches it; therefore, we believe it. However, for some this can raise the question as to whom to look to for direction and strength in their Christian walk. The answer is God. God the Father, God the Son, and God the Holy Spirit are one God. All three persons of the Godhead are divine and eternal, and exist in the divine essence. They are not three Gods but are the three persons of the one God. Though the word Trinity is not found in Scripture, it is used theologically to express the one essence eternally subsisting as three persons. These three are eternal, equal, and possess the same divine attributes. They are one in essence, in personality, and in will—three persons but one God. The one intelligence and the one will of the one God are expressed and exercised by the three persons. Each of the three has their office and are revealed in Scripture in a certain order of operation. The Father sends and works through the Son. The Father and Son send and work through the Spirit. Therefore, the One who indwells believers is the Holy Spirit, who is God in His fullness.

We speak of asking Christ to come into our hearts, and He does as He sends His Holy Spirit to us. We also speak of being led by Christ or being led by God to do a certain thing. The Bible teaches that we are indwelt by all three persons in the sense that the three are One. Romans 8:9 and 1 Corinthians 6:19 are two of the verses that tell us that Christians are indwelt by the Holy Spirit. Some examples that indicate we are indwelt by the Father and the Son are as follows:

Paul and his companions traveled throughout the region of Phrygia and Galatia, having been kept by the Holy Spirit from preaching the word in the province of Asia. When they came to the border of Mysia, they tried to enter Bithynia, but the Spirit of Jesus would not allow them to. So they passed by Mysia and

went down to Troas. During the night Paul had a vision of a man of Macedonia standing and begging him, "Come over to Macedonia and help us." After Paul had seen the vision, we got ready at once to leave for Macedonia, concluding that God had called us to preach the gospel to them. (Acts 16:6-10)

Jesus replied, "If anyone loves me, he will obey my teaching. My Father will love him, and we will come to him and make our home with him." (John 14:23)

So then, just as you received Christ Jesus as Lord, continue to live in him, rooted and built up in him, strengthened in the faith as you were taught, and overflowing with thankfulness. (Colossians 2:6-7)

Now the Lord is the Spirit, and where the Spirit of the Lord is, there is freedom. And we, who with unveiled faces all reflect the Lord's glory, are being transformed into his likeness with ever-increasing glory, which comes from the Lord, who is the Spirit. (2 Corinthians 3:17-18)

There is one body and one Spirit—just as you were called to one hope when you were called—one Lord, one faith, one baptism; one God and Father of all, who is over all and through all and in all. (Ephesians 4:4-6)

For in Christ all the fullness of the Deity lives in bodily form, and you have been given fullness in Christ, who is the head over every power and authority. (Colossians 2:9-10)

I have been crucified with Christ and I no longer live, but Christ lives in me. (Galatians 2:20a)

Remain in me, and I will remain in you. No branch can bear fruit by itself; it must remain in the vine. Neither can you bear fruit unless you remain in me. (John 15:4)

I think it is fair to conclude from Scripture that we are indwelt with the fullness of God. However, in the order of operation, we are indwelt by the person of the Holy Spirit. It is basically to Him that we should look to be led.

...because those who are led by the Spirit of God are sons of God. (Romans 8:14)

Characteristics of the Holy Spirit

We have seen that the Holy Spirit is not some impersonal force or power. He is God, the third person of the Trinity. The Holy Spirit has a personality in the same manner as the Father and the Son. Personal properties and actions are attributed to Him:

He has infinite intellect.

> For who among men knows the thoughts of a man except the man's spirit within him? In the same way no one knows the thoughts of God except the Spirit of God. (1 Corinthians 2:11)

He has a will.

> All these are the work of one and the same Spirit, and he gives them to each one, just as he determines. (1 Corinthians 12:11)

> God also testified to it by signs, wonders and various miracles, and gifts of the Holy Spirit distributed according to his will. (Hebrews 2:4)

He teaches.

> When you are brought before synagogues, rulers and authorities, do not worry about how you will defend yourselves or what you will say, for the Holy Spirit will teach you at that time what you should say. (Luke 12:11-12)

> This is what we speak, not in words taught us by human wisdom but in words taught by the Spirit, expressing spiritual truths in spiritual words. (1 Corinthians 2:13)

He speaks to people and through people.

> The Spirit clearly says that in later times some will abandon the faith and follow deceiving spirits and things taught by demons. (1 Timothy 4:1)

In those days Peter stood up among the believers (a group numbering about a hundred and twenty) and said, "Brothers, the Scripture had to be fulfilled which the Holy Spirit spoke long ago through the mouth of David concerning Judas, who served as guide for those who arrested Jesus.... (Acts 1:15-16)

While Peter was still thinking about the vision, the Spirit said to him, "Simon, three men are looking for you. So get up and go downstairs. Do not hesitate to go with them, for I have sent them." (Acts 10:19-20)

I only know that in every city the Holy Spirit warns me that prison and hardships are facing me. (Acts 20:23)

Be on your guard against men; they will hand you over to the local councils and flog you in their synagogues. On my account you will be brought before governors and kings as witnesses to them and to the Gentiles. But when they arrest you, do not worry about what to say or how to say it. At that time you will be given what to say, for it will not be you speaking, but the Spirit of your Father speaking through you.
(Matthew 10:17-20)

The Spirit told Philip, "Go to that chariot and stay near it." (Acts 8:29)

He can be lied to.

Then Peter said, "Ananias, how is it that Satan has so filled your heart that you have lied to the Holy Spirit and have kept for yourself some of the money you received for the land?" (Acts 5:3)

He exerts authority.

In the church at Antioch there were prophets and teachers: Barnabas, Simeon called Niger, Lucius of Cyrene, Manaen (who had been brought up with Herod the tetrarch) and Saul. While they were worshiping the Lord and fasting, the Holy Spirit said, "Set apart for me Barnabas and Saul for the work to which I have called them." So after they had fasted and prayed, they placed their hands on them and sent them off.

> The two of them, sent on their way by the Holy Spirit, went down to Seleucia and sailed from there to Cyprus. (Acts 13:1-4)

> And now, compelled by the Spirit, I am going to Jerusalem, not knowing what will happen to me there. (Acts 20:22)

> Keep watch over yourselves and all the flock of which the Holy Spirit has made you overseers. (Acts 20:28a)

He loves.

> I urge you, brothers, by our Lord Jesus Christ and by the love of the Spirit, to join me in my struggle by praying to God for me. (Romans 15:30)

He can be resisted.

> You stiff-necked people, with uncircumcised hearts and ears! You are just like your fathers: You always resist the Holy Spirit! (Acts 7:51)

He can be grieved.

> Yet they rebelled and grieved his Holy Spirit. (Isaiah 63:10)

> And do not grieve the Holy Spirit of God, with whom you were sealed for the day of redemption. (Ephesians 4:30)

Examples of the Holy Spirit in the Old Testament

The first reference to the Holy Spirit in the Bible is in the book of Genesis.

> Now the earth was formless and empty, darkness was over the surface of the deep, and the Spirit of God was hovering over the waters. (Genesis 1:2)

His work and influence are seen throughout the Old Testament. For example:

So Pharaoh asked them, "Can we find anyone like this man, one in whom is the spirit of God?" (Genesis 41:38)

Then the Lord said to Moses, "See, I have chosen Bezalel son of Uri, the son of Hur, of the tribe of Judah, and I have filled him with the Spirit of God, with skill, ability and knowledge in all kinds of crafts...." (Exodus 31:1-3)

I will come down and speak with you there, and I will take of the Spirit that is on you and put the Spirit on them. They will help you carry the burden of the people so that you will not have to carry it alone. (Numbers 11:17)

The Spirit of the Lord came upon him, so that he became Israel's judge and went to war. (Judges 3:10a)

Then the Spirit of the Lord came upon Jephthah. (Judges 11:29a)

The Spirit of the Lord will come upon you in power, and you will prophesy with them; and you will be changed into a different person. Once these signs are fulfilled, do whatever your hand finds to do, for God is with you. (1 Samuel 10:6-7)

The Spirit of the Lord spoke through me; his word was on my tongue. (2 Samuel 23:2)

You gave your good Spirit to instruct them. You did not withhold your manna from their mouths, and you gave them water for their thirst. (Nehemiah 9:20)

Do not cast me from your presence or take your Holy Spirit from me. (Psalm 51:11)

Teach me to do your will, for you are my God; may your good Spirit lead me on level ground. (Psalm 143:10)

"Woe to the obstinate children," declares the Lord, "to those who carry out plans that are not mine, forming an alliance, but not by my Spirit, heaping sin upon sin...." (Isaiah 30:1)

Examples of the Holy Spirit in the New Testament

In the New Testament, we see much of the work and the power of the Holy Spirit. John the Baptist was filled with (controlled by) the Holy Spirit while still in his mother's womb.

...for he will be great in the sight of the Lord. He is never to take wine or other fermented drink, and he will be filled with the Holy Spirit even from birth. (Luke 1:15)

Elizabeth (John's mother) and Zechariah (John's father) were filled with the Holy Spirit.

When Elizabeth heard Mary's greeting, the baby leaped in her womb, and Elizabeth was filled with the Holy Spirit. (Luke 1:41)

His father Zechariah was filled with the Holy Spirit and prophesied.... (Luke 1:67)

The Holy Spirit revealed to Simeon that he would not die before he had seen Christ.

Now there was a man in Jerusalem called Simeon, who was righteous and devout. He was waiting for the consolation of Israel, and the Holy Spirit was upon him. It had been revealed to him by the Holy Spirit that he would not die before he had seen the Lord's Christ. (Luke 2:25-26)

The Holy Spirit in the Life of Christ

He was instrumental in the conception of Christ and in His life and ministry.

The angel answered, "The Holy Spirit will come upon you, and the power of the Most High will overshadow you. So the holy one to be born will be called the Son of God." (Luke 1:35)

But after he had considered this, an angel of the Lord appeared to him in a dream and said, "Joseph son of David, do not be afraid to take Mary home as your wife, because what is conceived in her is from the Holy Spirit." (Matthew 1:20)

Christ was anointed with the Holy Spirit.

> ...how God anointed Jesus of Nazareth with the Holy Spirit and
> power, and how he went around doing good and healing all
> who were under the power of the devil, because God was with
> him. (Acts 10:38)

Christ was full (under the control) of the Holy Spirit, and was led
by the Holy Spirit when He faced Satan.

> Jesus, full of the Holy Spirit, returned from the Jordan and
> was led by the Spirit in the desert, where for forty days he was
> tempted by the devil. He ate nothing during those days, and at
> the end of them he was hungry. (Luke 4:1-2)

Christ, after facing Satan, returned to Galilee in the power of the
Holy Spirit.

> Jesus returned to Galilee in the power of the Spirit, and news
> about him spread through the whole countryside. (Luke 4:14)

Christ performed His ministry in the power of the Holy Spirit.

> The scroll of the prophet Isaiah was handed to him. Unrolling
> it, he found the place where it is written: "The Spirit of the
> Lord is on me, because he has anointed me to preach good
> news to the poor. He has sent me to proclaim freedom for the
> prisoners and recovery of sight for the blind, to release the
> oppressed, to proclaim the year of the Lord's favor." Then he
> rolled up the scroll, gave it back to the attendant and sat
> down. The eyes of everyone in the synagogue were fastened on
> him, and he began by saying to them, "Today this scripture is
> fulfilled in your hearing." (Luke 4:17-21)

Christ offered Himself on the cross, through the power of the Holy
Spirit.

> How much more, then, will the blood of Christ, who through
> the eternal Spirit offered himself unblemished to God, cleanse
> our consciences from acts that lead to death, so that we may
> serve the living God! (Hebrews 9:14)

Christ was resurrected by the Holy Spirit.

...and who through the Spirit of holiness was declared with power to be the Son of God by his resurrection from the dead: Jesus Christ our Lord. (Romans 1:4)

And if the Spirit of him who raised Jesus from the dead is living in you, he who raised Christ from the dead will also give life to your mortal bodies through his Spirit, who lives in you. (Romans 8:11)

Christ gave instructions through the Holy Spirit.

...until the day he was taken up to heaven, after giving instructions through the Holy Spirit to the apostles he had chosen. (Acts 1:2)

The Holy Spirit was sent to glorify Christ.

He will bring glory to me by taking from what is mine and making it known to you. (John 16:14)

The Indwelling Holy Spirit

One way the Holy Spirit glorifies Christ is by His work in and through Christians. He is the counselor or helper that Christ promised to send.

And I will ask the Father, and he will give you another Counselor to be with you forever—the Spirit of truth. The world cannot accept him, because it neither sees him nor knows him. But you know him, for he lives with you and will be in you. (John 14:16-17)

But the Counselor, the Holy Spirit, whom the Father will send in my name, will teach you all things and will remind you of everything I have said to you. (John 14:26)

Now I am going to him who sent me, yet none of you asks me, 'Where are you going?' Because I have said these things, you are filled with grief. But I tell you the truth: It is for your good that I am going away. Unless I go away, the Counselor will not come to you; but if I go, I will send him to you. When he comes, he will convict the world of guilt in regard to sin and righteousness and judgment: in regard to sin, because men do

not believe in me; in regard to righteousness, because I am going to the Father, where you can see me no longer; and in regard to judgment, because the prince of this world now stands condemned.

I have much more to say to you, more than you can now bear. But when he, the Spirit of truth, comes, he will guide you into all truth. He will not speak on his own; he will speak only what he hears, and he will tell you what is yet to come. (John 16:5-13)

After Christ ascended to heaven, the Holy Spirit was sent to not only be upon God's people but to be within them. When Christ walked the earth as man, He said He came to seek and save the lost. Now He indwells His people, through the Holy Spirit. He works in and through them, in order to continue His work of seeking and saving.

Being indwelt by the Holy Spirit is one thing, being controlled by the Holy Spirit is another. All Christians are indwelt by the Holy Spirit, yet, all Christians sin. When a Christian sins he is in control of his desires and actions. The Holy Spirit will not lead him to sin. While under His control, he can be tempted to sin but will not succumb to the temptation. The Holy Spirit will never empower him to sin but will always empower him to resist sin and to do good works. Just as the unbeliever must trust Christ to be saved, the believer must trust the Holy Spirit to control his thoughts, desires, and actions—in order to live a fruitful Christian life. Without trust, the unbeliever will not be saved; without trust, the believer will not be controlled.

Just as the unbeliever must come to the realization that without Christ, he is a lost sinner and that Christ alone can save him, so must the Christian come to the realization that in his own strength, he is utterly unable to live the Christian life in a manner pleasing to God. The Holy Spirit alone can provide the power and enable the Christian to please God.

Carnal Christian—Controlled by the Flesh

There are many Christians who understand very little about the work of the Holy Spirit in their lives. There are others who do not put into practice the knowledge and understanding that they have—often ignoring or resisting the prompting of the Spirit. As a result, there are many Christians who fall into the category that is known as the Carnal Christian. The Carnal Christian is one who is worldly and as such acts much like those of the world.

Brothers, I could not address you as spiritual but as worldly—mere infants in Christ. I gave you milk, not solid food, for you were not yet ready for it. Indeed, you are still not ready. You are still worldly. For since there is jealousy and quarreling among you, are you not worldly? Are you not acting like mere men? (1 Corinthians 3:1-3)

The Carnal Christian is one who is more influenced by the flesh than the Spirit; therefore, he thinks and acts so much like the unbeliever that one can see little, if any, difference in them.

They are both living by the dictates of sinful human nature. The unsaved man does not have the Holy Spirit. He is motivated by his human nature, which by human standards may seem to be good, but the Bible makes it clear that our human nature is sinful, and actions that stem from it cannot please God. That is also why, most of the time, the Carnal Christian does not please God. Although indwelt by the Spirit, he lives most of the time governed by his human nature rather than by the Spirit. Because the trend of the Carnal Christian's life is one of doing his own thing, he lives a life of guilt and defeat. Although he has a relationship with God, he seldom enjoys fellowship with Him nor the peace and joy that only comes with submission to God's Holy Spirit.

On the other hand, the spiritual man is seeking to live as the Holy Spirit leads him. He does not do this perfectly though, as his sinful nature is prone to exert itself from time to time. However, the trend of his life is one of living under the control of the Holy Spirit.

We often see new Christians who, having just received Christ, are so elated that they blindly charge out to do something for God. Often they think they are winning favor in God's eyes. Humanly speaking, these intentions are good; however, even when in ignorance, we charge out in our own strength to do what we think is a good thing, it does not please God because we are not being led by the Holy Spirit.

Works done in the flesh do not please God before we are saved, and they do not please God after we are saved. Only works done in faith please God. If we could not earn our salvation with our works of the flesh but were saved by the regenerating work of the Holy Spirit, then does it not follow that only those works done under the guidance and enabling of the Holy Spirit will please Him now?

Paul understood it to be this way and tells us in Galatians that as we were regenerated by the Spirit, we are to walk (live) under the control of the Holy Spirit.

> **Since we live by the Spirit, let us keep in step with the Spirit.** (Galatians 5:25)

With so much dependent on our understanding and practice of letting the Holy Spirit control our lives, let us look further at His work in our lives.

The Holy Spirit in Salvation

The teaching of Scripture is that we were once spiritually dead and that God gave us spiritual life.

> **...he saved us, not because of righteous things we had done, but because of his mercy. He saved us through the washing of rebirth and renewal by the Holy Spirit....** (Titus 3:5)

> **But because of his great love for us, God, who is rich in mercy, made us alive with Christ even when we were dead in transgressions—it is by grace you have been saved.** (Ephesians 2:4-5)

At the time of spiritual birth, the Holy Spirit regenerates man and brings about the new birth. Just as there was a time when we did not have physical life but were born into the world without any effort on our part, there was also a time when we did not have spiritual life but were given it without effort on our part. This is often referred to as being born again or being saved.

> **In reply Jesus declared, "I tell you the truth, no one can see the kingdom of God unless he is born again."**
> **"How can a man be born when he is old?" Nicodemus asked. "Surely he cannot enter a second time into his mother's womb to be born!"**

> Jesus answered, "I tell you the truth, no one can enter the kingdom of God unless he is born of water and the Spirit. Flesh gives birth to flesh, but the Spirit gives birth to spirit. You should not be surprised at my saying, 'You must be born again.' The wind blows wherever it pleases. You hear its sound, but you cannot tell where it comes from or where it is going. So it is with everyone born of the Spirit." (John 3:3-8)

In the above verses, Jesus tells us that the regeneration of man is the work of the Holy Spirit. The Holy Spirit applies the Word of God to our lives and brings about our spiritual birth. The Apostle John also points out that our spiritual birth is the work of God.

> Yet to all who received him, to those who believed in his name, he gave the right to become children of God—children born not of natural descent, nor of human decision or a husband's will, but born of God. (John 1:12-13)

We see that those who are children of God are not children because of who their ancestors were, or because their parents were Christians. They are not children by human decision (a human plan, human sex drive, a husband's will to have an heir to his name), but because they have been born of God the Holy Spirit.

Several things happen at the time of our spiritual birth:

1.   The moment we are born again (saved), the Holy Spirit comes to actually dwell within the body and life of the Christian.

> You, however, are controlled not by the sinful nature but by the Spirit, if the Spirit of God lives in you. And if anyone does not have the Spirit of Christ, he does not belong to Christ. (Romans 8:9)

> Do you not know that your body is a temple of the Holy Spirit, who is in you, whom you have received from God? (1 Corinthians 6:19)

> We know that we live in him and he in us, because he has given us of his Spirit. (1 John 4:13)

2. We receive the Holy Spirit as a gift from God.

> On one occasion, while he was eating with them, he gave them
> this command: "Do not leave Jerusalem, but wait for the gift
> my Father promised, which you have heard me speak about.
> For John baptized with water, but in a few days you will be
> baptized with the Holy Spirit." (Acts 1:4-5)

> Peter replied, "Repent and be baptized, every one of you, in the
> name of Jesus Christ for the forgiveness of your sins. And you
> will receive the gift of the Holy Spirit." (Acts 2:38)

> While Peter was still speaking these words, the Holy Spirit
> came on all who heard the message. The circumcised believers
> who had come with Peter were astonished that the gift of the
> Holy Spirit had been poured out even on the Gentiles.
> (Acts 10:44-45)

3. The Holy Spirit seals every Christian into Christ.

> And you also were included in Christ when you heard the word
> of truth, the gospel of your salvation. Having believed, you were
> marked in him with a seal, the promised Holy Spirit....
> (Ephesians 1:13)

4. The Holy Spirit is the deposit or guarantee of the inheritance
   that each Christian will one day receive.

> Now it is God who has made us for this very purpose and has
> given us the Spirit as a deposit, guaranteeing what is to come.
> (2 Corinthians 5:5)

> ...who is a deposit guaranteeing our inheritance until the
> redemption of those who are God's possession—to the praise
> of his glory. (Ephesians 1:14)

5. We are baptized into the body of Christ by Christ, who uses the
   Holy Spirit as His agent.

> I baptize you with water, but he will baptize you with the Holy
> Spirit. (Mark 1:8)

> For we were all baptized by one Spirit into one body—whether Jews or Greeks, slave or free—and we were all given the one Spirit to drink. (1 Corinthians 12:13)

The baptism of the Holy Spirit is something that is done at the time we are saved. It has nothing to do with whether or not we speak in tongues. At the moment we are saved, we are regenerated, indwelt, sealed, guaranteed, and baptized by the Holy Spirit.

In bringing us to accept Christ, the Holy Spirit works in us in such a manner that we are totally unaware that it is being done. He does not force us to do anything against our wills; rather, He brings about a change of our wills. Without the Spirit's work, we would never come to Christ.

There are many well-taught people whom the Spirit has never drawn to Christ. They know the books, history, and characters of the Bible but do not know its truth. They do not know Christ and will not know Him unless God the Holy Spirit reveals Him to them.

> "Stop grumbling among yourselves," Jesus answered. "No one can come to me unless the Father who sent me draws him, and I will raise him up at the last day. It is written in the Prophets: 'They will all be taught by God.' Everyone who listens to the Father and learns from him comes to me." (John 6:43-45)

Regardless of how clearly the Gospel is presented to people or how many times they hear it, they will not believe it unless the Holy Spirit applies it to their hearts. In fact, even if someone returns from the dead to witness to them, they still will not believe if they do not believe God's Word. Christ tells us this is the case in the story of the rich man and Lazarus.

> There was a rich man who was dressed in purple and fine linen and lived in luxury every day. At his gate was laid a beggar named Lazarus, covered with sores and longing to eat what fell from the rich man's table. Even the dogs came and licked his sores.
> The time came when the beggar died and the angels carried him to Abraham's side. The rich man also died and was buried. In hell, where he was in torment, he looked up and saw Abraham far away, with Lazarus by his side. So he called

to him, 'Father Abraham, have pity on me and send Lazarus to dip the tip of his finger in water and cool my tongue, because I am in agony in this fire.'

But Abraham replied, 'Son, remember that in your lifetime you received your good things, while Lazarus received bad things, but now he is comforted here and you are in agony. And besides all this, between us and you a great chasm has been fixed, so that those who want to go from here to you cannot, nor can anyone cross over from there to us.'

He answered, 'Then I beg you, father, send Lazarus to my father's house, for I have five brothers. Let him warn them, so that they will not also come to this place of torment.'

Abraham replied, 'They have Moses and the Prophets; let them listen to them.'

'No, father Abraham,' he said, 'but if someone from the dead goes to them, they will repent.'

He said to him, 'If they do not listen to Moses and the Prophets, they will not be convinced even if someone rises from the dead.' (Luke 16:19-31)

This story brings home how truly helpless we are to come to Christ and how totally dependent we are on the Holy Spirit to give us spiritual life. Just as the physically dead do not respond to physical stimuli, so the spiritually dead do not respond to spiritual stimuli. The physically dead can be cut, poked, exposed to loud noise, heat, and cold with no response. The spiritually dead can hear good preaching, read the Bible, be witnessed to, and listen to Christian tapes with no spiritual response. They are dead, and the dead do not respond. Being dead they can do nothing to gain life—it must be given to them by the regenerating work of the Holy Spirit.

The more understanding we have of this truth the more we can appreciate the miracle of the new birth. Raising the spiritually dead to spiritual life requires the supernatural work of God, just as raising the physically dead to physical life does. Both of these show the power of God. It is this same power that indwells us and works in and through us. It is the same power that raised Christ from the dead.

...and his incomparably great power for us who believe. That power is like the working of his mighty strength, which he exerted in Christ when he raised him from the dead and seated him at his right hand in the heavenly realms.... (Ephesians 1:19-20)

Enabling Power of the Holy Spirit

Just as our salvation is a miracle, so is the sustaining of our Christian life. One becomes a Christian through the supernatural work of God, and one remains a Christian through His supernatural work.

His divine power has given us everything we need for life and godliness through our knowledge of him who called us by his own glory and goodness. (2 Peter 1:3)

There is not a reader who belongs to Christ, who came to that relationship except through the work of the Holy Spirit. Also, there is not a reader who can live as God commands except by the power of the Holy Spirit. Apart from the Spirit, the Christian can do nothing.

I am the vine; you are the branches. If a man remains in me and I in him, he will bear much fruit; apart from me you can do nothing. (John 15:5)

The Spirit is the enabling power of the Christian.

But you will receive power when the Holy Spirit comes on you; and you will be my witnesses in Jerusalem, and in all Judea and Samaria, and to the ends of the earth. (Acts 1:8)

Christ carried out His work and performed His miracles in God's power.

Don't you believe that I am in the Father, and that the Father is in me? The words I say to you are not just my own. Rather, it is the Father, living in me, who is doing his work. Believe me when I say that I am in the Father and the Father is in me; or at least believe on the evidence of the miracles themselves. (John 14:10-11)

> **Men of Israel, listen to this: Jesus of Nazareth was a man accredited by God to you by miracles, wonders and signs, which God did among you through him, as you yourselves know.** (Acts 2:22)

If Christ did His work and miracles in the power of the Holy Spirit, can we expect to accomplish anything apart from the Holy Spirit working in our lives?

We have numerous commands from God on what to do and what not to do. In fact, we have so many that often Christians do not know where or how to start living their new lives. However, if we obey the command to be filled with the Spirit, He will lead us and empower us to obey the others. Our obedience to this one command is the key to our obedience to all the others. With this being true, it is easy to see that the biggest obstacle to our living as God would have us live, and doing the work that God would have us do, is ourselves. It is our failure to yield the control of our lives to the Holy Spirit. God is perfectly capable of handling all external circumstances. He can open and close doors. He can cause people and events to work in cooperation with us and to assist us. It is our own selfish hearts, our refusal to deny self and follow Him in a consistent manner, that hinders His work. Due to our sinful nature, living life under the control of the Holy Spirit is difficult, even when we are making a real effort to do so. It will not happen if we are not willing to work at it—it must be given top priority. If it is, all else will follow as God intends.

> **But seek first his kingdom and his righteousness, and all these things will be given to you as well.** (Matthew 6:33)

The Holy Spirit and Righteous Living

We should not only seek to enter the kingdom but also seek the righteousness expected of those who do. Heaven should be our destination, and holiness should be the road we travel.

> **...without holiness no one will see the Lord.** (Hebrews 12:14b)

Too often, we Christians have a false sense of what it means to be righteous. As a result, we substitute the energy of the flesh, the wisdom of the flesh, and the excitement of the flesh for the righteousness of God. Works done in the flesh are works that are done without the Spirit's command, direction, or permission. From the human perspective, they may be successful, but they do not please God—to Him they are like filthy rags. They are sin.

...and all our righteous acts are like filthy rags.... (Isaiah 64:6)

The only way we can live a righteous life is by the Holy Spirit. The command to be controlled by the Holy Spirit is not an abstract spiritual phrase—it is a concrete spiritual reality. Just as salvation is available to and commanded of the unsaved, being controlled by the Holy Spirit is available to and commanded of the Christian. In both cases, those who reject the offer and refuse to obey the command are held accountable by God.

The Spirit of Christ within Us

We know that Christ lives in His people to continue His work on earth. Therefore, we need to realize that each of us shares his body with Christ.

I have been crucified with Christ and I no longer live, but Christ lives in me. The life I live in the body, I live by faith in the Son of God, who loved me and gave himself for me. (Galatians 2:20)

When we are under the control of our human natures, we are using our bodies and denying Christ the use of them. When we are under the control of the Holy Spirit, Christ is using our bodies, and we enjoy the benefits and blessings that come with His use. It is truly a blessing to be controlled by the Holy Spirit but more than that, it is our duty to be. The Holy Spirit is not here to empower us to do what we choose to do for God; He is here to empower us to do what God wants done. We do not use the Holy Spirit—He uses us. God does not need us to do anything for Him—we need Him to do everything for us. As the Israelites were dependent on God for the manna from heaven to maintain their physical life, we are dependent on God the Holy Spirit to maintain our spiritual life. When we seek to do that which we feel led to do in His power, we are only limited in what we can do by what God has decreed. And that becomes a real adventure.

Quenching the Holy Spirit

The Holy Spirit is our only hope for living the Christian life; therefore, we certainly want to be careful not to do anything that will prevent His working in us.

Do not put out the Spirit's fire.... (1 Thessalonians 5:19)

We can quench the Spirit's fire by sinful thoughts and actions. However, what can also be crippling to our Christian walk, and is so commonplace among Christians today, is just letting the fire diminish for lack of fuel. If we ignore the Spirit's presence, do not act at His prompting, neglect church, prayer, Bible study and other graces that strengthen our faith, the fire will abate and our spiritual life will atrophy. We can be spiritual Christians at times. At other times we can quench the Spirit's work in our lives—even to the degree that we think, talk, and act so differently that we seem to be two different people. In essence, we are led by two different persons at different times. We are either led by our sinful nature (the flesh) or by God the Holy Spirit. The one leading us determines our actions. We either suffer the consequences or enjoy the rewards, depending on who is doing the leading.

Those who live according to the sinful nature have their minds set on what that nature desires; but those who live in accordance with the Spirit have their minds set on what the Spirit desires. (Romans 8:5)

When we live according to the flesh we not only rationalize and make allowances for our sins, but we actually make provision for them. To live according to the Spirit we must yield to the Spirit, and He will lead us from there.

The Holy Spirit and Bible Study

Of one thing we can be sure, the Spirit will lead us to study the Word. And when we study we should ask the Spirit to give us understanding. Studying the Word without the illumination of the Holy Spirit profits us very little. However, studying under the guidance and light of the Spirit is life changing. The Holy Spirit uses the Word of God to mold our character much as a craftsman uses an instrument. In fact, the Word is called the sword of the Spirit.

Take the helmet of salvation and the sword of the Spirit, which is the word of God. (Ephesians 6:17)

For the word of God is living and active. Sharper than any double-edged sword, it penetrates even to dividing soul and spirit, joints and marrow; it judges the thoughts and attitudes of the heart. (Hebrews 4:12)

God's Word is the truth, and the Holy Spirit teaches us the truth.

Sanctify them by the truth; your word is truth. (John 17:17)

But when he, the Spirit of truth, comes, he will guide you into all truth. (John 16:13a)

The Holy Spirit and Discernment

We look to the Spirit not only to show us the truth but also to point out what is not truth. Everyone is exposed to much that is false in this world, and Christians are no exception. In fact, there are so many false teachers and so much false doctrine in the marketplace that Christians really have to be careful not to be taken in. Scripture warns us about this and tells us to test the spirits, to discern if they are true or false.

Dear friends, do not believe every spirit, but test the spirits to see whether they are from God, because many false prophets have gone out into the world. (1 John 4:1)

I know that after I leave, savage wolves will come in among you and will not spare the flock. Even from your own number men will arise and distort the truth in order to draw away disciples after them. (Acts 20:29-30)

If we are to discern the spirits, we certainly cannot depend on our sinful human nature to do it. It could not do it before we were saved, and it cannot do it now. No, we must look to the Holy Spirit for discernment, and ask Him to show us what is true and what is false.

The Holy Spirit and Prayer

The Spirit leads us to study the Bible so that we might hear what God has to say. He also leads us to pray so that we might talk to God and tell Him what is on our hearts. We are to pray at His prompting and under His guidance.

And pray in the Spirit on all occasions with all kinds of prayers and requests. With this in mind, be alert and always keep on praying for all the saints. (Ephesians 6:18)

But you, dear friends, build yourselves up in your most holy faith and pray in the Holy Spirit. (Jude 20)

In prayer, what we say is more important than how we say it. A poorly expressed prayer from the heart is more important to God than a well-expressed one that is not. Our prayers often reflect our spirituality. Some Christians spend time in prayer asking God to heal their bodies but never ask Him to heal their spirits. They are unhappy if they have to live with their physical ailments but seem perfectly content to live with their spiritual infirmities—their sins.

Overcoming Sin by the Holy Spirit

The lure of sin is often so strong that man will pursue it even when his conscience loudly proclaims that it is wrong, and his reason warns him of the high cost. For most people, the temptation to sin is even greater if they think they can conceal the sin. Often if the sin is hidden from man they seem to think it is hidden from God. Sin done in secret may be punished out in the open as happened to David.

This is what the Lord says: 'Out of your own household I am going to bring calamity upon you. Before your very eyes I will take your wives and give them to one who is close to you, and he will lie with your wives in broad daylight. You did it in secret, but I will do this thing in broad daylight before all Israel.' (2 Samuel 12:11-12)

In one of his Psalms, David tells of his unbearable guilt over unconfessed sin and his relief when he did confess it.

When I kept silent,
my bones wasted away
through my groaning all day long.
For day and night
your hand was heavy upon me;
my strength was sapped
as in the heat of summer.
Then I acknowledged my sin to you
and did not cover up my iniquity.
I said, "I will confess
my transgressions to the Lord"—
and you forgave
the guilt of my sin.
(Psalm 32:3-5)

The pull of sin on the Christian can only be effectively overcome by the filling of the Holy Spirit. Being filled does away with the desire we have to sin because the Holy Spirit hates sin. Christians who fail to make being filled with the Spirit a way of life find themselves making numerous attempts to subdue their sinful natures and conquer sin. Sometimes they attain a high degree of success for a brief period, only to fall back again into their old ways.

Scripture teaches and experience proves that, in his own strength, the believer is unable to live the Christian life called for in the Bible. We must look to the indwelling Spirit of Christ for the enabling if we hope to succeed.

I can do everything through him who gives me strength. (Philippians 4:13)

If we are serious about not wanting to sin, we will ask God for the strength to resist it. The more time we spend asking God to keep us from sin, the less time we spend asking God to forgive sin. Yielding to the control of the Holy Spirit will lead to spiritual growth and strength because He will apply the means of grace which bring this about.

We do not have to be Christians a long time before we can be filled. The new Christian, as well as the Christian of many years, can be filled with the Spirit. Being filled is not based on how long one has been a Christian or what one knows about the Bible but on being yielded to the Spirit. As we yield to the Spirit and are

filled, we have a closer walk with God. The closer we walk with
God, the more sensitive we become to sin, both in the knowledge
of it and the abhorrence of it. Also, we are more prepared to do
battle with the spiritual powers that we face.

We may not be able to see Satan and his demons, but they are
as real as anything we can see, and much more destructive. The
only way we can fight against spiritual power is with spiritual
power. As we fight our battles in the power of the Holy Spirit, we
can be confident of victory.

**You, dear children, are from God and have overcome them,
because the one who is in you is greater than the one who is in
the world.** (1 John 4:4)

The Holy Spirit and the Church

The Holy Spirit works in the individual believer to bring about
God's purpose for that individual's life. He works through the
combined lives of all believers to bring about His purpose for His
church. He works to build, encourage, and strengthen the church.

**Then the church throughout Judea, Galilee and Samaria
enjoyed a time of peace. It was strengthened; and encouraged
by the Holy Spirit, it grew in numbers, living in the fear of the
Lord.** (Acts 9:31)

His church is the invisible church, those whom God indwells
by saving grace. They comprise His temple. We know that God is
everywhere; however, the temple of God is God's earthly dwelling
place. In the Old Testament, it was a physical building, with
physical properties, that was made by hands. Since the cross, the
temple of God is a spiritual building, with spiritual properties,
made without hands. Being indwelt by God, there is a sense in
which each believer and each local congregation of believers is a
temple of God. However, collectively, we are the temple of God.
As believers, we are all building blocks in God's temple—living
stones in a living building.

**What agreement is there between the temple of God and idols?
For we are the temple of the living God. As God has said: "I**

will live with them and walk among them, and I will be their God, and they will be my people." (2 Corinthians 6:16)

Consequently, you are no longer foreigners and aliens, but fellow citizens with God's people and members of God's household, built on the foundation of the apostles and prophets, with Christ Jesus himself as the chief cornerstone. In him the whole building is joined together and rises to become a holy temple in the Lord. And in him you too are being built together to become a dwelling in which God lives by his Spirit. (Ephesians 2:19-22)

Don't you know that you yourselves are God's temple and that God's Spirit lives in you? (1 Corinthians 3:16)

As you come to him, the living Stone—rejected by men but chosen by God and precious to him—you also, like living stones, are being built into a spiritual house to be a holy priesthood, offering spiritual sacrifices acceptable to God through Jesus Christ. (1 Peter 2:4-5)

Unity in the Holy Spirit

As we think of being living stones in a spiritual building, we must remember that this is not just any old building, and we are not just any old stones put in any old place. This building is designed by God. We are stones chosen by God, and the Holy Spirit is working to shape us so that we fit into our particular place exactly right. Often, this shaping process requires a good bit of cutting, chiseling, and grinding. It can be painful at times. However, it is necessary in order that we fit properly into our slot. As each of us is made to fit, there is a unity that makes for strength. This unity is in the Holy Spirit. It is given to us by the Holy Spirit, and we are to make every effort to keep it.

Make every effort to keep the unity of the Spirit through the bond of peace. (Ephesians 4:3)

This unity is not external. It does not mean that all of us are to do the same thing or do things the same way. It is not a unity in the method or mode of our worship. It is a unity of spirit produced by the Holy Spirit. It is a oneness with God and, through

God, a oneness with each other. We have the same God as our Father, the same Christ as our Savior, and the same Spirit as our Counselor. The same Spirit has renewed us and imparted faith to us. We have all been baptized into and are now members of one body—the body of Christ. We are all servants of the same Master, soldiers in the same army, and live for the same purpose—to glorify God.

When we think of the different temperaments of man, the different backgrounds he comes from, and the different cultures he lives in, we realize that only the Holy Spirit can maintain our unity. However, it is up to each of us to yield to Him in order for this to be done. We are to do our best to keep the unity. We do this through the bond of peace. Having made peace with God through Jesus Christ, we keep at peace with God through obedience. If we are at peace with God we will be at peace with each other. This peace is more than an absence of conflict—it springs from an internal spirit of love that is expressed in outward acts of love.

Our Home and the Holy Spirit

Think what it would be like if Christians continually exemplified Christian love. Think of the decrease in conflicts, arguments, and other acts of sin that would take place. It is so much easier not to sin when in the company of believers who have their hearts and minds on God. Most of us have been to a Christian gathering or retreat where everyone professed to know Christ, where there were sermons and teachings about Christ, and the music and conversation centered around Christ. In this environment it was much easier to show love to others and to be at peace with others. There was less temptation to sin, and it was easier to resist sin than it is in the atmosphere of the everyday world.

That being the case, think what it would be like to have a truly Christ-centered home. I say "truly" because too often the term "Christ-centered" means nothing more than that those living there have accepted Christ. They may be in Christ but they are not living for Christ. Neither their home nor their lives are under the control of the Holy Spirit—they operate under the influence of the flesh. Just think what a home could be like if everyone in it got serious about their Christian commitment. For husbands, wives, parents and children, a good place to start would be God's commands in Ephesians.

> Wives, submit to your husbands as to the Lord. For the husband is the head of the wife as Christ is the head of the church, his body, of which he is the Savior. Now as the church submits to Christ, so also wives should submit to their husbands in everything.
> Husbands, love your wives, just as Christ loved the church and gave himself up for her to make her holy, cleansing her by the washing with water through the word, and to present her to himself as a radiant church, without stain or wrinkle or any other blemish, but holy and blameless. In this same way, husbands ought to love their wives as their own bodies. He who loves his wife loves himself. After all, no one ever hated his own body, but he feeds and cares for it, just as Christ does the church—for we are members of his body.
> "For this reason a man will leave his father and mother and be united to his wife, and the two will become one flesh." This is a profound mystery—but I am talking about Christ and the church. (Ephesians 5:22-32)

> Children, obey your parents in the Lord, for this is right. "Honor your father and mother"—which is the first commandment with a promise—"that it may go well with you and that you may enjoy long life on the earth."
> Fathers, do not exasperate your children; instead, bring them up in the training and instruction of the Lord. (Ephesians 6:1-4)

In any home, there is unlimited potential for just one committed believer to be used by the Holy Spirit to bring about love, joy, and peace. Each of us needs to ask: Am I that committed believer being used by the Holy Spirit to make it easier for others in my home to maintain a close walk with Him? If not, why not?

Problem of Surrendering to the Holy Spirit

Surrendering our lives totally to the control of the Holy Spirit is easier said than done. Our human nature rebels at the thought of someone else controlling us—using us to do their work in order to accomplish their purpose. We all have a desire to do our own thing. We want to feel free and to be free to do what pleases us. To deny ourselves and surrender it all is a big step.

Often the thoughts that cause us to hesitate to give up control of our lives are questions such as: What will He want me to be? What will He want me to do? Where will He want me to go? Not knowing the answers, some Christians are afraid to surrender their lives totally for fear that God will take advantage of them, and they will have to do what they do not want to do. They fear that God will send them to their "Nineveh."

That being the case, they should first realize that, like Jonah, they are sinning by trying to avoid doing God's will. Secondly, God can get them to their "Nineveh" the hard way, just as He did Jonah. Thirdly, they fail to understand that once we have made a total surrender and the Holy Spirit is in complete control, His ways become our ways, His thoughts our thoughts, and His will our will. It becomes a privilege to have His commands and a blessing to obey them. It is in our obedience that we experience His peace and joy.

A subtle and self-deceiving substitute for turning our lives over to the Holy Spirit is the giving of things. For most Christians, it is easier to surrender things to God than it is to surrender oneself. Christians can give possessions and money, even tithe, without giving themselves to the control of the Holy Spirit. Some will give their time but are not willing to surrender a particular sin or sinful thought. It is up to us as Christians to be aware of the fact that the time we spend not living under the control of the Holy Spirit is time spent in sin. Moreover, it shows that we either have forgotten or are not concerned that we are called to live our lives for the Christ who died for us.

> **And he died for all, that those who live should no longer live for themselves but for him who died for them and was raised again.** (2 Corinthians 5:15)

Drawn Closer in Suffering

There is one thing that causes most Christians to seek to draw closer to God—suffering. It is in our trials and suffering that we are more ready to listen to Him and to obey. Until troubles come, some Christians seem to think of God as being in heaven far removed from them, as opposed to the reality that He is right there with them and in them. They spend little time thinking of Him and less time in communion with Him. As long as their health is good, their finances fine, and their loved ones are okay, they live as though their purpose in life is to seek to be happy rather than to glorify God. But when troubles come they turn to Him. Because He is faithful, they find the comfort of His presence with them.

If we confess our sins, he is faithful and just and will forgive us our sins and purify us from all unrighteousness. (1 John 1:9)

If we are faithless, he will remain faithful, for he cannot disown himself. (2 Timothy 2:13)

You are forgiving and good, O Lord,
abounding in love to all who call to you.
Hear my prayer, O Lord;
listen to my cry for mercy.
In the day of my trouble I will call to you,
for you will answer me. (Psalm 86:5-7)

How wonderful it is to know that God remains faithful. The most faithful of men are subject to moments of unfaithfulness, but God is eternally faithful. However, let us not be presumptuous about God's faithfulness—thinking that we can make it a habit to live for self in good times, seeking to draw close to God only in time of trouble. We cannot profess Christ with our lips but deny Him in our hearts and by our deeds. That would be mockery, and God will not be mocked.

Fools mock at making amends for sin, but goodwill is found among the upright. (Proverbs 14:9)

Do not be deceived: God cannot be mocked. A man reaps what he sows. The one who sows to please his sinful nature, from that nature will reap destruction; the one who sows to please the Spirit, from the Spirit will reap eternal life. (Galatians 6:7-8)

Professing Christ but living for self is deceiving, and the one doing this will reap destruction. Paul says it brings spiritual death.

> **Therefore, brothers, we have an obligation—but it is not to the sinful nature, to live according to it. For if you live according to the sinful nature, you will die; but if by the Spirit you put to death the misdeeds of the body, you will live....**
> (Romans 8:12-13)

The degree to which one lives for the flesh is the degree to which one endangers the soul. Notice in verse 12 that this is addressed to brothers—those professing Christ. However, the statement Paul makes is without exception, "If you live according to the sinful nature, you will die."

All through Scripture we see that true faith, producing a true profession, is expected to result in obedience. And it will. Although it will not be perfect, it will be a trend toward obedience. The true professor will not just mean to be obedient, but he will strive to be obedient. Knowing that Scripture teaches that the saved love Christ, and that those who love Christ keep His commands, we are left with only one conclusion concerning those who profess but do not truly seek to keep His commands—they are not saved. They do not love Christ. He says that if they did, they would keep His commands.

This is the teaching throughout Scripture. We must do more than just taste of the Holy Spirit. We must live and work in obedience to Him, showing that we possess Him and that He possesses us. We can only do this in His power. However, we are not to just sit in our easy chair and expect the Spirit to do good works through us. The grace of the Spirit is not an excuse for us to shirk our responsibility. His working does not reduce the need for us to work but rather increases it. We must work to give expression to His work—both in us and through us. We are to actively seek His will; moreover, we are to carry it out under His direction and in His strength. Then the work we do becomes work that will stand the test of fire.

> **...his work will be shown for what it is, because the Day will bring it to light. It will be revealed with fire, and the fire will test the quality of each man's work.** (1 Corinthians 3:13)

Of course there are many Christians who walk close to God most of the time, not just when they are troubled. They not only experience the blessings of peace and joy that come as a result of obedience, but they also have confidence that when trials come into their lives, they are not there for disciplinary reasons.

It is the common lot of all men in this corrupt world to undergo some degree of trials and suffering. However, no one has ever suffered or will ever suffer as our Lord Jesus Christ did. He not only suffered and resisted the temptations of this world, while at the same time undergoing the persecution and rejection of the world, but He suffered for the sins of the world. We cannot even begin to imagine how awful His suffering was, but He knew what He faced. Knowing what was ahead of Him, His human nature was reluctant but compliant. He was stressed and wanted to avoid the tremendous suffering that lay ahead. However, He came for that purpose—to suffer in our place. As the God-man, He would let nothing stop Him. In obedience to the Father and in the power of the Holy Spirit, He willingly went to the cross.

> They went to a place called Gethsemane, and Jesus said to his disciples, "Sit here while I pray." He took Peter, James and John along with him, and he began to be deeply distressed and troubled. "My soul is overwhelmed with sorrow to the point of death," he said to them. "Stay here and keep watch."
> Going a little farther, he fell to the ground and prayed that if possible the hour might pass from him. "Abba, Father," he said, "everything is possible for you. Take this cup from me. Yet not what I will, but what you will." (Mark 14:32-36)

> He withdrew about a stone's throw beyond them, knelt down and prayed, "Father, if you are willing, take this cup from me; yet not my will, but yours be done." An angel from heaven appeared to him and strengthened him. And being in anguish, he prayed more earnestly, and his sweat was like drops of blood falling to the ground. (Luke 22:41-44)

> During the days of Jesus' life on earth, he offered up prayers and petitions with loud cries and tears to the one who could save him from death, and he was heard because of his reverent submission. Although he was a son, he learned obedience from what he suffered.... (Hebrews 5:7-8)

We read in Luke 22:43 that an angel strengthened Jesus. Being man, Jesus suffered as man, and His heavenly Father sent an angel to strengthen Him. This same heavenly Father is our Father, and He will also strengthen us in our time of need.

> **God is our refuge and strength, an ever-present help in trouble.** (Psalm 46:1)

> **The salvation of the righteous comes from the Lord; he is their stronghold in time of trouble.** (Psalm 37:39)

> **I pray that out of his glorious riches he may strengthen you with power through his Spirit in your inner being....** (Ephesians 3:16)

> **So do not fear, for I am with you;**
> **do not be dismayed, for I am your God.**
> **I will strengthen you and help you;**
> **I will uphold you with my righteous right hand.**
> (Isaiah 41:10)

> **Cast your cares on the Lord and he will sustain you; he will never let the righteous fall.** (Psalm 55:22)

> **The Lord is good, a refuge in times of trouble. He cares for those who trust in him....** (Nahum 1:7)

> **He heals the brokenhearted and binds up their wounds.**
> (Psalm 147:3)

The Scriptures never tell that us we will not suffer; rather they make it clear that we will. Moreover, they are not as concerned with our being relieved of our suffering as they are with how we bear up under it. We know that everything is working for our good (Romans 8:28), and that includes our suffering. We are to glorify God not only in our easier times but also in the times of trials. It is in the times of trials that we find out how much faith we have and how strongly we are committed. Through trials we develop perseverance.

> **If you falter in times of trouble, how small is your strength!**
> (Proverbs 24:10)

> We are hard pressed on every side, but not crushed; perplexed, but not in despair; persecuted, but not abandoned; struck down, but not destroyed. (2 Corinthians 4:8-9)

> ...because you know that the testing of your faith develops perseverance. (James 1:3)

Being persecuted because of our stand for Christ is a form of suffering and trial that all Christians undergo. When we are persecuted for Christ's sake, we are told to rejoice. We do not rejoice because of the suffering itself but because it is due to our identity with Christ. Our confidence that we belong to Him is strengthened, and we can rejoice knowing that we will one day be rewarded by going to be with Him.

> Dear friends, do not be surprised at the painful trial you are suffering, as though something strange were happening to you. But rejoice that you participate in the sufferings of Christ, so that you may be overjoyed when his glory is revealed. If you are insulted because of the name of Christ, you are blessed, for the Spirit of glory and of God rests on you. If you suffer, it should not be as a murderer or thief or any other kind of criminal, or even as a meddler. However, if you suffer as a Christian, do not be ashamed, but praise God that you bear that name. For it is time for judgment to begin with the family of God; and if it begins with us, what will the outcome be for those who do not obey the gospel of God? (1 Peter 4:12-17)

> Blessed are you when people insult you, persecute you and falsely say all kinds of evil against you because of me. Rejoice and be glad, because great is your reward in heaven, for in the same way they persecuted the prophets who were before you. (Matthew 5:11-12)

> His speech persuaded them. They called the apostles in and had them flogged. Then they ordered them not to speak in the name of Jesus, and let them go. The apostles left the Sanhedrin, rejoicing because they had been counted worthy of suffering disgrace for the Name. Day after day, in the temple courts and from house to house, they never stopped teaching and proclaiming the good news that Jesus is the Christ. (Acts 5:40-42)

Christians need to be on guard against Satan at all times, but particularly during a time of suffering. Many of our troubles originate with him, but he will also attempt to use to his advantage those that do not. If he can catch us in a weakened condition with our guard down, he may get us engulfed in sin.

James tells us to resist the devil. How do we do that? Knowing what we do about his power, surely no human thinks of himself as his equal. The only way we can resist him is in God's power.

Submit yourselves, then, to God. Resist the devil, and he will flee from you. (James 4:7)

The more we submit to God, the easier we will find it is to resist the devil. As we humble ourselves and seek to do God's will, He gives us the necessary grace with which to do it.

But he gives us more grace. That is why Scripture says:
"God opposes the proud
but gives grace to the humble." (James 4:6)

We see God's grace at work in the lives of some Christians who suffer much more than most of us ever will. Yet, in His grace they are strengthened as they accept His will for their lives. They can even pray that He will glorify Himself in their suffering. That cannot be done in the flesh. It takes the enabling of the Holy Spirit to pray that way. We should thank God for these people and for the example of faith they set for us. It is an encouragement to us to see what God has done in their lives—the peace and joy He has given them in their adversity, and the way He has sustained them. It gives us hope that if we find ourselves in a situation similar to theirs, He will do the same for us. God uses their example of faith to strengthen us.

Paul thanks God for the Thessalonian Christians whose faith and love were increasing under persecution and trials.

We ought always to thank God for you, brothers, and rightly so, because your faith is growing more and more, and the love every one of you has for each other is increasing. Therefore, among God's churches we boast about your perseverance and faith in all the persecutions and trials you are enduring.

> All this is evidence that God's judgment is right, and as a result you will be counted worthy of the kingdom of God, for which you are suffering. (2 Thessalonians 1:3-5)

The Holy Spirit will always supply the grace we need to accomplish the task He has laid before us. This holds true in our suffering. If our suffering becomes more severe, He supplies us with more grace. We are as dependent on God for the increase of grace as we are to receive grace at first. It is comforting to know that our suffering is not for naught, but that God makes it work to our good and to the good of others. He uses it to draw us closer to Himself, to strengthen our faith, and to give us a firmer hope of heaven.

> Before I was afflicted I went astray,
>   but now I obey your word.
> It was good for me to be afflicted
>   so that I might learn your decrees.
> (Psalm 119:67,71)

> Not only so, but we also rejoice in our sufferings, because we know that suffering produces perseverance; perseverance, character; and character, hope. And hope does not disappoint us, because God has poured out his love into our hearts by the Holy Spirit, whom he has given us. (Romans 5:3-5)

> My comfort in my suffering is this:
>   Your promise preserves my life.
> (Psalm 119:50)

Christian Works and the Holy Spirit

Another important reason why the Christian needs to understand the work of the Holy Spirit and to let Him control his or her life is that the Spirit knows the work the Christian is to do. God has already determined what the works are that each Christian will do, and only as the Christian yields to the Holy Spirit will he or she know what to do.

> For we are God's workmanship, created in Christ Jesus to do good works, which God prepared in advance for us to do. (Ephesians 2:10)

Often, Christians hear it being said that they need to go to Bible study, witness, work on church committees, visit the sick, paint a widow's house, help the poor, raise funds for a paraminstry, etc. All these things are considered good things to do. Now if the non-Christian undertakes to do these things, we know that as good as it seems, it does not please God. It is not of faith. The same is true when the Christian does these things without seeking the guidance of the Holy Spirit and being sensitive to His leading. We are not to do the good works of our choice but those we feel led by Him to do.

Having faith when we accept Christ is one thing, but are we not suppose to act in faith when ten years later we go full-time into a Christian ministry? Should we not be seeking God's guidance in a decision of this nature? Certainly we should. And we should also seek His guidance in decisions about which church to attend, what line of work to pursue, etc. Then why not in so-called lesser decisions? Something that we think is a small matter may be very important to God— someone's eternal life may hinge on its outcome. If we look to God to lead us in only certain decisions or situations then, in essence, we determine what we will let God do and what we will do. In other words, we only look to Him for guidance some of the time, making all the other decisions ourselves, in the flesh. Scripture makes it clear that what we do in the flesh is sin. All that we do is to be done in faith, and to the best of our discernment it is to be what we think God wants us to do.

> **...and everything that does not come from faith is sin.**
> (Romans 14:23b)

In the flesh, the Christian could very well go paint the widow's house while the Holy Spirit wanted him to witness to a friend. Or someone could go to Bible study when at that particular time the Holy Spirit wanted her to visit the sick. How would a Christian know what to do, when to do it, or how to do it unless the Holy Spirit directed and empowered him or her? It becomes more apparent that being filled with the Spirit is not a spiritual luxury but a spiritual necessity.

Commanded To Be Filled with the Spirit

The realization that we are commanded to be controlled by the Holy Spirit, and that we are in sin when we are not, gives us even more reason to be concerned with the ministry of the Holy Spirit. Let us look at the command to be filled in more detail.

Do not get drunk on wine, which leads to debauchery. Instead, be filled with the Spirit. (Ephesians 5:18)

Being filled with the Holy Spirit means being controlled by Him. I do not read Greek, but from what I understand by reading those who do, there are four grammatical rules in the Greek language which lead us to four truths in this command to be filled with the Spirit.

1. The verb is in the imperative mode; it is a command similar to the command to be baptized.

2. The tense of the verb is present, and this tense in the imperative mode always represents action going on continually, not spasmodic action.

3. The verb is in the plural, making it a command to all Christians.

4. It is in the passive voice which means that the subject of the verb is inactive but is being acted upon. It is a work of God, not of man.

We are commanded by God to be controlled and to remain controlled by the Holy Spirit. That is, we are to maintain a state of being controlled by the Holy Spirit—be controlled by Him and continue to be controlled by Him. In other words, we are to live our lives in all we think, say, and do under the control of the Holy Spirit.

We do not want to confuse being filled with the Spirit as a need to have more of the Spirit. No, the Spirit is all-powerful God. We do not need more of Him; He needs more of us. We need to be more committed to Him, more surrendered to Him, and more submissive to Him. We need to place not only our Sunday school and church life under His control, but we need to place our life as father or mother, son or daughter, husband or wife, single person, business executive, factory worker or homemaker under His control. He is to be in control of our hobbies whether it is photography, gardening or travel. We need to place our entertainment and recreational activities under Him. This includes the movies, TV, and the videos we watch, as well as the books and magazines we read. Our sex life is to be under His control. I mention these areas of our lives to help illustrate the fact that our total life, all aspects of our life, are to be lived under the control of the Holy Spirit twenty-four hours a day, every day. That is our target. None of us can hit it, but by God's grace it is what we are to strive for.

It is sad to say, but many Christians put forth effort to obey the first part of Ephesians 5:18 but give little, if any, thought to the second part. You can obey the first without obeying the second, but you cannot obey the second without obeying the first. While many unbelievers do not get drunk, it is only believers who have the privilege of being controlled by the Holy Spirit. And although it is a privilege and a blessing, we must never lose sight of the fact that first of all it is our duty.

Being controlled by the Holy Spirit is easier said than done. Not only does the sinful nature impede it, but often we are hindered because we do not understand what it means to be controlled. However, if we consider how often we use the terms "filled with anger" or "full of hate" to describe someone who is under the influence or control of anger or hatred, we may understand it better. The Bible speaks of sinful man as being filled with wickedness and full of envy. Those filled with wickedness are controlled by wickedness.

> **They have become filled with every kind of wickedness, evil, greed and depravity. They are full of envy, murder, strife, deceit and malice.** (Romans 1:29)

While under the control of anger, most of us have spoken words or committed deeds that we later regretted. Violence and murder are often committed while a person is controlled by a raging jealousy or a burning desire for revenge. When controlled by anger or hatred we will do things we would not otherwise do. When controlled by the Holy Spirit the same thing is true—we do things we would not otherwise do. However, they are always good things—spiritual things.

As we seek to understand more fully how to be controlled by the Holy Spirit, we will find that we will question ourselves as to our motivation for doing different things. Is it for materialistic gain, fame, power, an ego trip, or is it because, as best I can discern, God is leading me to do it?

Some Christians may wonder if there is a difference in being full of the Holy Spirit and being filled with the Holy Spirit. There is no difference. To be full of the Holy Spirit means the same thing as to be filled with the Holy Spirit. Both denote that the person is under the control of the Holy Spirit. We have seen that Jesus lived His life under the control and in the power of the Holy Spirit. Luke 4:1 tells us that Jesus was full of the Holy Spirit. In the following verses we find that the apostles and other believers were spoken of as being either full or filled with the Holy Spirit.

> When the day of Pentecost came, they were all together in one place. Suddenly a sound like the blowing of a violent wind came from heaven and filled the whole house where they were sitting. They saw what seemed to be tongues of fire that separated and came to rest on each of them. All of them were filled with the Holy Spirit and began to speak in other tongues as the Spirit enabled them. (Acts 2:1-4)

> Then Peter, filled with the Holy Spirit, said to them.... (Acts 4:8a)

> After they prayed, the place where they were meeting was shaken. And they were all filled with the Holy Spirit and spoke the word of God boldly. (Acts 4:31)

> In those days when the number of disciples was increasing, the Grecian Jews among them complained against the Hebraic Jews because their widows were being overlooked in the daily distribution of food. So the Twelve gathered all the disciples together and said, "It would not be right for us to neglect the ministry of the word of God in order to wait on tables. Brothers, choose seven men from among you who are known to be full of the Spirit and wisdom. We will turn this responsibility over to them and will give our attention to prayer and the ministry of the word." (Acts 6:1-4)

But Stephen, full of the Holy Spirit, looked up to heaven and saw the glory of God, and Jesus standing at the right hand of God. (Acts 7:55)

Then Ananias went to the house and entered it. Placing his hands on Saul, he said, "Brother Saul, the Lord—Jesus, who appeared to you on the road as you were coming here—has sent me so that you may see again and be filled with the Holy Spirit." (Acts 9:17)

News of this reached the ears of the church at Jerusalem, and they sent Barnabas to Antioch. When he arrived and saw the evidence of the grace of God, he was glad and encouraged them all to remain true to the Lord with all their hearts. He was a good man, full of the Holy Spirit and faith, and a great number of people were brought to the Lord. (Acts 11:22-24)

Then Saul, who was also called Paul, filled with the Holy Spirit, looked straight at Elymas and said.... (Acts 13:9)

Professing without Possessing the Holy Spirit

All Christians should concern themselves with living their lives under the control of the Holy Spirit. However, there are some who profess to be Christians whose first concern should be the question, Am I really indwelt by the Holy Spirit?

The Bible makes it clear that if we belong to God we are indwelt by His Holy Spirit; moreover, if we do not have the Holy Spirit, we do not belong to God (Romans 8:9). A problem arises when some people who are not saved, and therefore do not have the Holy Spirit, become so entwined with true Christians that they are able to talk and act as if they were Christians. They accomplish works in the flesh. Some go as far as being part of a Christian ministry—even becoming leaders.

Not all of these are hypocrites or charlatans. Many are people who are sincere in what they believe. They think of themselves as being Christians. Like the Jews whom Paul speaks of in Romans 10:2, they have a zeal for God, but not according to knowledge. Theirs is a system of self-righteousness rather than Christ's righteousness. They may believe all around the truth, but they do not believe the truth. They have never trusted in the One who is truth. However, they appear so genuine that others accept them for real, and that makes it even easier for them to be self-deluded. It is sad when you realize that they seem to come so close to heaven and yet miss it. In the Parable of the Ten Virgins we see an example of something of this nature.

> At that time the kingdom of heaven will be like ten virgins who took their lamps and went out to meet the bridegroom. Five of them were foolish and five were wise. The foolish ones took their lamps but did not take any oil with them. The wise, however, took oil in jars along with their lamps. The bridegroom was a long time in coming, and they all became drowsy and fell asleep.
>
> At midnight the cry rang out: 'Here's the bridegroom! Come out to meet him!'
>
> Then all the virgins woke up and trimmed their lamps. The foolish ones said to the wise, 'Give us some of your oil; our lamps are going out.'
>
> 'No,' they replied, 'there may not be enough for both us and you. Instead, go to those who sell oil and buy some for yourselves.'
>
> But while they were on their way to buy the oil, the bridegroom arrived. The virgins who were ready went in with him to the wedding banquet. And the door was shut.
>
> Later the others also came. 'Sir! Sir!' they said, 'Open the door for us!'
>
> But he replied, 'I tell you the truth, I don't know you.'
>
> Therefore keep watch, because you do not know the day or the hour. (Matthew 25:1-13)

To help us better understand the parable, let us assume the position that is popular with most expositors: The bridegroom represents our Lord Jesus Christ; the ten virgins represent those who profess Christ; the lamps represent their professions, and the oil represents the Holy Spirit.

We see in the parable that the ten went out together. By being together and going out together it appears they shared some common interests. They certainly had in common the fact that they were going out to meet the same person—the bridegroom. It seems that night weddings were a common thing in that part of the world. Because the ten virgins were going to meet the bridegroom and accompany him to the wedding feast, they would need lamps. This is another thing they all had in common—each had her lamp.

But now we come to a difference—a crucial difference: The parable tells us that the foolish virgins had lamps, but no oil. That is why they are called foolish. The wise ones not only had their lamps, but they also took jars of oil. The foolish virgins had a profession of Christ, but it was hollow and without substance. It was not a true profession; therefore, they lacked the Holy Spirit. They were unprepared to meet the bridegroom. On the other hand, the wise virgins had a genuine profession, were indwelt by the Holy Spirit, and were prepared. Those who recite the same creeds, sing the same hymns, and attend the same Bible studies often appear the same to their fellow man; however, they may be totally different in God's sight.

By God's grace, the Holy Spirit is in the world striving with man (Genesis 6:3) and convicting the world of sin and judgment (John 16:8). The Bible speaks of those who have been enlightened, who have tasted the heavenly gift, who have shared in the Holy Spirit, who have tasted the goodness of the Word of God, and yet they are not truly converted (Hebrews 6:4-6). Think of the Israelites, they had seen the cloud by day and the fire by night, had been freed from bondage in Eqypt, crossed the Red Sea, eaten the manna from heaven, and been taught God's Word. They had much enlightenment but look at the vast numbers of them who were lost.

The Jews of Christ's day had God's Word, and some of them searched the Scriptures diligently. Yet, they did not receive Christ.

> You diligently study the Scriptures because you think that by them you possess eternal life. These are the Scriptures that testify about me, yet you refuse to come to me to have life. (John 5:39-40)

Being enlightened does not imply being saved. Many people are enlightened to the facts of the Gospel, but do not believe its message. There are varying degrees of enlightenment among unbelievers, one of which would include an unsaved seminary professor. As natural man he may have a great degree of natural enlightenment but still be unsaved.

Many people who spend time in a sound church where there are a number of true Christians have an opportunity to taste the heavenly gift (Christ). They also have an opportunity to share in the Holy Spirit and to taste that the Word of God is good. Just as one would taste food to see if it is good before serving a plate full, they have an opportunity to taste Christ by hearing about Him from those in the pulpit and from those in the pew. They get to see Him work in and through those who know Him. They are in places where the Holy Spirit is working and with people whom the Holy Spirit indwells. Therefore, they share in the Holy Spirit in the sense that they see Him work, feel He is present in the group, share in His blessing of the group, and are actually influenced by Him to lead a more moral and selfless life. Upon being given a certain degree of understanding of Scripture, they taste it and see that God's Word is good. Experiencing all of this, they react and make a profession of Christ. However, their profession is based only on head knowledge, and lacks commitment. Such might have been the case of the five foolish virgins. Also, it might have been the case of those whom Jesus knew did not truly believe, even though they had professed to believe.

Now while he was in Jerusalem at the Passover Feast, many people saw the miraculous signs he was doing and believed in his name. But Jesus would not entrust himself to them, for he knew all men. He did not need man's testimony about man, for he knew what was in a man. (John 2:23-25)

Apparently there were many who were impressed with the miracles that Jesus did and, in the flesh, were ready to rally around His ministry. Jesus knew that they did not have faith but were caught up in the excitement of the miracles—take these away and they would leave. Man can be fickle; the cause he so fervently supports today is often forgotten tomorrow. Even true converts can begin their Christian lives with a flourish, and later see their enthusiasm begin to wane.

We see that the ten virgins had a long wait, and they all fell asleep. They had been watching and waiting, but it seems the bridegroom was taking longer than they had expected. At midnight, they were awakened by a cry that the bridegroom was coming, and they all lit their lamps. However, the foolish virgins had failed to bring oil, and a wick burning without oil soon goes out. They now realized they were unprepared to meet the bridegroom. Being prepared involves more than getting prepared—it indicates a state of preparedness, one of staying prepared.

The foolish virgins wanted the wise ones to give them some of their oil, but the wise ones had only enough for themselves. Man cannot give the Holy Spirit—only God can. The wise virgins told the foolish to go buy oil. (The foolish virgins would not need money if they went to the right source to buy oil.)

Come, all you who are thirsty,
    come to the waters;
and you who have no money,
    come, buy and eat!
Come, buy wine and milk
    without money and without cost.
(Isaiah 55:1)

However, while they were on their way to buy oil the bridegroom arrived. The virgins who were prepared went in with him to the wedding banquet, and the door was shut. When the foolish virgins returned they asked the bridegroom to open the door; however, he told them he did not know them. Many people think that no one will be excluded from the banquet, but the parable makes it clear that some will be. While the door is open, mercy and forgiveness may be found; however, once the door is closed, the time of mercy and forgiveness is past, and judgment is at hand. When Christ returns we will not only be concerned that we have our lamps, but that we have oil for them. For it is only by the indwelling Holy Spirit that our lamps will continue to burn, and that we will be prepared to meet Him.

The Fruit of the Spirit

The term "fruit of the Spirit" is confusing to some people because they relate it to the fruit of the Christian's life or to the gifts of the Spirit. It is neither.

The fruit of the Christian's life consists of those things done by the Christian. It is true that to be pleasing to God they must be done at the direction and in the power of the Holy Spirit. However, they are still done by the Christian and are fruit of the Christian's life.

The gifts of the Spirit are given to the Christian to be used for the edification of the church, and to convert people to Christ. They then are gifts that are given in order to enable the Christian to do things that are fruitful in God's service. They are gifts from the Spirit, but are not to be confused with the fruit of the Spirit.

In order to make a practical distinction between the fruit of the Spirit, the fruit of the Christian's life, and the gifts of the Spirit, let us use as an example a Bible teacher. The teacher feels led of the Holy Spirit to conduct a Bible study with some fellow Christians, and in obedience he does so. The act of obedience in holding the study is fruit of the teacher's life. Let us assume that he is such a good teacher that it seems he has a gift for teaching. We might say he has been given the gift of teaching as a gift of the Spirit. When he is teaching the class, things come up from time to time that show the teacher to be a very kind person. We might say he manifests the virtue of kindness as fruit of the Spirit.

The fruit of the Spirit is work done within us by the Spirit. This work by the Spirit produces a character change within the Christian. As our character determines our deeds, we associate the fruit of the Spirit more with what kind of person the Christian is, rather than with what the Christian does. If we were to attempt to discern a Christian's spirituality, we would be on much safer ground to look for the fruit of the Spirit as opposed to the gifts of the Spirit.

The carnal Christian can display the use of spiritual gifts as did those in the church at Corinth. Although all Christians do not have the same spiritual gifts, all Christians do have the same fruit of the Spirit. The degree to which a Christian yields to the Holy Spirit will determine the degree to which the fruit of the Spirit is manifested in his life. The only person within whom this fruit is found in perfection is Jesus Christ.

Let us look at the fruit as it is listed in Galatians, and each consider to what degree it is present in our own life.

But the fruit of the Spirit is love, joy, peace, patience, kindness, goodness, faithfulness, gentleness and self-control. Against such things there is no law. (Galatians 5:22-23)

The fruit of the Spirit is not only a personal blessing to us and an enhancement to our walk with God, but it is also very much a factor in our behavior toward man, and our witness to man.

Love

The first virtue listed as fruit of the Spirit is love. We are to love God and man.

> **Jesus replied: "Love the Lord your God with all your heart and with all your soul and with all your mind.' This is the first and greatest commandment. And the second is like it: 'Love your neighbor as yourself.'"** (Matthew 22:37-39)

The love that is produced within us by the Holy Spirit is agape love (a higher love than that which is common to natural man). It is a supernatural love that comes from God.

> **Dear friends, let us love one another, for love comes from God. Everyone who loves has been born of God and knows God. Whoever does not love does not know God, because God is love. This is how God showed his love among us: He sent his one and only Son into the world that we might live through him. This is love: not that we loved God, but that he loved us and sent his Son as an atoning sacrifice for our sins. Dear friends, since God so loved us, we also ought to love one another. No one has ever seen God; but if we love one another, God lives in us and his love is made complete in us.**
> **(1 John 4:7-12)**

We see from the above verses that God is love and that He has shown us His perfect love by sending His Son to die for us. We are told that we should love one another because God loves us so much and indwells us. Actually the only reason we can love either God or man is because God loved us first. With this being the case, if we do not love each other something is wrong. John says our love for each other is an indication that we have been born of God.

If we have been born again, God will produce agape love within us and we will love our fellow believers. Scripture encourages us to cultivate that love so that it becomes stronger.

> **We know that we have passed from death to life, because we love our brothers. Anyone who does not love remains in death.**
> **(1 John 3:14)**

> Now that you have purified yourselves by obeying the truth so that you have sincere love for your brothers, love one another deeply, from the heart. (1 Peter 1:22)

> Now about brotherly love we do not need to write to you, for you yourselves have been taught by God to love each other. (1 Thessalonians 4:9)

Although Christians are to manifest a special love for one another, they are also to show love to unbelievers. There are a number of ways that Christians do this, but none is more important than telling them about Christ: who He is, what He has done, and what He can and will do for them if they will turn to Him. However, Christian love is to go still further. We are commanded to love our enemies. Because obedience to God is the surest sign of our love for Him, if we love our enemies it should increase our confidence that we truly love God.

> But I tell you who hear me: Love your enemies, do good to those who hate you....
> If you love those who love you, what credit is that to you? Even sinners love those who love them. (Luke 6:27,32)

> If you love me, you will obey what I command. (John 14:15)

We see how dependent we are on God's Holy Spirit to produce love in us and enable us to show that love to others. Our dependence on the Holy Spirit is further emphasized when we seek to love as Paul defined love in 1 Corinthians.

> And now I will show you the most excellent way. If I speak in the tongues of men and of angels, but have not love, I am only a resounding gong or a clanging cymbal. If I have the gift of prophecy and can fathom all mysteries and all knowledge, and if I have a faith that can move mountains, but have not love, I am nothing. If I give all I possess to the poor and surrender my body to the flames, but have not love, I gain nothing.
> Love is patient, love is kind. It does not envy, it does not boast, it is not proud. It is not rude, it is not self-seeking, it is not easily angered, it keeps no record of wrongs. Love does not delight in evil but rejoices with the truth. It always protects, always trusts, always hopes, always perseveres.

Love never fails. But where there are prophecies, they will cease; where there are tongues, they will be stilled; where there is knowledge, it will pass away. For we know in part and we prophesy in part, but when perfection comes, the imperfect disappears. When I was a child, I talked like a child, I thought like a child, I reasoned like a child. When I became a man, I put childish ways behind me. Now we see but a poor reflection as in a mirror; then we shall see face to face. Now I know in part; then I shall know fully, even as I am fully known.

And now these three remain: faith, hope and love. But the greatest of these is love. (1 Corinthians Chapter 13)

Joy

The joy the Holy Spirit produces within the Christian is a spiritual joy. It is not like the joy of the world—joy that is here today if things are going well but gone tomorrow if things fall apart. The joy the Holy Spirit gives us is rooted in the fact that we belong to God, and heaven is our destination. This stabilizes our joy so that we are not dependent on our circumstances, but rather we have joy in the bad times as well as the good. We do not alternate between moods of joy and gloom. This is a strengthening factor in our Christian walk.

Nehemiah said, "Go and enjoy choice food and sweet drinks, and send some to those who have nothing prepared. This day is sacred to our Lord. Do not grieve, for the joy of the Lord is your strength." (Nehemiah 8:10)

The Bible speaks of joy in spite of suffering.

You became imitators of us and of the Lord; in spite of severe suffering, you welcomed the message with the joy given by the Holy Spirit. (1 Thessalonians 1:6)

...sorrowful, yet always rejoicing.... (2 Corinthians 6:10)

Although joy is produced in us by the Holy Spirit, our conduct greatly affects the degree to which we benefit from it. If we are obedient we will experience it in abundance, but if we are disobedient we will lose it. Then we must repent and ask God to restore our joy, as David did.

> **Restore to me the joy of your salvation and grant me a willing spirit, to sustain me.** (Psalm 51:12)

When things are going well for us let us remember that our situation can change. It is not the circumstances of the moment upon which we are to base our joy but on the fact that Christ has saved us. Nothing can compare with salvation as a reason for joy. This is pointed out by Christ to the seventy-two disciples.

> **The seventy-two returned with joy and said, "Lord, even the demons submit to us in your name." He replied, "I saw Satan fall like lightning from heaven. I have given you authority to trample on snakes and scorpions and to overcome all the power of the enemy; nothing will harm you. However, do not rejoice that the spirits submit to you, but rejoice that your names are written in heaven."** (Luke 10:17-20)

Peter confirms the joy that believers have in their salvation.

> **Though you have not seen him, you love him; and even though you do not see him now, you believe in him and are filled with an inexpressible and glorious joy, for you are receiving the goal of your faith, the salvation of your souls.** (1 Peter 1:8-9)

Peace

Like joy, the peace given the Christian is different from that of the world.

> **Peace I leave with you; my peace I give you. I do not give to you as the world gives. Do not let your hearts be troubled and do not be afraid.** (John 14:27)

When we come to Christ, we make peace with God.

> **Therefore, since we have been justified through faith, we have peace with God through our Lord Jesus Christ....** (Romans 5:1)

Having made peace with God we are to live in peace with fellow Christians and with all men, if possible.

> **Live in peace with each other.** (1 Thessalonians 5:13b)

Make every effort to live in peace with all men....
(Hebrews 12:14a)

Turn from evil and do good; seek peace and pursue it.
(Psalm 34:14)

When we came to God through Christ, we not only ceased hostility toward Him but began communion with Him. We not only were made to be at peace with Him but were given peace by Him. However, if we are to continue to experience this peace and benefit from it, we must walk in obedience. We must be controlled by the Holy Spirit.

...but the mind controlled by the Spirit is life and peace....
(Romans 8:6)

One of the benefits of this peace is that we no longer have to fret and worry about anything—health, finances, family, job, people, events, etc. We are not to be anxious over these things but are to put them before God in prayer. As we do this, we can have peace.

Do not be anxious about anything, but in everything, by prayer and petition, with thanksgiving, present your requests to God. And the peace of God, which transcends all understanding, will guard your hearts and your minds in Christ Jesus.
(Philippians 4:6-7)

Cast all your anxiety on him because he cares for you.
(1 Peter 5:7)

These verses do not mean that we are not to have concern or exercise care; however, our faith in God's love for us, and in His sovereignty over all that touches us, will keep us from anxiety. We can face life in calm dependence on Him, knowing that He will work all things to our good.

And we know that in all things God works for the good of those who love him, who have been called according to his purpose. (Romans 8:28)

You will keep in perfect peace him whose mind is steadfast, because he trusts in you. (Isaiah 26:3)

Having been given peace by the God of peace (Romans 15:33), we should endeavor to foster peace. We should not just remain at peace with others but encourage peace between others—between family members, friends, and fellow believers. We should look to God to use us to be peacemakers, to help bring peace between man and man, and between God and man.

Blessed are the peacemakers, for they will be called sons of God. (Matthew 5:9)

Peacemakers who sow in peace raise a harvest of righteousness. (James 3:18)

Patience

Patience is next in the list of the fruit of the Spirit. This entails being patient under all circumstances, but particularly in the face of adversity and ill will. We are to be patient when provoked, and not retaliate. As Christ is our perfect example of all that is good, He is our example for patience.

But for that very reason I was shown mercy so that in me, the worst of sinners, Christ Jesus might display his unlimited patience as an example for those who would believe on him and receive eternal life. (1 Timothy 1:16)

The Lord is not slow in keeping his promise, as some understand slowness. He is patient with you, not wanting anyone to perish, but everyone to come to repentance. (2 Peter 3:9)

We are admonished to be patient with everyone. And, whether in affliction or under persecution, we are to be patient as we wait for the Lord's coming.

Be patient, then, brothers, until the Lord's coming. See how the farmer waits for the land to yield its valuable crop and how patient he is for the autumn and spring rains. You too, be patient and stand firm, because the Lord's coming is near.

Don't grumble against each other, brothers, or you will be
judged. The Judge is standing at the door!
    Brothers, as an example of patience in the face of
suffering, take the prophets who spoke in the name of the
Lord. As you know, we consider blessed those who have
persevered. You have heard of Job's perseverance and have
seen what the Lord finally brought about. The Lord is full of
compassion and mercy. (James 5:7-11)

Be joyful in hope, patient in affliction, faithful in prayer.
(Romans 12:12)

And we urge you, brothers, warn those who are idle, encourage
the timid, help the weak, be patient with everyone.
(1 Thessalonians 5:14)

The Book of Proverbs compares patience with a quick temper.

A patient man has great understanding, but a quick-tempered
man displays folly. (Proverbs 14:29)

A hot-tempered man stirs up dissension, but a patient man
calms a quarrel. (Proverbs 15:18)

Better a patient man than a warrior, a man who controls his
temper than one who takes a city. (Proverbs 16:32)

We see that Abraham waited patiently for the promise of
God.

When God made his promise to Abraham, since there was no
one greater for him to swear by, he swore by himself, saying,
"I will surely bless you and give you many descendants." And
so after waiting patiently, Abraham received what was
promised. (Hebrews 6:13-15)

We, too, are to wait patiently on Christ. We are to cling to our
hope of salvation, which is not the kind of hope the world knows,
but a hope that rests in Christ—a hope that is sure.

For our light and momentary troubles are achieving for us an
eternal glory that far outweighs them all. So we fix our eyes

not on what is seen, but on what is unseen. For what is seen is temporary, but what is unseen is eternal. (2 Corinthians 4:17-18)

But if we hope for what we do not yet have, we wait for it patiently. (Romans 8:25)

Kindness

Kindness suggests a mild or sweet temper, kind acts motivated by a regard for need, a politeness that goes beyond good manners, and manifests consideration for the fragile nature of human personality. God exercises kindness on earth, and His kindness is shown in His giving to and providing for mankind.

This is what the Lord says: "Let not the wise man boast of his wisdom or the strong man boast of his strength or the rich man boast of his riches, but let him who boasts boast about this: that he understands and knows me, that I am the Lord, who exercises kindness, justice and righteousness on earth, for in these I delight...." (Jeremiah 9:23-24)

Yet he has not left himself without testimony: He has shown kindness by giving you rain from heaven and crops in their seasons; he provides you with plenty of food and fills your hearts with joy. (Acts 14:17)

We should tell about God's kindness and praise Him for it. His kindness leads men toward repentance.

I will tell of the kindnesses of the Lord, the deeds for which he is to be praised, according to all the Lord has done for us.... (Isaiah 63:7)

Or do you show contempt for the riches of his kindness, tolerance and patience, not realizing that God's kindness leads you toward repentance? (Romans 2:4)

We are examples of God's kindness which is shown by His having saved us by grace.

> And God raised us up with Christ and seated us with him in the heavenly realms in Christ Jesus, in order that in the coming ages he might show the incomparable riches of his grace, expressed in his kindness to us in Christ Jesus. (Ephesians 2:6-7)

> But when the kindness and love of God our Savior appeared, he saved us.... (Titus 3:4-5a)

With God as our example of kindness and the indwelling Spirit producing the fruit of kindness within us, we certainly should seek to show God's kindness to others. Furthermore, God's Word tells us to be kind.

> And the Lord's servant must not quarrel; instead, he must be kind to everyone.... (2 Timothy 2:24)

> The king asked, "Is there no one still left of the house of Saul to whom I can show God's kindness?" (2 Samuel 9:3)

> Be kind and compassionate to one another, forgiving each other, just as in Christ God forgave you. (Ephesians 4:32)

> Make sure that nobody pays back wrong for wrong, but always try to be kind to each other and to everyone else. (1 Thessalonians 5:15)

Goodness

Goodness indicates being both morally and spiritually good and will lead to doing good as a result of being good. As a good tree produces good fruit so a good person does good deeds.

> The good man brings good things out of the good stored up in his heart.... (Luke 6:45)

As Christians, we are recipients of God's goodness.

> How great is your goodness, which you have stored up for those who fear you, which you bestow in the sight of men on those who take refuge in you. (Psalm 31:19)

How can I repay the Lord for all his goodness to me?
(Psalm 116:12)

As recipients of divine goodness and in obedience to divine will, we should strive to do good in both word and deed.

And do not forget to do good and to share with others, for with such sacrifices God is pleased. (Hebrews 13:16)

Command them to do good, to be rich in good deeds, and to be generous and willing to share. (1 Timothy 6:18)

In everything set them an example by doing what is good. (Titus 2:7a)

Therefore, as we have opportunity, let us do good to all people, especially to those who belong to the family of believers. (Galatians 6:10)

May our Lord Jesus Christ himself and God our Father, who loved us and by his grace gave us eternal encouragement and good hope, encourage your hearts and strengthen you in every good deed and word. (2 Thessalonians 2:16-17)

It becomes obvious that, if we are going to exemplify the fruit of goodness, we must concern ourselves with being helpful and seeking to benefit others by word and deed. We should even encourage other Christians to do good.

And let us consider how we may spur one another on toward love and good deeds. (Hebrews 10:24)

We should live such good lives and do such good deeds among unbelievers that our lives would give them nothing to be critical of; whereby, some of them may be won to Christ. It would only be out of ignorance or malice that they could accuse us of wrongdoing.

For it is God's will that by doing good you should silence the ignorant talk of foolish men. (1 Peter 2:15)

Live such good lives among the pagans that, though they accuse you of doing wrong, they may see your good deeds and glorify God on the day he visits us. (1 Peter 2:12)

We are even commanded to do good to our enemies. This becomes a real test of goodness in the Christian's life, and our response to this command shows whether or not we are being controlled by the Holy Spirit. As God is kind to the ungrateful and wicked, we are to be also.

But love your enemies, do good to them, and lend to them without expecting to get anything back. Then your reward will be great, and you will be sons of the Most High, because he is kind to the ungrateful and wicked. (Luke 6:35)

We are not to repay evil for evil but are to repay evil with good. One very positive aspect to doing good is that in so doing, we can overcome evil.

Do not be overcome by evil, but overcome evil with good. (Romans 12:21)

This verse makes it clear that we are not to just resist being overcome by evil but that we are to achieve victory over evil by doing good. This applies to all situations. In particular, it applies when someone has wronged us, and we are tempted to respond in a wrongful and unloving way. Instead, we are to love them and do good to them. Only as we allow the Holy Spirit to produce the fruit of goodness in us will we be able to respond in this manner.

Faithfulness

The fruit of faithfulness includes faithfulness to man as well as faithfulness to God. Faithfulness to God, though based on faith in God, is our faithfulness to serve God—our faithful obedience to God.

Now fear the Lord and serve him with all faithfulness. (Joshua 24:14a)

Paul tells us that Tychicus was faithful in his service to the Lord.

> **Tychicus, the dear brother and faithful servant in the Lord, will tell you everything, so that you also may know how I am and what I am doing.** (Ephesians 6:21)

God is our example of perfect faithfulness.

> **Know therefore that the Lord your God is God; he is the faithful God, keeping his covenant of love to a thousand generations of those who love him and keep his commands.** (Deuteronomy 7:9)

> **For great is his love toward us, and the faithfulness of the Lord endures forever.** (Psalm 117:2)

With God as our source and our example, we should seek to be faithful to our fellow man. A Christian who is faithful is someone who manifests fidelity, can be trusted to keep his word, and lives up to his promises. If we are faithful to God, it follows that by so being, we will be faithful to man. We will be faithful in the discharge of our duties, in taking care of our responsibilities, in fulfilling our commitments, in keeping our word and vows, in living up to our contracts, and in our relationships to others. As Christians we should strive to be faithful and to remain faithful.

> **Let love and faithfulness never leave you; bind them around your neck, write them on the tablet of your heart.** (Proverbs 3:3)

Gentleness

A gentle person does not give up his rights as a way of life, but may do so on occasion. However, when retaining and defending his rights, he always does so with gentleness. When in a superior position, one who is gentle may yield to one beneath him. He may not press a legal right to its fullest, in order to avoid causing the other party a problem. A gentle person is not violent, quarrelsome or harsh, but is friendly and considerate of others. The Bible tells us that God is gentle. Christ says for us to take His yoke because He is gentle.

> **He tends his flock like a shepherd: He gathers the lambs in his arms and carries them close to his heart; he gently leads those that have young.** (Isaiah 40:11)

> **Take my yoke upon you and learn from me, for I am gentle and humble in heart, and you will find rest for your souls.** (Matthew 11:29)

Paul appealed to the Corinthians in the gentleness of Christ.

> **By the meekness and gentleness of Christ, I appeal to you....** (2 Corinthians 10:1)

Scripture makes it clear that gentleness is expected of the Christian.

> **Brothers, if someone is caught in a sin, you who are spiritual should restore him gently.** (Galatians 6:1a)

> **Let your gentleness be evident to all. The Lord is near.** (Philippians 4:5)

Self-control

Self-control is the last virtue listed as the fruit of the Spirit. Being listed last in no way implies it is any less a virtue or any less needed than the others. We have only to look at Scripture to see how prevalent lack of self-control is among those who belong to the Lord. This evidence is backed up by our own personal experience and observation of our fellow believers. Self-control is a virtue to be sought. Lack of self-control is a sin to be discarded. Like all the other virtues of the fruit of the Spirit, self-control can only be achieved in the power of the Holy Spirit. In one sense, it is the new self in us having control over the old self—our sinful nature.

There was a time when high walls were built around cities as protection against enemies. God says if we lack self-control we are like a city without walls, defenseless against the enemy. We are defenseless against temptation and against the enticement of Satan.

> **Like a city whose walls are broken down is a man who lacks self-control.** (Proverbs 25:28)

> **Be self-controlled and alert. Your enemy the devil prowls around like a roaring lion looking for someone to devour.** (1 Peter 5:8)

Self-control involves having control over our thoughts, desires, natural impulses, emotions, and actions. It encompasses not only resisting the desires of the flesh but restraint of any form of behavior such as anger and temper. It further includes moderation in those things that are neutral. A neutral thing out of control is no longer neutral but can be disruptive and even destructive to our Christian walk. This would include eating, watching TV, reading, etc. Paul and Peter both wrote of the need for self-controlled lives.

> **So then, let us not be like others, who are asleep, but let us be alert and self-controlled.** (1 Thessalonians 5:6)

> **Therefore, prepare your minds for action; be self-controlled....** (1 Peter 1:13)

Self-control calls for self-discipline. The writer of Proverbs tells us that one of the reasons for writing Proverbs was to help people acquire a disciplined life.

> **The proverbs of Solomon son of David, king of Israel: for attaining wisdom and discipline; for understanding words of insight; for acquiring a disciplined and prudent life, doing what is right and just and fair....** (Proverbs 1:1-3)

Biblical self-control can be attained only if self is yielded to, and operating in the power of, the Holy Spirit. If we look to God to make self-control a reality in our lives, He will bring it about.

> **For God did not give us a spirit of timidity, but a spirit of power, of love and of self-discipline.** (2 Timothy 1:7)

Paul says there is no law against the fruit of the Spirit. These things are good, and there is no law against being good or doing good. There is not only no law against them, but the law could not bring them into being. It could not cause them to be manifested. It is only by the work of the Holy Spirit that they come about.

Gifts of the Spirit

Whereas the fruit of the Spirit has to do with our character, the gifts of the Spirit have bearing on our works. All Christians have at least one gift; some have more than one. These gifts are given to us to equip us to do the work that is necessary to add to and build up the church, and should be exercised at the direction of the Holy Spirit and in His strength.

> Each one should use whatever gift he has received to serve others, faithfully administering God's grace in its various forms. If anyone speaks, he should do it as one speaking the very words of God. If anyone serves, he should do it with the strength God provides, so that in all things God may be praised through Jesus Christ. To him be the glory and the power for ever and ever. Amen. (1 Peter 4:10-11)

The Holy Spirit has different work for each of us to do, and He gives His gifts and grace to us as needed to accomplish His purpose.

> There are different kinds of gifts, but the same Spirit. There are different kinds of service, but the same Lord. There are different kinds of working, but the same God works all of them in all men.
> Now to each one the manifestation of the Spirit is given for the common good. To one there is given through the Spirit the message of wisdom, to another the message of knowledge by means of the same Spirit, to another faith by the same Spirit, to another gifts of healing by that one Spirit, to another miraculous powers, to another prophecy, to another distinguishing between spirits, to another speaking in different kinds of tongues, and to still another the interpretation of tongues. All these are the work of one and the same Spirit, and he gives them to each one, just as he determines.
> (1 Corinthians 12:4-11)

> Now you are the body of Christ, and each one of you is a part of it. And in the church God has appointed first of all apostles, second prophets, third teachers, then workers of miracles, also those having gifts of healing, those able to help others, those with gifts of administration, and those speaking in different kinds of tongues. Are all apostles? Are all prophets? Are all

teachers? Do all work miracles? Do all have gifts of healing?
Do all speak in tongues? Do all interpret? But eagerly desire
the greater gifts. (1 Corinthians 12:27-31)

For by the grace given me I say to every one of you: Do not
think of yourself more highly than you ought, but rather think
of yourself with sober judgment, in accordance with the
measure of faith God has given you. Just as each of us has one
body with many members, and these members do not all have
the same function, so in Christ we who are many form one
body, and each member belongs to all the others. We have
different gifts, according to the grace given us. If a man's gift
is prophesying, let him use it in proportion to his faith. If it is
serving, let him serve; if it is teaching, let him teach; if it is
encouraging, let him encourage; if it is contributing to the
needs of others, let him give generously; if it is leadership, let
him govern diligently; if it is showing mercy, let him do it
cheerfully. (Romans 12:3-8)

Paul brings out a point in Romans 12:3 that we all should
heed: Whatever our gift or gifts, we are not to think more highly
of ourselves than is warranted. We are not to think, much less
claim, that we have gifts and abilities that we do not possess. On
the other hand, we should not go too far in the other direction and
deny gifts and abilities that the Holy Spirit has given to us. Either
way is wrong. Our task is to take a realistic look at what our gifts
are and, by His grace, use them as He directs. If we do not, the
work and edification of the church suffer.

It appears that there are seventeen to twenty gifts of the Spirit
listed in the Bible, depending on who is doing the counting.
However, we do not know if there are gifts that are not listed.
Whatever gift or gifts we have we should seek to develop and use.
At the same time, we should not close our minds to the fact that
the Holy Spirit may give us a new task five years from now, and a
new gift by which to accomplish it. Let us not forget that He
determines what will be done, and He gives the gifts at His own
pleasure.

Blasphemy Against the Holy Spirit

Blasphemy against the Holy Spirit is often referred to as the
unpardonable sin. Gospel references to it are Matthew 12:31-32,

Mark 3:28-29, and Luke 12:10. Expositors have different opinions as to what constitutes blasphemy against the Spirit because these verses do not spell it out in absolute fashion. Let us look at how this is stated in Matthew.

> Then they brought him a demon-possessed man who was blind and mute, and Jesus healed him, so that he could both talk and see. All the people were astonished and said, "Could this be the Son of David?"
>
> But when the Pharisees heard this, they said, "It is only by Beelzebub, the prince of demons, that this fellow drives out demons."
>
> Jesus knew their thoughts and said to them, "Every kingdom divided against itself will be ruined, and every city or household divided against itself will not stand. If Satan drives out Satan, he is divided against himself. How then can his kingdom stand? And if I drive out demons by Beelzebub, by whom do your people drive them out? So then, they will be your judges. But if I drive out demons by the Spirit of God, then the kingdom of God has come upon you.
>
> Or again, how can anyone enter a strong man's house and carry off his possessions unless he first ties up the strong man? Then he can rob his house.
>
> He who is not with me is against me, and he who does not gather with me scatters. And so I tell you, every sin and blasphemy will be forgiven men, but the blasphemy against the Spirit will not be forgiven. Anyone who speaks a word against the Son of Man will be forgiven, but anyone who speaks against the Holy Spirit will not be forgiven, either in this age or in the age to come." (Matthew 12:22-32)

Some expositors say that the blasphemy is the failure to believe the message of the Holy Spirit about Christ. Others put it stronger and say it is a willful and defiant disbelief of the Holy Spirit. In both cases those who do not believe are condemned to hell; that is a stated fact throughout Scripture. However, blasphemy against the Spirit seems to be something more specific. Some say it is calling good bad and bad good. I feel that this is a little broad and somewhat vague. Others say it is attributing the work of Christ, in calling out the demons, to Satan instead of to the Holy Spirit. I believe this is more in line with what is said, but possibly too specific.

It is easier for me to accept the exposition of those who say it is attributing any of the miraculous works of Christ to Satan instead of to the Holy Spirit. However, regardless of what blasphemy against the Spirit is, one thing is certain: A child of God will not commit it. Those who commit it are eternally lost, but a child of God is eternally saved. If we are saved it is because we are of the Elect. God chose to save us; therefore, those whom God has chosen to save will be saved. Otherwise, God is limited in what He can do, and if limited, He is not God. No, if we are Christians we do not have to worry about committing the unpardonable sin. By God's grace, that is another blessing we enjoy. We are saved and will remain saved—we cannot be lost. God is the one who saved us, and He is the one who will keep us saved. It is true that we must endure to the end, but it is equally true that God's Holy Spirit will see that we do.

Praise be to the God and Father of our Lord Jesus Christ! In his great mercy he has given us new birth into a living hope through the resurrection of Jesus Christ from the dead, and into an inheritance that can never perish, spoil or fade —kept in heaven for you, who through faith are shielded by God's power until the coming of the salvation that is ready to be revealed in the last time. (1 Peter 1:3-5)

To him who is able to keep you from falling and to present you before his glorious presence without fault and with great joy.... (Jude 24)

He will keep you strong to the end, so that you will be blameless on the day of our Lord Jesus Christ. God, who has called you into fellowship with his Son Jesus Christ our Lord, is faithful. (1 Corinthians 1:8-9)

Sanctification and the Holy Spirit

From a perspective of both doctrine and experience, a number of Christians know much about salvation but little about sanctification. Sanctification is the ongoing work of the Holy Spirit in the lives of believers. How successful it is depends on our willingness to yield to His control. As our thoughts, words, and deeds reflect what is in our hearts, our lives should not only show that we have been justified before God but that we are being sanctified by God.

Make a tree good and its fruit will be good, or make a tree bad and its fruit will be bad, for a tree is recognized by its fruit. (Matthew 12:33)

Fruit cannot make the tree good or bad; it can only indicate that it is so. The tree comes first and the type of tree will determine the type of fruit. A lack of fruit indicates a useless tree—one that is taking up space without producing fruit.

Then he told this parable: "A man had a fig tree, planted in his vineyard, and he went to look for fruit on it, but did not find any. So he said to the man who took care of the vineyard, 'For three years now I've been coming to look for fruit on this fig tree and haven't found any. Cut it down! Why should it use up the soil?'

'Sir,' the man replied, 'leave it alone for one more year, and I'll dig around it and fertilize it. If it bears fruit next year, fine! If not, then cut it down.'" (Luke 13:6-9)

Because the tree comes before the fruit, we should concern ourselves not as much with our "doing" as with our "being." If the tree is good, it will not only bear fruit but it will bear good fruit. All Christians are expected to bear good fruit; moreover, in the process of sanctification, the Holy Spirit is pruning us to make us even more fruitful.

I am the true vine, and my Father is the gardener. He cuts off every branch in me that bears no fruit, while every branch that does bear fruit he prunes so that it will be even more fruitful. (John 15:1-2)

Our sanctification, like our salvation, is a work of God.

May God himself, the God of peace, sanctify you through and through. May your whole spirit, soul and body be kept blameless at the coming of our Lord Jesus Christ. The one who calls you is faithful and he will do it. (1 Thessalonians 5:23-24)

Although sanctification is the work of the Holy Spirit, it is our responsibility to desire it, pray for it, and strive after it. We are called to be receptive to the work of the Holy Spirit; moreover, we are to be actively responsive to it. Our action is in response to the prompting of the Holy Spirit, but equally important, it is to be at His direction and in His power. In sanctification God is totally active, and we are to be totally active. He is continually working in us to will and to do, and we are to continually will and do that which He works in us. As we do this we are working out our salvation, not working for it.

> For this very reason, make every effort to add to your faith goodness; and to goodness, knowledge; and to knowledge, self-control; and to self-control, perseverance; and to perseverance, godliness; and to godliness, brotherly kindness; and to brotherly kindness, love. For if you possess these qualities in increasing measure, they will keep you from being ineffective and unproductive in your knowledge of our Lord Jesus Christ. (2 Peter 1:5-8)

> Therefore, my dear friends, as you have always obeyed—not only in my presence, but now much more in my absence—continue to work out your salvation with fear and trembling.... (Philippians 2:12)

The Holy Spirit does not lead us to just want to be saved, He leads us to want to serve God. He causes us to seek to know God's will and then to seek to do it. If we do not want to do God's will, we are not under the control of the Holy Spirit—we may not even have the Spirit.

How To Be Filled with the Spirit

As our conviction for the necessity of living the Spirit-filled life grows, let us look closely at what we must do for this to be a reality in our lives.

First, we must want the Holy Spirit to control our lives, regardless of what that brings. It will mean doing God's will—not our will, doing what God wants and denying self, doing things God's way—not our way, and doing things in God's strength instead of in the flesh. It will mean taking a totally different view of those so-called little sins that many Christians consider harmless. God says for us to be holy for He is holy (1 Peter 1:16), and a holy God cannot tolerate <u>any</u> sin.

Second, it will mean exerting our will. We must will to do God's will. We must not only want the Holy Spirit to control us, but we must actively will to have the Holy Spirit in control. We must confess our sins and ask God to control us by His Holy Spirit. We do this through faith, believing what God's Word says:

By faith we believe our sins are forgiven.

> **If we confess our sins, he is faithful and just and will forgive us our sins and purify us from all unrighteousness.**
> **(1 John 1:9)**

By faith we believe God wants us to be controlled by the Holy Spirit.

> **Do not get drunk on wine, which leads to debauchery. Instead, be filled with the Spirit.** (Ephesians 5:18)

By faith we believe God will control us through His Holy Spirit if we ask Him.

> **This is the confidence we have in approaching God: that if we ask anything according to his will, he hears us. And if we know that he hears us—whatever we ask—we know that we have what we asked of him.** (1 John 5:14-15)

We act in faith to please God and to receive the promise of being controlled by the Holy Spirit.

> **And without faith it is impossible to please God, because anyone who comes to him must believe that he exists and that he rewards those who earnestly seek him.** (Hebrews 11:6)

> **But when he asks, he must believe and not doubt, because he who doubts is like a wave of the sea, blown and tossed by the wind. That man should not think he will receive anything from the Lord; he is a double-minded man, unstable in all he does.** (James 1:6-8)

We know it is His will that we be filled. If, in obedience to His will, we ask to be filled and we ask in faith, then what will happen? We will be filled—we will be controlled by the Holy Spirit. God promises this to be the result. When we ask according to His will He will give us what we ask.

You may ask, once I am controlled, then what? My answer would be, do your best to see that the Holy Spirit stays in control of your life. Then He will guide and direct you to do that which pleases Him.

Will that be the way it is from now on? No, not if you are like the writer and all the other Christians I have known. I believe the teaching of the Bible is that our sinful nature will exert itself, and we will take over control of our lives from the Holy Spirit. This will grieve Him and break the fellowship we were enjoying with God. We always have our relationship as a child of God, but our fellowship is dependent on our obedience. Unless we are being controlled by the Holy Spirit, we are being disobedient. We are failing to obey a command from God. We are sinning, and as a result, our fellowship with God is broken. However, we are not to be discouraged, but are to turn to God, confess that we have taken over control, and once again ask His Holy Spirit to control our lives. We can then know that the Holy Spirit is back in control, that we have fellowship with God, and that as long as He is in control, we will not sin.

Every time we realize that we have resumed control of our lives (and sometimes we resume control in very subtle ways), we need to go through the process of actively confessing our sins and asking God to control our lives through His Holy Spirit. As we make a practice of doing this, we will find that we grow spiritually and do not have to go through the process as often as we once did. However, if at first we need to do it every thirty minutes, we should do so. The important thing is to will to do it, make the commitment to do it, and start now—before you lay this book down.

Just as unbelievers can pray in faith to be saved, believers can pray in faith to be controlled by the Holy Spirit. You may want to pray the following prayer or something similar, as you feel led:

Dear God, I confess I have sinned and I ask you to please forgive my sins and to control and empower me by your Holy Spirit. I ask this in Jesus' name. Amen.

We should pray like this each time we realize we are in control of our lives or when we have doubts as to who is in control. If we have failed for a period of time to check ourselves to see who is in control, we may have doubts about who is. However, when we pray and ask God to take control, we should never doubt, but always trust that He will do what He has promised. Keep in mind that we are not controlled by the Holy Spirit because we feel controlled, nor are we not controlled because we do not feel controlled. It is not a matter of how we feel. It is a matter of what God has willed and what God has promised to do when we respond in obedience to His will. It will happen when we ask in faith according to His will.

Evidence that We Are Filled

If being controlled by the Holy Spirit does not depend on how we feel (it does not depend on feelings anymore than our salvation depends on our "feeling saved"), then we may wonder if there are any indications that we are really being controlled by the Holy Spirit. Yes, there are. We begin to actually see our lives changing more than before. Changes in values, desires, and attitudes are greater and more rapid. There is a greater appreciation for what the Bible calls good, and a greater dislike of what the Bible calls sin. We are conscious of sinning less, and begin to develop an intolerance for sin in our lives. There is a greater desire to read and study God's Word, and a real concern to know and to do God's will.

As we practice walking in the Spirit, we better understand God, His written Word, and ourselves. We see God changing us, and this glorifies Him because we know He has done it. We see Him working through us, using us as instruments or mere tools to accomplish His work in others. We begin to receive a much greater degree of pleasure when we are used by God. We derive a greater pleasure from reading His Word, watching Him work, and seeing Him glorified.

As time passes, we find that we rely more on Him and less on ourselves. A rough idea of walking in the Spirit would be the following illustration I once heard: Imagine you are painting a picture, and you know absolutely nothing about art. As a result, you are making somewhat of a mess of the painting. But, along comes a master artist who reaches over your shoulder and takes your wrist. You still hold the brush, but the artist tells you to let your arm be limber. Then he begins to move your arm so that a beautiful picture is being formed. If you decide you want to help or you think the artist is not doing it right and you stiffen your arm and make some strokes, you begin to make a mess of the painting again. Only as you let your arm remain limber and allow the artist to move it, is the picture painted correctly. Only then does it become the picture it is possible for it to be.

This is true of our walk with God. Only as we keep our wills limber and let God direct our thoughts, words, and actions will our lives be lived correctly. Only then will they become what it is possible for them to be.

Live Under the Control of the Holy Spirit

As we come to the close of our discussion of the Holy Spirit, it is my hope that each of us is aware of our need to live continually under His control. It is our only hope of pleasing God and our only hope of overcoming sin. The alternative to being under the control of the Spirit is to be under the control of our sinful nature. Because nothing but evil comes from the sinful nature and nothing but good comes from the Holy Spirit, it becomes readily apparent why being controlled by the Spirit is so vital. We must look to the Holy Spirit to guide us in how we spend our time, where we spend it, and with whom we spend it.

The Spirit leads us, not as one going before us to show us the way, but as one holding on to us and guiding us along. He is not showing us how to get where we want to go but is taking us where He chooses. We are like a blind man; we cannot see where we are to go or how to get there. The Spirit must pick our destination and then lead us by the hand. We can think of ourselves as children holding our heavenly Father's hand. As long as we are holding His hand, the Holy Spirit is in control of our lives and we will not stumble. However, when we let go of His hand by taking over control of our lives, we will stumble and must reach up to grab His hand again. In our own strength and wisdom, we are unable to live a fruitful Christian life. That can only be accomplished as we live under the control of the Holy Spirit.

What is election?

Who originated it?

Is it fair?

Does it make man a robot?

Objections refuted.

And he will send his angels and gather his elect from the four winds, from the ends of the earth to the ends of the heavens. (Mark 13:27)

Election

The doctrine of Election is one of the most misunderstood doctrines in the Bible. Many people have a false idea about the meaning of Election. They have never made an in-depth study of it by searching the Scriptures to see what God says. Instead, they have formed their opinion based on something they heard someone say. Too often, that someone was in error. Because of their false understanding of Election, they object to it. There are others who have some understanding of the doctrine but find it difficult to believe that man has no part in his salvation. Let me state what I think God says about Election, and then we will look at verses from the Bible, to see if this is so.

Election Briefly Stated

I believe the Bible teaches that before we are saved, we are all lost sinners; we are all spiritually dead, and we are all headed to hell. We may be religious, but we do not know God. We cannot understand things of God and do not really care to. As a result, if left to ourselves, we will never come to a saving faith in Jesus

Christ. However, God acts to regenerate a people that He has purposed to save. He does this by working in them so that, without violating their wills, they freely believe and accept Christ as Savior and Lord. He does not do this because of any good He sees in the people. He does this out of His mercy, because it pleases Him to do so, and it brings glory to Himself.

Election is stated in many ways in Scripture, but I call your attention to two words that are frequently used to express the doctrine: "elect" and "chosen." In the American Heritage Dictionary (Second College Edition), we find the following definitions for "elect": "to choose, pick out, chosen deliberately, one that is chosen or selected, one selected by divine will for salvation." We also find the following definitions for "chosen": "selected from or preferred above others, one of the elect, the elect collectively." We need to keep these definitions in mind as we read the Bible. Now let us look at some verses pertaining to Election.

> If the Lord had not cut short those days, no one would survive. But for the sake of the elect, whom he has chosen, he has shortened them. (Mark 13:20)

> And he will send his angels and gather his elect from the four winds, from the ends of the earth to the ends of the heavens. (Mark 13:27)

> Not only that, but Rebekah's children had one and the same father, our father Isaac. Yet, before the twins were born or had done anything good or bad—in order that God's purpose in election might stand: not by works but by him who calls—she was told, "The older will serve the younger." Just as it is written: "Jacob I loved, but Esau I hated."
> What then shall we say? Is God unjust? Not at all! For he says to Moses, "I will have mercy on whom I have mercy, and I will have compassion on whom I have compassion."

> It does not, therefore, depend on man's desire or effort, but on God's mercy. For the Scripture says to Pharaoh: "I raised you up for this very purpose, that I might display my power in you and that my name might be proclaimed in all the earth." Therefore God has mercy on whom he wants to have mercy, and he hardens whom he wants to harden.
> One of you will say to me: "Then why does God still blame us? For who resists his will?" But who are you, O man, to talk

back to God? "Shall what is formed say to him who formed it, 'Why did you make me like this?'" Does not the potter have the right to make out of the same lump of clay some pottery for noble purposes and some for common use?

What if God, choosing to show his wrath and make his power known, bore with great patience the objects of his wrath—prepared for destruction? What if he did this to make the riches of his glory known to the objects of his mercy, whom he prepared in advance for glory—even us, whom he also called, not only from the Jews but also from the Gentiles? (Romans 9:10-24)

He was in the world, and though the world was made through him, the world did not recognize him. He came to that which was his own, but his own did not receive him. Yet to all who received him, to those who believed in his name, he gave the right to become children of God—children born not of natural descent, nor of human decision or a husband's will, but born of God. (John 1:10-13)

I am not referring to all of you; I know those I have chosen. (John 13:18a)

If the world hates you, keep in mind that it hated me first. If you belonged to the world, it would love you as its own. As it is, you do not belong to the world, but I have chosen you out of the world. (John 15:18-19a)

And you also are among those who are called to belong to Jesus Christ. (Romans 1:6)

Therefore, as God's chosen people, holy and dearly loved, clothe yourselves with compassion, kindness, humility, gentleness and patience. (Colossians 3:12)

But you are a chosen people, a royal priesthood, a holy nation, a people belonging to God, that you may declare the praises of him who called you out of darkness into his wonderful light. Once you were not a people, but now you are the people of God; once you had not received mercy, but now you have received mercy. (1 Peter 2:9-10)

But we ought always to thank God for you, brothers loved by the Lord, because from the beginning God chose you to be saved through the sanctifying work of the Spirit and through belief in the truth. (2 Thessalonians 2:13)

If those days had not been cut short, no one would survive, but for the sake of the elect those days will be shortened. At that time if anyone says to you, 'Look, here is the Christ!' or, 'There he is!' do not believe it. For false Christs and false prophets will appear and perform great signs and miracles to deceive even the elect—if that were possible. (Matthew 24:22-24)

Lord, they have killed your prophets and torn down your altars; I am the only one left, and they are trying to kill me. And what was God's answer to him? "I have reserved for myself seven thousand who have not bowed the knee to Baal." (Romans 11:3-4)

Therefore I endure everything for the sake of the elect, that they too may obtain the salvation that is in Christ Jesus, with eternal glory. (2 Timothy 2:10)

Therefore, my brothers, be all the more eager to make your calling and election sure. (2 Peter 1:10a)

Paul, a servant of God and an apostle of Jesus Christ for the faith of God's elect and the knowledge of the truth that leads to godliness.... (Titus 1:1)

In him we were also chosen, having been predestined according to the plan of him who works out everything in conformity with the purpose of his will.... (Ephesians 1:11)

For many are invited, but few are chosen. (Matthew 22:14)

He was not seen by all the people, but by witnesses whom God had already chosen—by us who ate and drank with him after he rose from the dead. (Acts 10:41)

And we know that in all things God works for the good of those who love him, who have been called according to his purpose. For those God foreknew he also predestined to be conformed to the likeness of his Son, that he might be the firstborn among many brothers. And those he predestined, he also called; those he called, he also justified; those he justified, he also glorified. (Romans 8:28-30)

Who will bring any charge against those whom God has chosen? It is God who justifies. (Romans 8:33)

For we know, brothers loved by God, that he has chosen you.... (1 Thessalonians 1:4)

They will make war against the Lamb, but the Lamb will overcome them because he is Lord of lords and King of kings—and with him will be his called, chosen and faithful followers. (Revelation 17:14)

Two Main Objections to Election

I doubt if any doctrine stirs up more controversy among true believers than the doctrine of Election. There are several objections that people raise to this doctrine and we will examine each of them. However, in my experience, there are two primary objections, and we will look at these first:

1. Election is unfair.
2. Election makes man a robot and does away with his free will.

I believe there is ample scriptural evidence to prove these objections invalid. Our finite minds may not be able to explain or understand Election; even so, we must believe, by faith, what God's Word has to say, and accept it as truth. (We cannot explain the Trinity, but we believe it.) Because something seems unfair to our finite minds, does not make it so. History shows us that what man considers to be right and just is, many times, later determined to be wrong and unjust. Look at our present world—we have many issues where opinions are divided, with each group claiming their way is right. If we had to understand everything that God said in His Word before we believed it, we would be in trouble. We would have a real problem with the incarnation of Christ and His resurrection.

Misconceptions Concerning Election

Before we look at whether or not Election is unfair, let me dispel two misconceptions. Many people think Election is something a man named John Calvin originated. John Calvin did not originate Election anymore than Martin Luther originated the idea that "The righteous will live by faith" (Romans 1:17b). Luther was writing and teaching about Election before Calvin. Before Luther, Saint Augustine was writing about the doctrine. One of the great Baptist preachers, C. H. Spurgeon, preached and taught Election. Of course, the original writings were by a man we know as the Apostle Paul and by other writers of both the Old and New Testaments. In the Gospel of John, Jesus Christ makes a number of statements which teach Election.

Some people think that the doctrine is a teaching of only the Presbyterian denomination—that too is incorrect. The Westminster Confession of Faith, which is used by several Presbyterian denominations, is only one place where Election is taught. Some of the older creeds of other denominations also teach it. Four examples are as follows:

1. The old Baptist Confession, which was written over a hundred years before Spurgeon's time, says the following:

> 3d Article: By the decree of God, for the manifestation of his glory, some men and angels are predestinated, or foreordained to eternal life through Jesus Christ, to the praise of his glorious grace; others being left to act in their sins to their just condemnation, to the praise of his glorious justice. These angels and men thus predestinated and foreordained, are particularly and unchangeably designed, and their number so certain and definite, that it cannot be either increased or diminished. Those of mankind that are predestinated to life, God, before the foundation of the world was laid, according to his eternal and immutable purpose, and the secret counsel and good pleasure of his will, hath chosen in Christ unto everlasting glory, out of his mere free grace and love, without any other thing in the creature as a condition or cause moving him thereunto.

2. The Waldensian Creed, which was probably written during the last half of the 12th century, says:

That God saves from corruption and damnation those whom he has chosen from the foundations of the world, not for any disposition, faith, or holiness that he foresaw in them, but of his mere mercy in Christ Jesus his Son, passing by all the rest, according to the irreprehensible reason of his own free-will and justice.

3. In the Articles of Religion of the Episcopal Church in the United States of America, the 17th Article states the following pertaining to Predestination and Election:

Predestination to life is the everlasting purpose of God, whereby (before the foundations of the world were laid) he hath constantly decreed by his counsel secret to us, to deliver from curse and damnation those whom he hath chosen in Christ out of mankind, and to bring them by Christ to everlasting salvation, as vessels made to honor. Wherefore they which be endued with so excellent a benefit of God be called according to God's purpose by his Spirit working in due season: they through grace obey the calling: they be justified freely: they be made sons of God by adoption: they be made like the image of his only-begotten Son Jesus Christ: they walk religiously in good works, and at length, by God's mercy, they attain to everlasting felicity.

4. A statement similar to the one above is made in the Thirty-nine Articles of the Church of England.

The fact that the above-mentioned men taught Election and that the above-mentioned denominations included Election in their Articles or Confessions does not make it true. However, if these great men of faith, and those who composed the Articles and Confessions, and many other Christians throughout the ages have believed in Election, that should be grounds enough for us to make a serious study of God's Word to see if we agree or disagree with them.

Is Election Unfair?

Let us now consider the first objection: Election is unfair. In doing so, we will assume that those who think Election is unfair also think that non-Election is fair. The following comparisons will help us get a clearer picture of the difference between Election and non-Election.

COMPARISON CHART #1

ELECTION	NON-ELECTION
1. Fall of man (Ro 5:12)	1. Fall of man (Ro 5:12)
2. Man is sinful (Ro 3:23)	2. Man is sinful (Ro 3:23)
3. Man is spiritually separated from God (Ro 6:23)	3. Man is spiritually separated from God (Ro 6:23)
4. God offers man salvation through Jesus Christ (Jn 3:16)	4. God offers man salvation through Jesus Christ (Jn 3:16)
5. In his natural state man does not understand (1 Cor 2:14)	5. In his natural state man does not understand (1 Cor 2:14)
6. Man is free to choose Christ but his sinful nature prevents him from doing so (Ro 8:5-8)	6. Man is free to choose Christ but his sinful nature prevents him from doing so (Ro 8:5-8)
7. With this situation no one will be saved (Jn 8:24)	7. With this situation no one will be saved (Jn 8:24)
8. God in His mercy chooses to regenerate some people and they freely turn to Christ and accept Him (Titus 3:4-7)	8. God waits on man to choose Christ but none do (Ro 3:10-11)
9. Results: some are saved, some are lost (Jn 3:18)	9. Results: all are lost (Ro 6:23)
10. God knew from eternity it would happen this way (Ps 139:1-4)	10. God knew from eternity it would happen this way (Ps 139:1-4)

In looking at Comparison Chart #1, we see that there is no difference in Election and non-Election until we get to item 8. Here we see that under Election, God, in His mercy, chooses to regenerate some people. As a result of His regenerating work, they turn to Christ and accept Him as Savior. Under non-Election, there are none who accept Christ. All are free to make the choice; however, due to their sinful natures, they do not understand things of God. They continue in either active rebellion or passive indifference toward God.

Item 9 shows that, under Election, some people are saved while others are lost. The saved being those in whom God does a regenerating work, without violating their wills. As a result of God's work, they freely "will" to accept Christ as Savior and Lord. Under non-Election, all people are lost because they choose to do evil. All people have a sinful nature and suppress the truth of God. Unless God performs a regenerative work in their hearts, they cannot come to an understanding of His plan of salvation. Left to themselves, they continue on the road to destruction and are eternally lost.

Under item 10 both show that, before the world was ever made, God knew what would happen. God has known from all eternity who would be saved.

In view of the above, on what grounds does one call Election unfair? If there is no Election, all are lost. If there is Election, some are saved and some are lost. Is it more fair to have all lost than to have some lost and others saved? Which way is the greater mercy shown? We must acknowledge that, under Election, God shows greater mercy.

COMPARISON CHART #2

ELECTION	NON-ELECTION
1. Fall of man	1. Fall of man
2. Man is sinful	2. Man is sinful
3. Man is spiritually separated from God	3. Man is spiritually separated from God
4. God offers man salvation through Jesus Christ	4. God offers man salvation through Jesus Christ
5. In his natural state man does not understand	5. Some men do not understand—some do
6. Man is free to choose Christ but his sinful nature prevents him from doing so	6. Man is free to choose Christ without the restraint of his sinful nature
7. With this situation no one will be saved	7. With this situation some may be saved
8. God in His mercy chooses to regenerate some people and they freely turn to Christ and accept Him	8. Of those men who understand the gospel, some may decide to choose Christ
9. Results: some are saved, some are lost	9. Results: if any choose Christ they are saved, the others are lost. If none choose Christ, all are lost
10. God knew from eternity it would happen this way	10. God knew from eternity it would happen this way

Let us now look at Comparison Chart #2. Notice that the items under Election are the same as those on Chart #1, but some of the items under non-Election will differ. The reason for this difference is that Chart #1 is an attempt to show what the true biblical result would be if there were no such thing as Election. On Chart #2, some things are shown to happen which actually would not take place. This allows us to follow certain ideas to their logical conclusions. For the sake of discussion, let us assume that on Chart #2, under both Election and non-Election, one hundred people are saved. Then let us follow the steps of each to help our understanding of what is "fair."

We see that in items 1 through 4, the two methods are in agreement, but when we reach item 5 they differ. Under Election, natural man does not understand the things of God. However, under non-Election it would be necessary for some to understand—if any are to be saved—so we allow that to happen.

Item 6 reflects another difference. Under Election, man is free to choose Christ; however, because of his sinful nature, he chooses evil. Under non-Election, man is free to choose Christ, and we remove the restraint of his sinful nature to allow him the ability to do so.

Item 7 points out that, under Election, left in this situation, no one will be saved. Under non-Election the possibility is there for some to be saved.

Item 8 tells us that, under Election, God chooses to save some people. Under non-Election, some may choose to accept Christ.

In item 9 we see the results. Under Election, some are saved for sure and others are lost. Under non-Election some may be saved and others lost.

In item 10 we come back into agreement. We are assuming, in each case, that one hundred people are saved. In both situations, God knew before the world was ever made that no more and no less than one hundred people would be saved. Now, there is no question that God knew this in Election. He chose the people, decreed it would happen, and brought it about—all in His sovereignty. Someone may question the "no more, no less" in non-Election. But, if we look closely, I believe we will see that it too is certain. We know that God is omniscient (all knowing). Before He made the world, even under non-Election, He would have known who would accept Christ and who would not. He then made the world, Adam, etc. Does anyone think that later some of those who God thought would believe changed their minds, or that unbelievers changed and believed? This would have caught God by surprise, and He would not be omniscient or sovereign. No, the one hundred is as certain under non-Election as under Election.

Let us go back still another step. Before God decided who would be the people who would inhabit the earth, do you suppose He decided how many believers and unbelievers He would have? As the Sovereign Creator, the One who made us all, He could have changed the ratio of believers to unbelievers and still have left the choice up to each person in non-Election. All He had to do was consider the countless other people He could create, and make some of them to replace some of those He did create. This way, He could swap out believers for unbelievers, or vice versa. If God chose to, He could continue going over all the possible people He could make and settle on only the believers. Thus, He could have made a world consisting of only believers. So we see that if non-Election were a fact, the number of saved and unsaved people would have been determined before the world was made. In Election, the number of each has also been determined beforehand.

This comparison leaves no room to call Election unfair. For under Election or non-Election, God determined how many people He would create. He also determined how many would go to heaven and how many to hell, whether it be through Election or non-Election.

But, some may say, it is not "fair" of God to work in the hearts of some, to save them, while others are condemned to hell. Let us consider that thought.

Under non-Election or Election, all deserve hell. All who do not accept Christ for the forgiveness of their sins will go there. We must acknowledge and agree with this fact of Bible teaching and Christian belief. Thus, we see that God is not unfair by sending to hell those who do not repent and trust Christ as Savior. According to God's Word, they receive what they deserve—they receive justice. Those whom God regenerates and saves, receive mercy. They also deserve hell, but God does not give them what they deserve—they go to heaven.

Considering that we all deserve hell, can it be unfair for some to go to hell and others to be saved? Because God saves some, is He obligated to save all? If He justly condemns some, is He obligated to condemn all? If you think so, I ask the question, Why? Are you for justice? Are you for mercy? If so, then where is the conflict? Do you think it unfair of God to send all who do not trust in Christ to hell? Is it unfair of God to take whomever He chooses into heaven? If you find God unfair in showing mercy to some, do you suggest that God not show mercy, and condemn all to hell? Remember, that "all" includes you. If you are against all going to hell and you want all treated alike, then you are suggesting that God save all. Do you say God is unfair if He does not save all?

Do we treat all others the same? Do we give the same amount to all who ask, do equally for all others, and show the same amount of love to all others, etc.? Even among the saved do we not find different degrees of trials and suffering? Because some of our Christian brothers and sisters were fed to the lions or burned at the stake, do we desire to suffer the same type death? Because some Christians suffer long and painful illnesses, should we all suffer likewise? Because the Holy Spirit bestows different gifts on different members of the Body of Christ, is He unfair? Does not God say,

I will have mercy on whom I have mercy, and I will have compassion on whom I have compassion. (Romans 9:15)

Does anyone dare to question God? I can tell you with certainty that I do not.

God, in His sovereign plan and purpose, chooses to save some while passing over others. He leaves them to their "just deserts." Those He chooses are not chosen because of any merits they have, but because it pleases God to show them mercy and save them. This is Election; this is mercy; this is God's grace; this is that "Amazing Grace" of which we sing.

Free Will or Robot

Now that we have discussed the objection that Election is unfair, let us look at the second major objection: Man is made a robot and does not have a free will.

First, we need to examine what is meant by free will. I think we could agree that "man being free to choose Christ or not to choose Christ" is a simple enough definition for the situation we are studying. In other words, if man wills to trust Christ, he is free to do so; if man wills to reject Christ, he is free to do so. Man is free to make his choice. But, what type of choice is man capable of making? Being "free" to choose something is one thing; however, being "able" to choose something is another.

I once heard an example which helps to illustrate this. A meat eater, such as the wolf, will starve to death if enclosed in a large pen with grass to eat but no meat. A sheep will starve in a concrete-floored pen with nothing but chickens running around. In the opposite pens they would both eat and live. Why is this so? Are they not free to choose the food at hand? Yes, they are. However, they are not able to choose that which is against their natures. God's Word tells us that natural man is much like that. He is free to choose, but by nature he is unable to choose things of God.

For the message of the cross is foolishness to those who are perishing, but to us who are being saved it is the power of God. (1 Corinthians 1:18)

The man without the Spirit does not accept the things that come from the Spirit of God, for they are foolishness to him, and he cannot understand them, because they are spiritually discerned. (1 Corinthians 2:14)

Natural Man's Will is Enslaved to Sin

Man comes into this world with a sinful nature. He does not sin against his will but sins because he wills to. The Bible tells us sin is fun for a period of time.

By faith Moses, when he had grown up, refused to be known as the son of Pharaoh's daughter. He chose to be mistreated along with the people of God rather than to enjoy the pleasures of sin for a short time. (Hebrews 11:24-25)

The Bible also tells us how wicked natural man is. His will is enslaved to sin; moreover he is in bondage to sin both by nature and by deed. He is totally depraved. This does not mean that man is as evil as he could be; it means he is evil throughout. The classical illustration of the glass of water helps us understand this fact: If someone stirs a few drops of poison into a glass of water, it will not be as poisonous as it could be; however, it will be poisonous throughout. God tells man how sinful he is and that he wants only to sin. Until he comes to Christ he is a slave to sin and, though he may not be conscious of it, he does the will of Satan.

Those who live according to the sinful nature have their minds set on what that nature desires; but those who live in accordance with the Spirit have their minds set on what the Spirit desires. The mind of sinful man is death, but the mind

controlled by the Spirit is life and peace; the sinful mind is hostile to God. It does not submit to God's law, nor can it do so. Those controlled by the sinful nature cannot please God. (Romans 8:5-8)

As for you, you were dead in your transgressions and sins, in which you used to live when you followed the ways of this world and of the ruler of the kingdom of the air, the spirit who is now at work in those who are disobedient. All of us also lived among them at one time, gratifying the cravings of our sinful nature and following its desires and thoughts. Like the rest, we were by nature objects of wrath. (Ephesians 2:1-3)

Put to death, therefore, whatever belongs to your earthly nature: sexual immorality, impurity, lust, evil desires and greed, which is idolatry. (Colossians 3:5)

For they mouth empty, boastful words and, by appealing to the lustful desires of sinful human nature, they entice people who are just escaping from those who live in error. (2 Peter 2:18)

Jesus said to them, "If God were your Father, you would love me, for I came from God and now am here. I have not come on my own; but he sent me. Why is my language not clear to you? Because you are unable to hear what I say. You belong to your father, the devil, and you want to carry out your father's desire. He was a murderer from the beginning, not holding to the truth, for there is no truth in him. When he lies, he speaks his native language, for he is a liar and the father of lies." (John 8:42-44)

In this sinful state, how can natural man ever come to Christ? The answer is obvious. If left to himself, he cannot; therefore he will not. None of us seek God. None of us do good. We do only evil.

As it is written: "There is no one righteous, not even one; there is no one who understands, no one who seeks God. All have turned away, they have together become worthless; there is no one who does good, not even one." (Romans 3:10-12)

All of us have become like one who is unclean, and all our righteous acts are like filthy rags; we all shrivel up like a leaf, and like the wind our sins sweep us away. (Isaiah 64:6)

Who can bring what is pure from the impure? No one!
(Job 14:4)

Can the Ethiopian change his skin or the leopard its spots?
Neither can you do good who are accustomed to doing evil.
(Jeremiah 13:23)

We make up our own religions.

While Paul was waiting for them in Athens, he was greatly
distressed to see that the city was full of idols. (Acts 17:16)

Paul then stood up in the meeting of the Areopagus and said:
"Men of Athens! I see that in every way you are very religious."
(Acts 17:22)

There is a way that seems right to a man, but in the end it
leads to death. (Proverbs 14:12)

Throughout the world, there are many religions that seem
right to those who embrace them, but they are not worshiping the
true God. Even in the nominal Christian religions, there are many
who are not born again—who are not Christians. They, too, are
not worshiping the true God. They are worshiping the god of their
imagination, or the imaginary god of some leader they are
following. God tells us, "...in the end it leads to death." If the
picture of the unsaved man is so dark, then what can he do? The
answer is, nothing.

Salvation is All of God

Natural man is spiritually dead. God must regenerate him and
renew his will. He must enable man to understand and choose
spiritual things. Just as the physically dead cannot respond to
physical stimuli, the spiritually dead cannot respond to spiritual
stimuli. Lazarus was made to come alive. He could contribute
nothing toward receiving life, nor could he do anything to prevent
being made alive. He had to be given physical life in order to
respond to the command, "Lazarus, come out."

Jesus, once more deeply moved, came to the tomb. It was a cave with a stone laid across the entrance. "Take away the stone," he said.

"But, Lord," said Martha, the sister of the dead man, "by this time there is a bad odor, for he has been there four days."

Then Jesus said, "Did I not tell you that if you believed, you would see the glory of God?"

So they took away the stone. Then Jesus looked up and said, "Father, I thank you that you have heard me. I knew that you always hear me, but I said this for the benefit of the people standing here, that they may believe that you sent me."

When he had said this, Jesus called in a loud voice, "Lazarus, come out!" The dead man came out, his hands and feet wrapped with strips of linen, and a cloth around his face.

Jesus said to them, "Take off the grave clothes and let him go." (John 11:38-44)

Just as Lazarus could not respond without the supernatural work of God, natural man cannot respond without the supernatural work of God. God, through Christ, did not choose to raise all the physically dead, but He did raise Lazarus. He also, for reasons known only to Him, does not choose to make spiritually alive all who are spiritually dead, but He does give spiritual life to the Elect.

When you were dead in your sins and in the uncircumcision of your sinful nature, God made you alive with Christ. (Colossians 2:13a)

Then he said: 'The God of our fathers has chosen you to know his will and to see the Righteous One and to hear words from his mouth.' (Acts 22:14)

God offers man the gift of salvation (John 3:16), but man does not have it in him to accept the gift. Man in his sinful state says, I do not need it; I do not believe it; I will do it my way. The Bible tells us that while we were yet at enmity toward God, He loved us and died for us.

But God demonstrates his own love for us in this: While we were still sinners, Christ died for us. (Romans 5:8)

He loved us first.

We love because he first loved us. (1 John 4:19)

God, the Father, gave the Elect to Christ.

Jesus answered, "I did tell you, but you do not believe. The miracles I do in my Father's name speak for me, but you do not believe because you are not my sheep. My sheep listen to my voice; I know them, and they follow me. I give them eternal life, and they shall never perish; no one can snatch them out of my hand. My Father, who has given them to me, is greater than all; no one can snatch them out of my Father's hand. I and the Father are one." (John 10:25-30)

After Jesus said this, he looked toward heaven and prayed: "Father, the time has come. Glorify your Son, that your Son may glorify you. For you granted him authority over all people that he might give eternal life to all those you have given him." (John 17:1-2)

Father, I want those you have given me to be with me where I am, and to see my glory, the glory you have given me because you loved me before the creation of the world. (John 17:24)

God is able to save.

Surely the arm of the Lord is not too short to save, nor his ear too dull to hear. (Isaiah 59:1)

God regenerates us and God saves us. Salvation is all of God—He does it all!

Jesus answered, "I tell you the truth, no one can enter the kingdom of God unless he is born of water and the Spirit. Flesh gives birth to flesh, but the Spirit gives birth to spirit. You should not be surprised at my saying, 'You must be born again.' The wind blows wherever it pleases. You hear its sound, but you cannot tell where it comes from or where it is going. So it is with everyone born of the Spirit." (John 3:5-8)

For just as the Father raises the dead and gives them life, even so the Son gives life to whom he is pleased to give it. (John 5:21)

But when the kindness and love of God our Savior appeared, he saved us, not because of righteous things we had done, but because of his mercy. He saved us through the washing of rebirth and renewal by the Holy Spirit, whom he poured out on us generously through Jesus Christ our Savior, so that, having been justified by his grace, we might become heirs having the hope of eternal life. (Titus 3:4-7)

He puts a new heart in us.

I will give you a new heart and put a new spirit in you; I will remove from you your heart of stone and give you a heart of flesh. (Ezekiel 36:26)

He gives us the ability to understand the truth of the Gospel, the ability to see our need for Christ, and the ability to accept Him. His work within us results in our repenting of our sinful ways and our trusting Christ as Savior and Lord.

No one can come to me unless the Father who sent me draws him, and I will raise him up at the last day. It is written in the Prophets: 'They will all be taught by God.' Everyone who listens to the Father and learns from him comes to me. (John 6:44-45)

"The Spirit gives life; the flesh counts for nothing. The words I have spoken to you are spirit and they are life. Yet there are some of you who do not believe." For Jesus had known from the beginning which of them did not believe and who would betray him. He went on to say, "This is why I told you that no one can come to me unless the Father has enabled him." (John 6:63-65)

When Jesus came to the region of Caesarea Philippi, he asked his disciples, "Who do people say the Son of Man is?"
They replied, "Some say John the Baptist; others say Elijah; and still others, Jeremiah or one of the prophets."
"But what about you?" he asked. "Who do you say I am?"
Simon Peter answered, "You are the Christ, the Son of the living God."
Jesus replied, "Blessed are you, Simon son of Jonah, for this was not revealed to you by man, but by my Father in heaven." (Matthew 16:13-17)

> Everyone who believes that Jesus is the Christ is born of God,
> and everyone who loves the father loves his child as well.
> (1 John 5:1)

> For you have been born again, not of perishable seed, but of
> imperishable, through the living and enduring word of God.
> (1 Peter 1:23)

God Does Not Violate Our Wills

God does this without violating our wills. Some years ago, a
very dear lady led my wife and me to the Lord. I did not come
against my will—I wanted to come. I heard the Gospel and
realized that I was a lost sinner. I knew my only hope was to trust
Christ to forgive my sins, and I did this freely and gladly. Did I feel
the slightest bit like a robot? No. Did I feel forced against my will?
No. Did I feel manipulated in any way? No. Was I aware that God
had worked in me to bring this about? Not at all. Sometime later,
I came to understand that God had produced in me the faith with
which to believe in Him.

> But because of his great love for us, God, who is rich in mercy,
> made us alive with Christ even when we were dead in
> transgressions—it is by grace you have been saved.
> (Ephesians 2:4-5)

It was still later before God brought me to the place where I
could understand and accept the doctrine of Election. I began to
understand that God's grace is truly that—grace. It is unmerited
favor. It was through His grace alone that I was saved. I realized
that God bestows His grace on whomever He chooses. He
regenerates the Elect, gives them the faith with which to believe,
and brings them to a saving knowledge of His Son, Jesus Christ.
Now, I praise Him for the wonder of Election. There is
forgiveness, love, mercy, and security in it. I am so glad God chose
me, instead of leaving it up to me to choose Him.

It is all of God. Man contributes nothing just as an
unconscious person who is carried from a burning building
contributes nothing to being saved from the fire. If man
contributes even the smallest bit to his salvation, it is not all of
grace. If it is up to man, in his own strength, to provide faith and

to believe in the claims of the Gospel, then man cannot be saved by Christ alone. It is Christ <u>and</u> man; salvation will not take place unless man does his part. In doing his part, man merits something—even if his part is small. However, man's part looms very large when we consider the importance of his role.

Though Christ clothed Himself in human flesh, led a sinless life, suffered agony, died on the cross and was raised from the dead; it was all in vain unless <u>man</u> does his part. Man casts the deciding vote. Man has the final say. The Sovereign Lord of the Universe must wait on man, to see if he will choose to believe and accept His offer, or if His precious Son died for nothing. If man accepts Christ on those conditions, then that is not God bestowing His grace on man. That is man acting to save himself with God's help, or God acting to save man with man's help. Either way it is a joint effort. One could not do it without the other. In this case, man is deserving of something for he certainly has made a contribution to his own salvation. But God's grace is unmerited: It is bestowed on those who have not earned it and who do not deserve it.

> So too, at the present time there is a remnant chosen by grace. And if by grace, then it is no longer by works; if it were, grace would no longer be grace. (Romans 11:5-6)

> The grace of our Lord was poured out on me abundantly, along with the faith and love that are in Christ Jesus. (1 Timothy 1:14)

> So do not be ashamed to testify about our Lord, or ashamed of me his prisoner. But join with me in suffering for the gospel, by the power of God, who has saved us and called us to a holy life—not because of anything we have done but because of his own purpose and grace. This grace was given us in Christ Jesus before the beginning of time.... (2 Timothy 1:8-9)

God's Sovereignty in Election

God is sovereign in the life of the individual and in the history of the human race. In His sovereignty, salvation is offered to all men.

> For God so loved the world that he gave his one and only Son, that whoever believes in him shall not perish but have eternal life. (John 3:16)

In His sovereignty, salvation is given to the Elect by God.

> Every good and perfect gift is from above, coming down from the Father of the heavenly lights, who does not change like shifting shadows. He chose to give us birth through the word of truth, that we might be a kind of firstfruits of all he created. (James 1:17-18)

> For it is by grace you have been saved, through faith—and this not from yourselves, it is the gift of God—not by works, so that no one can boast. (Ephesians 2:8-9)

> For God did not appoint us to suffer wrath but to receive salvation through our Lord Jesus Christ.
> (1 Thessalonians 5:9)

> When the Gentiles heard this, they were glad and honored the word of the Lord; and all who were appointed for eternal life believed. (Acts 13:48)

Men are not condemned to hell because they are not elected. They are condemned because they are sinners.

> ...for all have sinned and fall short of the glory of God.... (Romans 3:23)

> For the wages of sin is death.... (Romans 6:23)

This is justice.

Men are not given eternal life because they are not sinners. They are given eternal life because they are elected.

> All things have been committed to me by my Father. No one knows the Son except the Father, and no one knows the Father except the Son and those to whom the Son chooses to reveal him. (Matthew 11:27)

Praise be to the God and Father of our Lord Jesus Christ, who has blessed us in the heavenly realms with every spiritual blessing in Christ. For he chose us in him before the creation of the world to be holy and blameless in his sight. In love he predestined us to be adopted as his sons through Jesus Christ, in accordance with his pleasure and will—to the praise of his glorious grace, which he has freely given us in the One he loves. (Ephesians 1:3-6)

This is mercy.

Election is a merciful act of God. It strips us clean and it humbles us. We are nothing, have nothing, and can do nothing. We are left with nothing but Jesus Christ. As God has chosen and appointed the Elect to be saved, He has also determined and foreordained the means by which it is accomplished. That "means" is His Son, Jesus Christ. It is by Him, in Him, and for Him, that we are saved.

Election can be explained very simply in today's vernacular. The chosen ones (the Elect), are the "choosees," and God (the one who chooses), is the "chooser." The "choosees" do not make a choice—instead, they are the objects of choice. The "chooser" is the one who makes the choice. The "chooser" determines who will be the "choosees."

When we read the Old Testament, we quickly find that the nation of Israel is an elect nation.

For you are a people holy to the Lord your God. The Lord your God has chosen you out of all the peoples on the face of the earth to be his people, his treasured possession.
(Deuteronomy 7:6)

But you, O Israel, my servant, Jacob, whom I have chosen, you descendants of Abraham my friend, I took you from the ends of the earth, from its farthest corners I called you. I said, 'You are my servant'; I have chosen you and have not rejected you.
(Isaiah 41:8-9)

Israel, at one time, was the only nation that had the Word of God. God was with them and blessed them greatly. He also punished them for their unfaithfulness. In His dealing with Israel, the Scriptures make it clear that all of the Jews were not saved—only the Elect. The same was true when God sent the Gospel to the Gentiles—only the Elect were saved. God is still saving elect Jews and elect Gentiles from nations around the world.

> It is not as though God's word had failed. For not all who are descended from Israel are Israel. Nor because they are his descendants are they all Abraham's children. On the contrary, "It is through Issac that your offspring will be reckoned." In other words, it is not the natural children who are God's children, but it is the children of the promise who are regarded as Abraham's offspring. (Romans 9:6-8)

God also has His Elect angels; therefore it follows that there are non-Elect angels.

> I charge you, in the sight of God and Christ Jesus and the elect angels, to keep these instructions without partiality, and to do nothing out of favoritism. (1 Timothy 5:21)

> And the angels who did not keep their positions of authority but abandoned their own home—these he has kept in darkness, bound with everlasting chains for judgment on the great Day. (Jude 6)

God's way of dealing with the angels differs from the way He deals with man. The Elect angels never fell. However, all of mankind fell, including the Elect. The fallen angels are not restored or saved. The teaching of the Bible is that they never will be and that they will suffer punishment. A portion of fallen man is saved—the Elect. All others are left in their fallen state to suffer the consequences of their sins.

The Elect are Predestined

In God's sovereignty, He has predestined, or decreed, all that happens, down to the most minute detail.

> The Lord said to him, "Who gave man his mouth? Who makes him deaf or mute? Who gives him sight or makes him blind? Is it not I, the Lord?" (Exodus 4:11)

Remember the former things, those of long ago;
   I am God, and there is no other;
   I am God, and there is none like me.
I make known the end from the beginning,
   from ancient times, what is still to come.
I say: My purpose will stand,
   and I will do all that I please.
From the east I summon a bird of prey;
   from a far-off land, a man to fulfill my purpose.
What I have said, that will I bring about;
   what I have planned, that will I do.
(Isaiah 46:9-11)

Are not two sparrows sold for a penny? Yet not one of them
will fall to the ground apart from the will of your Father. And
even the very hairs of your head are all numbered. So don't be
afraid; you are worth more than many sparrows.
(Matthew 10:29-31)

All the good and all the evil in the world takes place because
God has decreed it to happen. However, God does not make
anyone sin nor does He tempt anyone to sin; He is not the author
of sin.

Is it not from the mouth of the Most High that both calamities
and good things come? (Lamentations 3:38)

Though they are driven into exile by their enemies, there I will
command the sword to slay them. I will fix my eyes upon them
for evil and not for good. (Amos 9:4)

When tempted, no one should say, "God is tempting me." For
God cannot be tempted by evil, nor does he tempt anyone....
(James 1:13)

Predestination, like Election, creates a reaction in many
Christians. They feel they have no control over their lives. In one
sense, this is true. There is much over which we have no control:
who our parents are; how tall we are; the color of our skin, hair or
eyes; the country in which we are born; etc. On the other hand, we
have the freedom to choose and to change many things in our
lives. Most are free to seek an education, work hard, change jobs,
move to another city, join the military, read a book, go to a movie,

play a sport, watch TV, date, get married, have children, go to church, visit a friend, go jogging, etc. Man is free to choose these things, yet everything we do is done because God decreed it.

In his heart a man plans his course, but the Lord determines his steps. (Proverbs 16:9)

I know, O Lord, that a man's life is not his own; it is not for man to direct his steps. (Jeremiah 10:23)

The doctrine of Predestination is clearly taught in the Bible but is beyond the complete understanding of finite man. In His sovereignty, God decrees all that comes to pass, but man is fully responsible for his actions and is held accountable for his sins. We are not able to understand this anymore than we are able to comprehend the Trinity, the Creation, the Virgin Birth, or how Christ could be fully man and fully God at the same time. But, these truths are taught in the Bible, and we must believe them —even though we do not understand them. The same is true of Predestination and Election. I accept them in the same manner as I do the others; I hope you will also. For further information on Predestination, see the chapter on the Sovereignty of God.

Man is free to seek after God. He is free to make a choice—to live or not to live up to the knowledge of God he has attained. Scripture tells us we are all given a knowledge of God. Even the heathen, in a heathen country, have a knowledge of God from looking at Creation. Their knowledge, however, is not as much as if they had God's Word, but it is enough so that they are without excuse for not living up to the knowledge they have.

The heavens declare the glory of God;
     the skies proclaim the work of his hands.
Day after day they pour forth speech;
     night after night they display knowledge.
There is no speech or language
     where their voice is not heard.
Their voice goes out into all the earth,
     their words to the ends of the world.
(Psalm 19:1-4)

The wrath of God is being revealed from heaven against all the godlessness and wickedness of men who suppress the truth by

their wickedness, since what may be known about God is plain
to them, because God has made it plain to them. For since the
creation of the world God's invisible qualities—his eternal
power and divine nature—have been clearly seen, being
understood from what has been made, so that men are without
excuse. (Romans 1:18-20)

From the fall of Adam, man comes into this world with a
sinful nature and a desire to do only evil in God's sight. Do not
confuse this with good and evil in man's sight, for corrupt man
often sees corrupt men do things that are, humanly speaking, good.
However, the One who judges the intent of the heart, the One who
is above all, the One who is over all, says, "Be ye holy, for I am
holy" (1 Peter 1:16). By His measuring stick, we fall short of His
glory. When we stand in His light, all of our imperfections show,
and our sins are laid bare. If we want to know what we are like
outwardly, we look into a mirror. If we want to know what we are
like inwardly, we look into God's Word. In His Word, He makes
it clear how evil we truly are.

The Lord saw how great man's wickedness on the earth had
become, and that every inclination of the thoughts of his heart
was only evil all the time. (Genesis 6:5)

What is man, that he could be pure,
    or one born of woman, that he could be righteous?
If God places no trust in his holy ones,
    if even the heavens are not pure in his eyes,
how much less man, who is vile and corrupt,
    who drinks up evil like water! (Job 15:14-16)

God looks down from heaven
    on the sons of men
to see if there are any who understand,
    any who seek God.
Everyone has turned away,
    they have together become corrupt;
there is no one who does good,
    not even one. (Psalm 53:2-3)

The heart is deceitful above all things and beyond cure. Who
can understand it? (Jeremiah 17:9)

**This is the verdict: Light has come into the world, but men
loved darkness instead of light because their deeds were evil.**
(John 3:19)

In this sinful state, it is not surprising that man does not
choose to come to Christ. Many who do not believe in Election are
not aware of the sinful nature of man, his utter lack of ability to
understand spiritual truth, and his lack of desire to even want to
understand. He is "free" to choose to understand, but he does not
have the "ability" to do so. For example, I am "free" to throw rocks
at the moon; however, I could throw for a thousand years and
never hit it. I do not have the ability. Though free to, without the
ability, man can never choose Christ. God must give him the
ability. God not only gives the ability to the Elect, but He also
moves them to act on that ability and trust Christ as Savior and
Lord.

**Turn my heart toward your statutes and not toward selfish
gain.** (Psalm 119:36)

**Therefore I tell you that no one who is speaking by the Spirit
of God says, "Jesus be cursed," and no one can say, "Jesus is
Lord," except by the Holy Spirit.** (1 Corinthians 12:3)

**I keep asking that the God of our Lord Jesus Christ, the
glorious Father, may give you the Spirit of wisdom and
revelation, so that you may know him better.**
(Ephesians 1:17)

**One of those listening was a woman named Lydia, a dealer in
purple cloth from the city of Thyatira, who was a worshiper of
God. The Lord opened her heart to respond to Paul's message.**
(Acts 16:14)

**Then he opened their minds so they could understand the
Scriptures.** (Luke 24:45)

When we look at our discussion of Election to this point, our
understanding of the doctrine becomes clearer. We see that all
men have a sinful nature and are lost in their sins. Humanly
speaking, they may be good and religious men, but they suppress
the truth of God and are by nature inclined only to sin. They do

not understand things of God; moreover they do not have the ability to understand God's plan of salvation. Therefore, if left alone, they cannot and will not come to Christ. God, in His mercy, elects to save some of these lost souls, and He does it without violating their wills. He enables them to understand His plan of salvation and to accept Christ. Those that God elects to save, He does so for reasons known only to Him. There is nothing in the Elect that would merit His special favor. They have nothing to boast about, other than how great God is! He leaves the others alone to do as they choose and to receive His justice for their sins.

> **Brothers, think of what you were when you were called. Not many of you were wise by human standards; not many were influential; not many were of noble birth. But God chose the foolish things of the world to shame the wise; God chose the weak things of the world to shame the strong. He chose the lowly things of this world and the despised things—and the things that are not—to nullify the things that are, so that no one may boast before him. It is because of him that you are in Christ Jesus, who has become for us wisdom from God—that is, our righteousness, holiness and redemption. Therefore, as it is written: "Let him who boasts boast in the Lord."**
> (1 Corinthians 1:26-31)

> **For who makes you different from anyone else? What do you have that you did not receive? And if you did receive it, why do you boast as though you did not?** (1 Corinthians 4:7)

You may wonder how God can cause the Elect to do something without violating their wills. But, does the Bible not teach us that God rules in the affairs of man? For that matter, look at the writers of the Bible. God is truly the author of the Bible, but He used human beings as His instruments to accomplish this. He worked in the mind of each writer to have him write what He wanted, yet He did not violate his will or his personality.

All through the Bible, we see God's sovereignty. He causes men to come, to go, and to do as He has decreed. We pray to God for answers to questions and trust He will guide us, but we do not think of Him as violating our wills in giving us an answer. He tells us that the Holy Spirit indwells each true believer; moreover that we are to surrender control of our lives to Him, and let Him direct our thoughts and actions. Without violating our wills, the Holy

Spirit gives us understanding of Scripture and leads us to do the good works that God has ordained we should do. In the same way, the Holy Spirit works to bring us to an understanding of spiritual things and causes us to accept Christ. The following verses will help us to better understand this:

> You, however, are controlled not by the sinful nature but by the Spirit, if the Spirit of God lives in you. And if anyone does not have the Spirit of Christ, he does not belong to Christ. (Romans 8:9)

> For who has known the mind of the Lord that he may instruct him? But we have the mind of Christ. (1 Corinthians 2:16)

> But the Counselor, the Holy Spirit, whom the Father will send in my name, will teach you all things and will remind you of everything I have said to you. (John 14:26)

> But when he, the Spirit of truth, comes, he will guide you into all truth. He will not speak on his own; he will speak only what he hears, and he will tell you what is yet to come. He will bring glory to me by taking from what is mine and making it known to you. (John 16:13-14)

> Do not get drunk on wine, which leads to debauchery. Instead, be filled with the Spirit. (Ephesians 5:18)

> ...for it is God who works in you to will and to act according to his good purpose. (Philippians 2:13)

Objection: God Foresees and Then Elects

There are people who say they believe in Election but that they believe the Elect are people who God has foreseen will accept Christ. They believe God foresees who will accept Christ and then elects them to be saved—as a result of His foreknowledge. They attempt to base this on the words "foreknew" and "foreknowledge"; however, at best, this is just a play on words.

We can say with certainty that God had foreknowledge of the earth, the birds, man, etc. But, this foreknowledge was not because He saw that these things would be, but because He decreed that they would be. They were not going to just happen—God brought them into being.

We know that Christ did not just happen to go to the cross; it was planned and known before the world was made, and it came about right on schedule. People tried to kill Jesus before the cross, but the Bible tells us they did not succeed because "His time had not come." No one could have nailed Jesus to the cross had He not consented to let them.

> **The reason my Father loves me is that I lay down my life—only to take it up again. No one takes it from me, but I lay it down of my own accord. I have authority to lay it down and authority to take it up again. This command I received from my Father.** (John 10:17-18)

> **They did what your power and will had decided beforehand should happen.** (Acts 4:28)

> **For you know that it was not with perishable things such as silver or gold that you were redeemed from the empty way of life handed down to you from your forefathers, but with the precious blood of Christ, a lamb without blemish or defect. He was chosen before the creation of the world, but was revealed in these last times for your sake.** (1 Peter 1:18-20)

Those people whom God foreknew are those whom God loves, and they were foreordained to be those He loved—they are the Elect. An event that is in the foreknowledge of God is one that is certain to happen; it is not just foreseen to happen. We find in the Bible that the words "foreknew" and "foreknowledge" carry a meaning of "foreordained" where they pertain to people and events relating directly to God. We see an example of this as Peter tells of the crucifixion of Christ on the Day of Pentecost.

> **Men of Israel, listen to this: Jesus of Nazareth was a man accredited by God to you by miracles, wonders and signs, which God did among you through him, as you yourselves know. This man was handed over to you by God's set purpose and foreknowledge; and you, with the help of wicked men, put him to death by nailing him to the cross.** (Acts 2:22-23)

The following are verses pertaining to the Elect where the word "foreknowledge" means foreordination or decree.

> **Peter, an apostle of Jesus Christ, To God's elect, strangers in the world, scattered throughout Pontus, Galatia, Cappadocia, Asia and Bithynia, who have been chosen according to the foreknowledge of God the Father, through the sanctifying work of the Spirit, for obedience to Jesus Christ and sprinkling by his blood: Grace and peace be yours in abundance.**
> (1 Peter 1:1-2)

These verses tell us that the Elect were chosen and ordained, by God, to be saved. There is no mention in these verses that man did anything, or that God elected anyone because of something he or she did. God did the choosing, according to His purpose. He applied the work of Christ to the lives of the Elect, through the Holy Spirit, so that the Elect would be obedient and be saved. The Holy Spirit enables us to understand the Gospel, and moves us to accept Christ and put our sins under His shed blood.

The meaning of "foreknew" in the following verses is foreordained.

> **For those God foreknew he also predestined to be conformed to the likeness of his Son, that he might be the firstborn among many brothers.** (Romans 8:29)

> **God did not reject his people, whom he foreknew. Don't you know what the Scripture says in the passage about Elijah—how he appealed to God against Israel....**
> (Romans 11:2).

It is obvious that God foreknew everyone who will ever live. However, He has not chosen to save everyone, therefore that cannot be the meaning of "foreknew" in the above verses. There is something special about the ones God "foreknew." It is not something special that they have done; we do not see them doing anything. They are special because God is doing something to them and for them. They are special because God loves them—they are His Elect.

In other verses we see the use of the word "know" meaning more than just "to know" someone.

> I am the good shepherd; I know my sheep and my sheep know me.... (John 10:14)

> I will give them a heart to know me, that I am the Lord. They will be my people, and I will be their God, for they will return to me with all their heart. (Jeremiah 24:7)

The use of the word in these verses denotes love and a real relationship between those that "know" and are "known." Another passage is:

> Not everyone who says to me, 'Lord, Lord,' will enter the kingdom of heaven, but only he who does the will of my Father who is in heaven. Many will say to me on that day, 'Lord, Lord, did we not prophesy in your name, and in your name drive out demons and perform many miracles?' Then I will tell them plainly, 'I never knew you. Away from me, you evildoers!' (Matthew 7:21-23)

We realize that Christ knows all things and knows all people (based upon the common usage of the word "know"). However, in these verses He tells some people that He never knew them. Again, we see that the word "know" ("knew" in the past tense) denotes relationship. In Matthew 7:23 the words "I never knew you" tell us there was not a relationship. In the case of Jeremiah, there was a relationship, as shown by the word "knew" in "I knew you."

> Before I formed you in the womb I knew you, before you were born I set you apart; I appointed you as a prophet to the nations. (Jeremiah 1:5)

Objection: Election Fosters Sinful Living

Another objection one encounters to Election is that the doctrine allows, and even fosters, sinful living. This arises from the misunderstanding that the Elect are going to be saved no matter what they do or how sinfully they live. This is not God's Election. Furthermore, one does not have to believe in Election to hold this erroneous view. From the days of the early church, there have been those who professed Christ with their lips but were libertines or antinomians at heart and perverted the Gospel by living as if they had a license to sin. In the book of Jude, the Lord tells us about people who think and live this way. He also tells us of their end.

> Dear friends, although I was very eager to write to you about the salvation we share, I felt I had to write and urge you to contend for the faith that was once for all entrusted to the saints. For certain men whose condemnation was written about long ago have secretly slipped in among you. They are godless men, who change the grace of our God into a license for immorality and deny Jesus Christ our only Sovereign and Lord. (Jude 3-4)

> These men are blemishes at your love feasts, eating with you without the slightest qualm—shepherds who feed only themselves. They are clouds without rain, blown along by the wind; autumn trees, without fruit and uprooted—twice dead. They are wild waves of the sea, foaming up their shame; wandering stars, for whom blackest darkness has been reserved forever. (Jude 12-13)

The Elect of God were not only elected to be saved, but they were also chosen to perform good works—which God ordained they would do.

> For we are God's workmanship, created in Christ Jesus to do good works, which God prepared in advance for us to do. (Ephesians 2:10)

The fact that they will perform these good works is as certain as the fact that they will be saved. Some Christians serve the Lord more faithfully than others; some do greater deeds; some bear more fruit; but all glorify God to one degree or another. Anyone who believes they can live as they please, ignoring God and following their own sinful desires, cannot expect to be thought of as one of God's Elect. This person is in grave danger of hell. A belief like this is not scriptural. Again, I say, this is not God's Election.

Objection: Universalism

The Universalists raise another objection. All who believe in Universalism object to Election because they believe that everyone is going to heaven—whether or not they have ever heard of Christ, much less accepted Him as Savior. The only way they can explain Election is through irrational thinking, declaring everyone who ever lived to be Elect. Those who believe in Universalism either do not understand or they refuse to accept what the Bible teaches in verses like Romans 3:23, Romans 6:23, John 1:12, Matthew 7:21-23, Matthew 11:27, John 5:21, 1 Corinthians 1:18, and John 8:42-44. The concept of the saved going to heaven and the lost going to hell is clearly taught throughout the Bible. However, the following five examples should be sufficient to show that Universalism is a false doctrine.

And this is the testimony: God has given us eternal life, and this life is in his Son. He who has the Son has life; he who does not have the Son of God does not have life.
(1 John 5:11-12)

Then Jesus went through the towns and villages, teaching as he made his way to Jerusalem. Someone asked him, "Lord, are only a few people going to be saved?"
He said to them, "Make every effort to enter through the narrow door, because many, I tell you, will try to enter and will not be able to. Once the owner of the house gets up and closes the door, you will stand outside knocking and pleading, 'Sir, open the door for us.'
But he will answer, 'I don't know you or where you come from.'
Then you will say, 'We ate and drank with you, and you taught in our streets.'
But he will reply, 'I don't know you or where you come from. Away from me, all you evildoers!'
There will be weeping there, and gnashing of teeth, when you see Abraham, Isaac and Jacob and all the prophets in the kingdom of God, but you yourselves thrown out."
(Luke 13:22-28)

For God so loved the world that he gave his one and only Son, that whoever believes in him shall not perish but have eternal life. For God did not send his Son into the world to condemn the world, but to save the world through him. Whoever believes in him is not condemned, but whoever does not believe stands condemned already because he has not believed in the name of God's one and only Son. (John 3:16-18)

Whoever believes in the Son has eternal life, but whoever rejects the Son will not see life, for God's wrath remains on him. (John 3:36)

Then I saw a great white throne and him who was seated on it. Earth and sky fled from his presence, and there was no place for them. And I saw the dead, great and small, standing before the throne, and books were opened. Another book was opened, which is the book of life. The dead were judged according to what they had done as recorded in the books. The sea gave up the dead that were in it, and death and Hades gave up the dead that were in them, and each person was judged according to what he had done. Then death and Hades were thrown into the lake of fire. The lake of fire is the second death. If anyone's name was not found written in the book of life, he was thrown into the lake of fire. (Revelation 20:11-15)

Objection: Election Hinders Evangelism and Missions

There are still others who object to Election on the grounds that it is a hindrance to evangelism and missions. They are afraid that those who embrace the doctrine will not feel the need to preach the Gospel or witness—thinking if someone is Elect, God will save them regardless. Nothing could be further from the truth. Those who embrace Bible Election also embrace Bible evangelism and missions.

As the Scripture says, "Anyone who trusts in him will never be put to shame." For there is no difference between Jew and Gentile—the same Lord is Lord of all and richly blesses all who call on him, for, "Everyone who calls on the name of the Lord will be saved."
How, then, can they call on the one they have not believed in? And how can they believe in the one of whom they have not heard? And how can they hear without someone preaching to them? And how can they preach unless they are sent? As it is written, "How beautiful are the feet of those who bring good news!" (Romans 10:11-15)

> Then Jesus came to them and said, "All authority in heaven and on earth has been given to me. Therefore go and make disciples of all nations, baptizing them in the name of the Father and of the Son and of the Holy Spirit, and teaching them to obey everything I have commanded you. And surely I am with you always, to the very end of the age."
> (Matthew 28:18-20)

Actually, belief in Election has a positive effect on evangelism and missions. It makes us aware that God has chosen certain people, throughout the world, to be saved; however, they must hear the Word in order to believe. We have no idea who they are or where they are; therefore our mission is to get the Word out to everyone. We know that only God can save them, but we should work as though their salvation depends on us.

Why Did You Choose Christ?

At this point I am going to ask a question; I suggest you tell God the answer. The question is, If you know Christ, why do you accept Him as your Savior when so many others do not? Please do not give an impulsive answer, or a shallow answer. Search your heart and mind, then tell God why you choose Christ when so many others do not. Compare yourself with others in terms of intelligence, family background, past lifestyles, present lifestyles, personal history, and moral values. Can you tell God it was one of these, or a combination of these, that was the deciding factor? Perhaps you could tell God that you are smarter than those who do not accept Christ. Or maybe you will tell Him that you are a nicer person, that you have higher morals, and that those who do not accept Christ are just not in your class. You must end up telling God that, in some way, you are better than the others since there has to be a reason for the difference in you and them. The only other alternative is that there is no difference in you and them, but God worked in you to cause you to come to Christ.

Is there anyone who has not considered that there are, ultimately, only two groups of people in this world—the saved and the unsaved? When we look at the two groups, we find many similarities. In each group we find rich, poor, intelligent, not so intelligent, all colors of skin, and all walks of life. However, the one dividing factor is that one group belongs to Christ while the other group is headed to hell. Perhaps, humanly speaking, you were a very moral person before you came to Christ. But what does that prove? There are many very moral people who never choose Christ. What about the social outcasts, the skid-row derelicts, the child abusers, and the murderers? It is, obviously, not high moral values that bring them to Christ. Yet, a number of these people do come, and their lives are changed. But why do some come and others do not? How can we account for the fact that, in response to the Gospel, a criminal comes to Christ and a respected banker does not? Another time, a banker comes and a criminal does not. Have you come up with an idea or explanation as to why you belong to Him? If you have then you will have some idea as to why the others belong in your group. As a result, you should have insight into why the lost are members of the unsaved group.

Although we have read much Scripture to the contrary, experience tells me that there are still some readers who will say that they are saved by grace but that their acceptance of Christ was their decision. God did not regenerate them first to bring this about. In essence, they are saying that Christ died to make it possible for them to be saved, but that they actually took the final step of salvation by themselves. This being the case, they really do have something about which they can boast. Even if they make an attempt at modesty, it was their decision that brought about their salvation. They will tell you how wonderful God's plan of salvation is and that it is all of grace, yet they cling to that one accomplishment—they accepted Christ. Those who believe this way remind me of a little boy who, upon seeing his daddy building a tool shed, runs and gets his toy hammer to help. The daddy patiently works over and around the boy, encouraging him all along. When the tool shed is finished, the little boy runs to tell his mother what he and his daddy built.

Most Christians who do not believe in Election do believe in praying to God for the salvation of a family member or a loved one. I have often wondered why one would pray to God if the decision is up to the individual. God cannot do anything—the person must make the choice. If God were dependent on human beings to respond, then it is possible that Christ died in vain. This would be the case if no one chose to trust Christ. Election removes that possibility. God's Election is absolutely unconditional. He has chosen His Elect—the number is set, certain, and unchangeable.

He will save the exact number of people He has purposed and planned to save. The beauty of Election is that God receives all the glory, for He has done it all. Man is humbled and stripped naked without even a fig leaf. He is left standing completely helpless and absolutely lost. It is then that God, in His mercy, saves him.

Only God can break the bonds that hold sinful man. Only God can soften his heart and open his understanding. Only God can regenerate him and cause him to repent, to seek God, and to trust Christ as Savior and Lord. And only God can do this without violating man's will. When you come to believe this, it will cause your heart to overflow with gratitude and praise to God. You will realize that you do not deserve to be saved any more than those whose destiny is hell. You did not respond to God because of something worthwhile in you, but God regenerated you and brought about your salvation with no help from you. God suffered and died for you, knowing all along that, left to yourself, you would not respond and be saved. Nevertheless, He had mercy upon you and caused you to respond. When you realize this, you will treasure your salvation more than ever, and you will have a new awareness of God's love and God's mercy.

Elect Saved, Non-Elect Condemned—Why?

As we come to the end of our study of Election, there are two things I want to make clear. First, one does not have to believe in Election to be saved. We are saved by accepting Christ as Savior and Lord, and trusting Him to forgive our sins. There are many saved people who do not believe God chose them; they believe they did the choosing—it was their decision to accept Christ. Once again, let us see what God says.

You did not choose me, but I chose you.... (John 15:16)

Second, not being one of the Elect does not condemn a person to hell. A person is condemned because of sin. The Elect go to heaven not because they are without sin, but because God, in His mercy, has forgiven their sins. You may ask, But what if some in my family are not Elect, will not they be condemned? I have to ask that same question for my family. The answer, from God's Word, is that all perish except the Elect. But again, they do not perish because they are not one of the Elect—they perish because of their sins. If there were not a doctrine of Election, they would still perish because of their sins. We all have family, friends, and loved ones whom we want to come to Christ. It behooves us to witness to them, set an example for them, and pray for them. Knowing the sinful nature of man, we know that they will not come unless God draws them; therefore, we do need to pray that God will save them. But if they pass away giving no indication of accepting Christ, we are not to despair or think God has done them (or us) an injustice. God can do no wrong. Because He showed us mercy, He is not obligated to do the same for them. They will receive justice.

Humanly speaking, we feel sorrow at their plight and wish we could have done more. It hurts to think of a loved one suffering in hell, and the dearer the loved one is to us, the greater our pain. But we must not put our love for anyone above our love for God. We are commanded to love God with all our heart, soul, and mind. We are to put our love for Him, and obedience to Him, above everything and everyone else.

> Do not suppose that I have come to bring peace to the earth. I did not come to bring peace, but a sword. For I have come to turn 'A man against his father, a daughter against her mother, a daughter-in-law against her mother-in-law—a man's enemies will be the members of his own household.'
>
> Anyone who loves his father or mother more than me is not worthy of me; anyone who loves his son or daughter more than me is not worthy of me; and anyone who does not take his cross and follow me is not worthy of me. Whoever finds his life will lose it, and whoever loses his life for my sake will find it. (Matthew 10:34-39)

We know that God can do no wrong and that His will is perfect. When we get to heaven, there will be no sorrow and no tears. We will have nothing but joy in our hearts. We know that all is right with God and He will make all right with us. We must believe this and hold firmly to this hope. We must remember that God loves us so much that He gave His only Son to suffer and die for us. We must trust Him and His Word when He tells us that all things work together for our good. We must bow before "The Lord of lords" and "The King of kings" and say with a humble heart, Yet not as I will, but as You will.

If you know Christ, aren't you grateful for His mercy, His love, and His saving grace? Aren't you thankful that you are one of the Elect? If you have not come to an understanding of the truth of unconditional Election, I suggest you keep an open mind, study God's Word, and pray that God will reveal to you that which pleases Him. As you study, keep in mind what God has said about man's sinful nature. We have seen, in His Word, that man (before he comes to Christ) cannot understand things of God, and not only does not try to understand but actually suppresses the truth. This being the case—if there were no Election, then what did Christ come in the flesh to do? If He came to die, what did He die for? If He came to save, whom did He save? If He came to save the world (all men), then He failed. If He came to make salvation possible for all men, He did that. But He has done only that; there is no guarantee that people will come to Christ if left to their choice. Actually, the teaching of Scripture is that none will come. But Scripture also says Christ came to save the lost.

For the Son of Man came to seek and to save what was lost. (Luke 19:10)

There is no contradiction. Under Election, though none will come on their own, the Elect will be brought by God to a saving faith in Christ.

I was found by those who did not seek me; I revealed myself to those who did not ask for me. (Romans 10:20)

Christ did not die just to make a way of salvation; He is The Way. He came to save the Elect, and He does exactly that. Under Election, Christ's death and resurrection made the way of salvation possible for all, but insures the salvation of the Elect.

I have revealed you to those whom you gave me out of the world. They were yours; you gave them to me and they have obeyed your word. (John 17:6)

I pray for them. I am not praying for the world, but for those you have given me, for they are yours. (John 17:9)

The Elect Will Persevere

God not only saves the Elect, He also causes them persevere. They can never be lost.

To him who is able to keep you from falling and to present you before his glorious presence without fault and with great joy....
(Jude 24)

He will keep you strong to the end, so that you will be blameless on the day of our Lord Jesus Christ.
(1 Corinthians 1:8)

What, then, shall we say in response to this? If God is for us, who can be against us? He who did not spare his own Son, but gave him up for us all—how will he not also, along with him, graciously give us all things? Who will bring any charge against those whom God has chosen? It is God who justifies. Who is he that condemns? Christ Jesus, who died—more than that, who was raised to life—is at the right hand of God and is also interceding for us. Who shall separate us from the love of Christ? Shall trouble or hardship or persecution or famine or nakedness or danger or sword? As it is written: "For your sake we face death all day long; we are considered as sheep to be slaughtered."
    No, in all these things we are more than conquerors through him who loved us. For I am convinced that neither death nor life, neither angels nor demons, neither the present nor the future, nor any powers, neither height nor depth, nor anything else in all creation, will be able to separate us from the love of God that is in Christ Jesus our Lord.
(Romans 8:31-39)

Praise be to the God and Father of our Lord Jesus Christ! In his great mercy he has given us new birth into a living hope through the resurrection of Jesus Christ from the dead, and into an inheritance that can never perish, spoil or fade—kept in heaven for you, who through faith are shielded by God's power until the coming of the salvation that is ready to be revealed in the last time. (1 Peter 1:3-5)

...being confident of this, that he who began a good work in you will carry it on to completion until the day of Christ Jesus.
(Philippians 1:6)

When the "Final Day" comes, and the truth is laid bare for all to see, the lost will know and understand that they, alone, are to blame for their being lost. The saved will know and understand that God, alone, is responsible for their being saved.

One final thought: If you are having difficulty understanding how natural man can have such a sinful nature and be in such bondage to sin that he not only will not accept Christ but he cannot accept Christ (without God bringing it about), then I invite you to turn over the coin. As one who is spiritual (who has accepted Christ and is His bondservant), would you want to turn to Satan and ask him to be your master? Could you deny Christ and worship Satan? You not only will not do that, you cannot do that. You are free to do it, but you do not have the ability to do it. You have the opportunity to choose Satan, but you do not have the ability to choose him. You want nothing to do with him. That is where you were on the other side of the coin, except it was God with whom you did not want anything to do. Then God regenerated you, and look where you are today. Praise God!

The Author's Testimony

Before I became a Christian, I thought I was one. I had always believed there was a God and that Jesus was the Son of God. I lived in a Christian country, was a member of a church, and I accepted the fact that Jesus died for the sins of the world. I felt this made me a Christian. I believed I would go to heaven when I died, although I had no real basis for believing it. I believed that some people would go to hell, but like most everyone, I thought it would always happen to the other fellow. I knew I was a sinner who did some wrong things. However, I knew that I tried to be a good citizen, husband, and father. I felt the good I did outweighed the bad. I thought that in comparing my good and bad deeds, I was keeping the scales tipped in my favor. I envisioned that when this world is brought to an end, if all the people who had ever lived stood in a long line before the gates of heaven and God made a cut-off, the people on one side going to heaven and those on the other side going to hell, I would be on the side that got into heaven. I did not expect to be at the front of the line, but I did expect to make the cut-off.

There came a time in my life when I realized how fortunate I was. I had a nice home, a good marriage, two fine children (too young to get into real trouble), and good health. My wife Peg and I both felt blessed. Sometimes we would sit in our kitchen drinking coffee and wonder what life is all about. We wondered if enjoying life, as we were, and then one day dying with the uncertain hope of going to heaven, was all there is to life. We became restless as we continued to wonder about the purpose of life.

While traveling in my work I would often listen to preachers on the car radio. Looking back, I feel sure some were good and some were not, but I did not know the difference. However, I heard and understood enough to make me question if I was truly a Christian. I found myself praying as I drove, asking God to please make me and my family Christians.

Peg started taking our children to Sunday school. She felt it would be good for them, and I certainly agreed. She would attend an adult class while the children were in their classes. She suggested that I might want to join them, and I did. With time, Peg and I became very religious—attending Sunday school and church on a regular basis. Peg became active in the women's work, and I became an officer of the church. We even helped to start a mission church. We were religious, but not saved. We still carried the guilt of sin and were still under the penalty of sin. We were religiously active but spiritually dead. If we had died while in that condition we would have gone straight to hell.

My younger sister Mitzi told us about a lady, Elizabeth Newbold, who was a Bible teacher. It seemed that Elizabeth said the Bible taught that to be a Christian a person had to have a personal relationship with Jesus Christ. Mitzi said that she now had this relationship. Peg and I did not understand what was meant by a personal relationship with Christ, but decided to find out.

One night, I called Elizabeth. I told her that I was Mitzi's brother, and that Peg and I would like to talk with her. She said that she had to go to Huntsville the next day to teach a Bible class but would come to our house that night when she got back. Wanting to be a gentleman and do the right thing, I told her we would come to her house. However, she insisted on coming to ours. The next night we got a phone call about 9:30. Elizabeth had just gotten back from Huntsville, and it would be 10:30 before she could get to our house. She wanted to know if that was too late for us. The time was fine with us, but I felt it was too late for her. However, again she insisted. The fact that she was so eager and willing to do this for strangers made us even more desirous of hearing what she had to say.

We had made a list of questions to ask Elizabeth and she obligingly answered them. However, she kept returning the conversation to the Gospel. She made us aware that we were counting on living lives good enough to deserve heaven. In other words, we were attempting to earn the right to go there when we died. She showed us where the Bible says that no one is saved by good deeds. We found that we could not tip the scales in our favor by doing good—our good deeds could not erase the sin on our record.

Elizabeth explained that God would not allow sin into heaven. She then pointed out that if we have committed just one sin, it is the same as breaking all of God's law. We realized that no matter how hard we tried, we could not live the life God required—life without any sin. And even if that were now possible, we were already condemned by our past sins. It became clear that we were lost sinners, without hope and headed to hell.

Elizabeth had given us the bad news. Next, she gave us the good. She told us that Christ had died for us. He had already paid for every sin we had ever committed in the past, and every one we would ever commit in the future. Christ had lived a sinless life, suffered and died for our sins, was resurrected, and had ascended to heaven. He offered us the free gift of salvation. We could go to heaven because of what Christ did for us, not because of anything we do. He did it all. We could contribute nothing. Our sin debt was paid in full; all we needed to do was accept the gift.

Elizabeth pointed out that it seems so simple, many people have trouble believing it. She explained that we should acknowledge that we were sinners, repent, ask Jesus Christ to forgive us and to come into our hearts and lives as our Savior and Lord. She explained that this involved more than an intellectual assent of fact about Jesus. It is a personal thing. A person must not only believe about Jesus, but must personally commit their life to Him, trusting and relying on Him to save them.

She then asked us if we would like to receive Christ as Savior and Lord. We were both only too glad to be able to do so, and about one o'clock in the morning, we knelt in our living room and asked Christ to save us. He did, and our lives were changed.

This was in the early part of 1966. We no longer had reason to wonder what life was all about. We soon learned we were to live and serve God in whatever way pleased Him. We were now Christians, and the purpose of the Christian life is to glorify God.

Before I became a Christian there were things that I knew were wrong to do, but I did them anyway. After Christ saved me, I began to try to stop doing those things. One of the first things I stopped was cursing. In time I found there were things that were sinful that I had never thought of before as being sinful. Like all Christians, I sinned even though I did not want to nor intend to. And like all Christians, I still sin today. We will not reach perfection and be without sin until we get to heaven. However, as times passes, I sin less and less as I learn, by God's grace, to walk more consistently in the control and power of His Holy Spirit.

When I do sin, I know I can turn to God and, in the name of His precious Son Jesus Christ, ask Him to forgive me—and He does. Having been forgiven so much by God I want to be forgiving of others. I would hope that any one I have wronged, intentionally or unintentionally, would forgive me too. However, all wrongdoing is actually sin against God, and it is His forgiveness that we must have. I am fully confident that I have that forgiveness based on the fact that Christ paid the penalty for my sins. I received the benefit of His payment when I accepted Him as my Savior and Lord. I have confidence that I will go to heaven when I die, not because I deserve to, but because God has promised salvation to all who put their trust in His Son. Knowing that I do not deserve heaven makes me very grateful to God for His love and mercy in saving me.

I think it is normal for Christians, having experienced the joy of salvation, to want to tell others how they might come to know Christ personally. We want our families, friends, and strangers to hear the Good News about salvation. That is one reason this book was written. It is my hope that, through this book, many who do not know Christ will come to a saving knowledge of Him. In addition, I hope that many who are saved will learn what it means to be filled with the Spirit. If you do not have a personal relationship with Christ, please read the chapter on salvation. If you know Christ as your Savior and Lord, please read the chapter on the Holy Spirit.

Reader's Response

Having written Let God Speak with the hopeful expectation that God would use it to save some and to work spiritual maturity in some, I would be most grateful for any confirmation that this is being done. My basic reason for wanting this confirmation is that in addition to selling the book, I am giving away a number of copies through my ministry of "Search the Scriptures." If the book is having a meaningful impact on people's lives, I would want to continue to give away copies as the Lord leads and provides.

If, as a result of reading this book, you have received Jesus Christ as your Lord and Savior, trusting Him to forgive your sins and save you, please let me know.

If you were saved before reading the book but now feel you have a better understanding of your dependency on the Holy Spirit to live the Christian life and are committed to making a conscience effort to have Him control your life day by day, moment by moment, please let me know.

If this book has enabled you to better understand the doctrines discussed, strengthened your resolve to walk in obedience, or been meaningful in any other manner, I would like to know. If you have any questions, I will attempt to answer them.

As a result of reading the book:

___ I received Christ as my Savior and Lord.

___ I am seeking to let the Holy Spirit control my life moment by moment.

Remarks and/or questions: _____

_____

_____

_____

_____

_____

Mail to: Ed McDavid
Search the Scriptures
P. O. Box 131447
Birmingham, Al. 35213

BIBLIOGRAPHY

Alleine, Joseph. *An Alarm to Unconverted Sinners*
Bates, William. *The Harmony of The Divine Attributes*
Boettner, Loraine. Studies in Theology
Boettner, Loraine. *The Reformed Doctrine of Predestination*
Bright, Bill. *The Holy Spirit The Key to Supernatural Living*
Briscoe, Stuart. *Beyond Limits*
Briscoe, Stuart. *The Fullness of Christ*
Bruce, F. F. *The New Testament Documents: Are they reliable?*
Buchanan, James. *The Office and Work of The Holy Spirit*
Bunyan, John. *A Holy Life The Beauty of Christianity*
Criswell, W. A. *Why I Preach That the Bible Is Literally True*
Custance, Arthur C. *The Sovereignty Of Grace*
Dabney, Robert L. *Discussions: Evangelical and Theological*
 Vol. 1
Epp, Theodore H. *The Other Comforter*
Flynn, Leslie B. *19 Gifts of the Spirit*
Gerstner, John H. *A Bible Inerrancy Primer*
Gerstner, John H. *Repent or Perish*
Gerstner, John H. *Jonathan Edwards: A Mini-Theology*
Girardeau, John L. *Calvinism and Evangelical Arminianism*
Graham, Billy. *The Holy Spirit*
Green, Michael. *I Believe in the Holy Spirit*
Griffiths, Michael. *Three Men filled With the Spirit*
Gutzke, Manford G. *Plain Talk About The Holy Spirit*
Gutzke, Manford George. *Living in the Spirit—Is It Real?*
Hammond, T. C. *In Understanding Be Men*
Harris, R Laird. *Inspiration and Canonicity Of The Bible*
Hodgkin, A. M. *Christ In All The Scriptures*
Howard, David M. *By the Power of the Holy Spirit*
Kendall, R. T. *Tithing A Call to Serious, Biblical Giving*
Kennedy, James D. *Truths That Transform*
Little, Paul E. *Know Why You Believe*
Lloyd-Jones, D. Martyn. *Sermon on the Mount*
Lockyer, Herbert. *The Holy Spirit Of God*
Luther, Martin. *The Bondage of the Will*
Manly, Basil. *The Bible Doctrine of Inspiration Explained and
 Vindicated*
McDowell, Josh. *Evidence That Demands A Verdict*

Mell, Patrick Hues. (President of the Southern Baptist Convention
    for 17 years) *A Southern Baptist Looks At Predestination*
Montgomery, John Warwick, editor. *God's Inerrant Word*
Montgomery, John Warwick. *History and Christianity*
Morris, Henry M. *Many Infallible Proofs*
Murray, Andrew. *The Believer's Secret of Obedience*
Murray, Andrew. *Absolute Surrender*
Murray, Andrew. *The Believer's Secret of the Master's Indwelling*
Nettles, Dr. Thomas J. editor. *Southern Baptist Sermons On
    Sovereignty and Responsibility*
Owen, John. *Sin & Temptation*
Pache, Rene. *The Person and Work of the Holy Spirit*
Packer, J. I. *Knowing God*
Packer, J. I. *God Has Spoken*
Packer, J. I. *Keep In Step With The Spirit*
Palmer, Edwin H. *The Holy Spirit*
Pentecost, J. Dwight. *Things Which Become Sound Doctrine*
Pink, A. W. *The Sovereignty of God*
Pink, A. W. *Gleanings From The Scriptures (Man's Total
    Depravity)*
Pink, Arthur W. *The Attributes of God*
Pink, A. W. *The Sovereignty of God*
Pink, Arthur W. *The Holy Spirit*
Pink, A. W. *The Doctrines of Election and Justification*
Rice, N. L. *God Sovereign and Man Free*
Ridout, Samuel. *The Person & Work of the Holy Spirit*
Robertson, Norvell. *Hand-Book Of Theology*
Ryle, J. C. *Holiness*
Ryrie, Charles Caldwell. *A Survey of Bible Doctrine*
Sanders, J Oswald. *The Holy Spirit And His Gifts*
Schaeffer, Francis A. *True Spirituality*
Scudder, Henry. *The Christian's Daily Walk*
Selph, Robert B. *Southern Baptists and the Doctrine of Election*
Sproul, R. C. *Chosen By God*
Spurgeon, C. H. *Spurgeon On Sovereignty*
Spurgeon, C. H. *Spurgeon On The Providence of God*
Spurgeon, C. H. *All of Grace*
Stott, John R. W. *The Baptism & Fullness of the Holy Spirit*
Stott, John R. W. *Men Made New*
Torrey, R. A. *What the Bible Teaches*

Trench, R. C. *Notes on the Parables of Our Lord*
Unknown Christian. *How To Live The Victorious Life*
Urquhart, John. *The Wonders of Prophecy*
Warfield, Benjamin B. *The Plan of Salvation*
Webb, Robert Alexander. *Christian Salvation Its Doctrine and Experience*
Wirt, Sherwood Eliot. *The Inner Life Of The Believer*
Yohn, Rick. *Discover Your Spiritual Gift and Use It*

COMMENTARIES

Brown, David. *The Four Gospels*
Bruce, F. F. *Tyndale New Testament Commentaries The Epistle of Paul to the Romans*
Erdman, Charles R. *The Epistle of Paul to the Romans*
Green, Michael. *2 Peter & Jude*
Greene, Oliver B. *Romans*
Haldane, Robert. *An Exposition of Romans*
Hendriksen, W. *More Than Conquerors*
Hendriksen, William. *New Testament Commentary The Gospel According to John*
Hendriksen, William. *New Testament Commentary Exposition of Galatians*
Hendriksen, William. *New Testament Commentary Exposition of the Gospel According to Matthew*
Hendriksen, William. *New Testament Commentary Exposition of Paul's Epistle on the Romans*
Hewitt, Thomas. *Tyndal New Testament Commentaries The Epistle To The Hebrews*
Hodge, Charles. *Commentary on the Epistle to the Romans*
Ironside, H. A. *Epistle to the Galatians*
Lenski, R. C. H. *Interpretation of Romans*
Leupold, H. C. *Exposition of Daniel*
Lloyd-Jones, D. M. *Romans Chapter 1*
Lloyd-Jones, D. M. *Romans Chapters 3:20-4:25*
Lloyd-Jones, D. Martyn. *Romans Chapter 5*
Lloyd-Jones D. Martyn. *Romans Chapter 6*
Lloyd-Jones, D. Martyn. *Romans Chapters 7:1-8:4*
Lloyd-Jones, D. Martyn. *Romans Chapter 8:5-17*

Lloyd-Jones, D. Martyn. *Romans Chapter 8:17-39*
Lloyd-Jones, D. Martyn. *God's Ultimate Purpose Eph. 1:1 to 1:23*
Lloyd-Jones, D. Martyn. *God's Way of Reconciliation
Eph. Chapter 2*
Lloyd-Jones, D. M. *Life in the Spirit an Exposition of
Ephesians 5:18 to 6:9*
Luther, Martin. *Commentary on St. Paul's Epistle to the Galatians*
MacArthur, John. *The MacArthur New Testament Commentary
Hebrews*
MacArthur, John. *The MacArthur New Testament Commentary
1 Corinthians*
McGee, J. Vernon. *Thru the Bible with J. Vernon
McGee, Vols. 1 thru 5*
Mills, Sanford C. *A Hebrew Christian looks at Romans*
Morris, Henry M. *The Revelation Record*
Murray, John. *Epistle to the Romans*
Newell, William R. *Romans Verse by Verse*
Newell William R. *Revelation: A Complete Commentary*
Philip, Rev. James. *The Epistle to the Romans A Commentary*
Pink, Arthur W. *Exposition of Hebrews*
Plumer, Wm. S. *Commentary on Romans*
Stibbs, Alan M. *Tyndale New Testament Commentaries The First
Epistle General of Peter*
Stott, John R. W. *The Message of Galatians*
Stott, John R. W. *The Message of Ephesians*
Wilson, Geoffrey B. *Romans*
Wuest, Kenneth S. *Wuest's Word Studies Romans*
Wuest, Kenneth S. *Wuest's Word Studies Hebrews*
Wuest, Kenneth S. *Wuest's Word Studies 1 Peter*

Calvin's New Testament Commentaries, Vols. 1 thru 12. David W.
Torrance; Thomas F. Torrance, editors
Barnes' Notes on the New Testament. Albert Barnes
Commentary on the Whole Bible. Matthew Henry
The New Bible Commentary: Revised. D. Guthrie; J. A. Motyer;
A. M. Stibbs; D. J. Wiseman
Commentary on the Whole Bible. Rev. Robert Jamieson; Rev. A.
R. Fausset; Rev. David Brown
The New Testament and Wycliffe Bible Commentary. The Iversen
Associates

Ellicott's Bible Commentary. Charles John Ellicott
Liberty Bible Commentary. Jerry Falwell; Edward E. Hindson;
Woodrow Michael Kroll

REFERENCE WORKS

Josephus Complete Works. Translated by William Whiston
Outlines Of Theology. A. A. Hodge
Westminster Confession of Faith
Readings in Calvin's Theology. Donald K. McKim, editor
Instruction in Christianity, A Summary of Calvin's "Institutes".
Translated into English by Joseph Pitts Willes
*Bible Characters From The Old Testament And The New
Testament.* Alexander Whyte
Everyone In The Bible. William P. Barker
Encyclopedia of Bible Difficulties. Gleason L. Archer
All The Parables Of The Bible. Dr. Herbert Lockyer
All The Miracles Of The Bible. Dr. Herbert Lockyer
Vines Expository Dictionary of New Testament Words. W. E. Vine
Layman's English-Greek Concordance. James Gall
The New Bible Dictionary. J. D. Douglas
Smith's Bible Dictionary. William Smith
Nave's Topical Bible. Orville J. Nave
The NIV Exhaustive Concordance. Edward W. Goodrick & John
R. Kohlenberg III
Strong's Exhaustive Concordance. James Strong

BIBLE TRANSLATIONS CONSULTED

New International Version
King James Version
New American Standard
Revised Standard Version
The New English Bible
The Amplified Bible
Young's Literal Translation
The Living Bible—Paraphrased

SCRIPTURE INDEX

The verses used in each chapter are listed by the books of the Bible from which they are taken. The listings are not in numerical order but in the order that they occur as used in the chapter.

VERSES USED IN WHY BELIEVE THE BIBLE

Genesis
3:15a
18:18

Exodus
19:3

Deuteronomy
29:29
28:68
18:15
34:10
4:27

Joshua
20:1-3

Psalms
41:9
69:4
22:16
22:6-8
69:21
22:18
34:20
16:10
68:18

Isaiah
40:8
55:9
48:3,5a
7:14
53:3

50:6
55:8

Jeremiah
1:4-7

Ezekiel
26:1-14
2:3-5

Micah
5:2
2:3

Habakkuk
2:2

Zephaniah
3:20

Zechariah
9:9
12:10b
1:1-6
7:11-14

Malachi
4:1

Matthew
26:56a
2:1
1:18
1:22-23

27:39-40
28:7-9
4:4
4:7
4:10
19:3-6

Mark
9:7
14:10
14:65
15:24

Luke
24:50-51
24:25-27
24:44-47

John
6:14
1:11
12:13-14
15:23-25
20:27
19:29
19:34
19:32-33
21:18-19
21:24-25

Acts
13:29
3:25
2:22-23

VERSES USED IN CHAPTER ON SOVEREIGNTY

VERSES USED IN CHAPTER ON SALVATION

Numbers
  32:23

2 Chronicles
  6:36a

Psalms
  51:5
  5:4
  22:14-18

Proverbs
  16:25
  19:3
  20:9

Ecclesiastes
  7:20

Isaiah
  29:13
  55:6
  64:6
  1:5
  53:6
  Chapter 53
  45:22

Jeremiah
  8:6

Ezekiel
  18:4b

Matthew
  13:41-42
  7:13-14
  10:38
  13:1-8
  13:18-23
  24:10
  1:18-25

5:17
27:27-40
26:37-38
26:39
26:42
26:50-54
28:5-7
7:21-23
25:31-34,41,46
13:24-30
13:36-43
23:13-15
23:27-28

Mark
  9:43-48
  8:34
  15:1-5
  8:31
  1:23-24
  1:34

Luke
  1:26-35
  18:31-33
  22:37
  22:44
  24:50-53
  18:9-14

John
  14:6
  6:38
  1:1-2
  10:30
  1:14
  19:23-24
  10:14-18
  11:25-26
  20:24-29
  3:16-18
  3:35-36

8:23-24
6:67-69
8:56
3:36
5:28-29
11:25-26
8:21-24
14:6
3:10-18
3:36
1:12
8:34-47
16:2-3
15:23
14:26
6:37
10:27-30

Acts
  16:30
  17:31
  1:21-22
  2:32
  10:37-41
  3:15
  16:30-31
  4:12
  3:19-20
  20:21

Romans
  3:11
  5:12
  6:23
  8:6
  8:7
  1:18-32
  2:5
  3:23
  8:1-3
  4:25
  3:20

VERSES USED IN CHAPTER ON OBEDIENCE

VERSES USED IN CHAPTER ON THE HOLY SPIRIT

James	5:7	1 John
1:3	2:15	4:13
4:7	2:12	4:1
4:6	5:8	4:4
3:18	1:13	1:9
5:7-11	4:10-11	4:7-12
1:6-8	1:3-5	3:14
		1:9
1 Peter	2 Peter	5:14-15
2:4-5	1:3	
4:12-17	3:9	Jude
1:22	1:5-8	20
1:8-9		24

VERSES USED IN CHAPTER ON ELECTION

Genesis	Jeremiah	Mark
6:5	13:23	13:27
	10:23	13:20
Exodus	17:9	13:27
4:11	24:7	
	1:5	Luke
Deuteronomy		24:45
7:6	Lamentations	13:22-28
	3:38	19:10
Job		
14:4	Ezekiel	John
15:14-16	36:26	1:10-13
		13:18a
Psalms	Amos	15:18-19a
19:1-4	9:4	8:42-44
53:2-3		11:38-44
119:36	Matthew	10:25-30
	24:22-24	17:1-2
Proverbs	22:14	17:24
14:12	16:13-17	3:5-8
16:9	11:27	5:21
	10:29-31	6:44-45
Isaiah	7:21-23	6:63-65
64:6	28:18-20	3:16
59:1	10:34-39	3:19
41:8-9		14:26
46:9-11		16:13-14